D0222791

DECONSTRUCTING DIGITAL NATIVES

There have been many attempts to define the generation of students who emerged with the Web and new digital technologies in the early 1990s. The term "Digital Native" refers to the generation born after 1980, which has grown up in a world where digital technologies and the Internet are a normal part of everyday life. Young people belonging to this generation are therefore supposed to be "native" to the digital lifestyle, always connected to the Internet and comfortable with a range of cutting-edge technologies.

Deconstructing Digital Natives offers the most balanced, research-based view of this group to date. Existing studies of digital natives lack application to specific disciplines or conditions, ignoring the differences of educational fields and gender. How, and how much, are learners changing in the digital age? How can a more pluralistic understanding of these learners be developed? Contributors to this volume produce an international overview of developments in digital literacy among today's young learners, offering innovative ways to steer a productive path between traditional narratives that offer only complete acceptance or total dismissal of digital natives.

Dr. Michael Thomas is Senior Lecturer in Language Learning Technologies and Digital Business Communication in the School of Languages and International Studies at the University of Central Lancashire, UK.

DECONSTRUCTING DIGITAL NATIVES

Young People, Technology and the New Literacies

Edited by
Michael Thomas

ROUTLEDGE
Routledge
Taylor & Francis Group
NEW YORK AND LONDON

First published 2011
by Routledge
711 Third Avenue, New York, NY 10017

Simultaneously published in the UK
by Routledge
2 Park Square, Milton Park, Abingdon, Oxon OX14 4RN

Routledge is an imprint of the Taylor & Francis Group, an informa business

© 2011 Taylor & Francis

The right of Michael Thomas to be identified as the author of the editorial material, and of the authors for their individual chapters, has been asserted in accordance with sections 77 and 78 of the Copyright, Designs and Patents Act 1988.

Typeset in Bembo and Stone Sans
by Florence Production Ltd, Stoodleigh, Devon

Printed and bound in the United States of America on acid-free paper
by Walsworth Publishing Company, Marceline, MO

All rights reserved. No part of this book may be reprinted or reproduced or utilized in any form or by any electronic, mechanical, or other means, now known or hereafter invented, including photocopying and recording, or in any information storage or retrieval system, without permission in writing from the publishers.

Trademark Notice: Product or corporate names may be trademarks or registered trademarks, and are used only for identification and explanation without intent to infringe.

Library of Congress Cataloging in Publication Data
Deconstructing digital natives: young people, technology, and the new literacies/edited by Michael Thomas.
p. cm.
Includes bibliographical references and index.
1. Internet in education—United States. 2. Technology and youth—United States. I. Thomas, Michael.
LB1028.5.D353 2011
371.33′44678—dc22 2010042832

ISBN13: 978-0-415-88993-3 (hbk)
ISBN13: 978-0-415-88996-4 (pbk)
ISBN13: 978-0-203-81884-8 (ebk)

The SFI label applies to the text stock.

CONTENTS

ILLUSTRATIONS

Figures

Tables

FOREWORD

The idea of a technological or media-related generation gap is by no means new. One can look back to the 1960s, when the idea of the "television generation" was popularly used as a shorthand means of explaining social change; and there is an extensive history of such claims being used in relation to earlier popular cultural forms. Such ideas are a staple element of "moral panics"; although they also typically invoke much more diffuse and generalized concerns about the impact of modernity. The idea of the generation gap entails a narrative of transformation, and even of rupture, in which fundamental continuities between the past and the future have been destroyed. Such arguments have considerable emotional appeal: by aligning claims about media and technology with ideas about childhood and youth, they provide a powerful vehicle for some of our most intense hopes and fears.

The contemporary idea of the "Digital Native"—and related formulations such as the "digital generation" and the "net generation"—generally place a more positive spin on this basic narrative. The problem here is not with the natives themselves, but rather with the rest of us, the "Digital Immigrants" who remain obstinately tied to older media, and who are failing to catch up with the times. Such arguments often entail an almost utopian view of technology—a fabulous story about technology liberating and empowering young people, enabling them to become global citizens, and to learn and communicate and create in free and unfettered ways.

Despite its popular appeal, the problems with this narrative are fairly apparent; and many of them are rehearsed by the contributors to this volume, which usefully brings together a range of empirical evidence on the issue. Proponents of the digital natives argument typically overstate the extent and effects of technological change and ignore elements of continuity. Yet the history of technology suggests that change, however rapid, is generally incremental rather than revolutionary. Only rarely do new technologies simply replace older ones; and there are often considerable overlaps and parallels between "old" and "new" media. Technologies do not appear from nowhere: they are developed, designed, and marketed in specific social contexts, which reflect broader economic, cultural, and social factors. Technologies have possibilities and limitations (or "affordances"), but they do not produce social change in themselves.

The digital natives argument also overstates the differences between generations, and understates the diversity within them. Many so-called digital natives are no more intensive users of digital media than many so-called digital immigrants. They are by no means as technologically fixated or as technologically proficient as is often assumed. They don't necessarily have the skills, the competency or the natural fluency that they are assumed to possess. Much of young people's use of digital technology is mundane rather than spectacular: it is characterized not by dramatic manifestations of innovation and creativity, but by relatively routine forms of communication and information retrieval. Contemporary children have many of the same interests, concerns, and preoccupations as children in previous generations—even if the ways in which they manifest these through their use of technology are likely to be rather different.

Ultimately, the digital natives argument tends to essentialize generations—and in the process to "exoticize" young people, to make them seem inherently strange and different. There is a familiar sentimentality about children and youth here, mixed up with a kind of fear about what might be going on in this younger generation. While it appears positive and celebratory, this characterization of young people is also strangely belittling: it assumes that young people spontaneously know everything they need to know about technology, rather than having to make the effort to learn about it. Growing up with a technology may well imply a different orientation towards it than coming to it later in life—but it is certainly debatable how lasting that kind of difference is. One of the most striking developments in the UK in recent years has been the rapid uptake of the Internet among middle-aged and elderly people: while there might be a time-lag between generations, it may prove to be rather less than significant.

While the notion of the generation gap does reflect some persistent hopes and fears about the future, it also takes on different forms in different historical and cultural settings. It may also have an economic dimension. We could certainly analyze contemporary claims about digital natives as a kind of sales pitch, promulgated by individuals and companies with goods and services to sell in an increasingly volatile commercial environment. Young people are a notoriously unpredictable market; and the pace of technological change appears to be accelerating. Consultants and experts who claim to have privileged insider knowledge of this market may well find themselves in great demand. The combination of fearful apprehension and wishful thinking about technology appears to be highly intoxicating for company executives—and indeed for governments—whose business appears ever more precarious.

Yet despite all this, the concept of generational change remains a relevant and productive one with which to work. There is a body of sociological and historical analysis here—for example, in Karl Mannheim's macro-level account of the construction of generations—that might usefully be applied to technological change. There are also productive analyses of how generations are constructed—and how people come to define themselves as members of generations—at the micro-level of everyday interactions. In the field of Childhood Studies, there has been considerable use of the notion of "generationing," the idea that (both as young people and as adults) we are constantly defining ourselves as members of generations through an ever-shifting *performance* of age identities. This process plays out in homes and in schools, not least in terms of how people use technology, in what they say about technology, and in terms of how the activity of using technology is produced, constructed, and regulated. So, for example, we could consider how parents construct their children as technology experts, while at the same time attempting to monitor and regulate what they are doing with technology. Technology often plays a complex and ambivalent role in this ongoing, mutual construction of generations.

However, this approach implies a more reflexive, critical use of the concept of generations than is typically the case in popular discussions of young people's use of technology. If we wish to understand the complex and uneven nature of social change, and the place of technology within it, we need more measured and careful investigations that pay close attention to the texture of lived experience. This timely book makes a significant contribution to these debates on digital technologies in education, underlining the value of a research-based approach by presenting empirical evidence and argument from international researchers in the field. If—despite its shortcomings—the "Digital Natives" debate has provoked this kind of international collaboration and discussion, then it may well have been worthwhile.

Professor David Buckingham
Institute of Education
University of London, UK

1

TECHNOLOGY, EDUCATION, AND THE DISCOURSE OF THE DIGITAL NATIVE

Between Evangelists and Dissenters

Michael Thomas

From Plato to Web 2.0, new technologies have always attracted both passionate advocates as well as an active dissenting tradition. Advocates, variously identified as technoevangelists, technoromantics, or enlightenment thinkers have long had to contend with the verbal or even physically destructive response of technophobes, antimodernists, or luddites. During the Industrial Revolution in England, factory owners installed mechanical looms to improve production but were perceived as threatening employment and causing a massive change in social relations. Luddites damaged and destroyed industrial machinery as an act of self-preservation. Two hundred years later, the Internet has brought greater global access to information, education, and commerce than ever before, but these benefits have to be balanced against cybercrime, cyber-bullying, information overload, violent video games, copyright infringement, and 24/7 online pornography.

While Warschauer argues new technologies are "bringing about a shift in literacy practices as dramatic as any since the development of the printing press" (2006, p. ix), it is not unusual to see self-proclaimed "digital luddites" (Young, 2010) lamenting the need to escape the constant and disruptive interference of email or hear them telling their students to switch off their mobile phones and laptop computers as they enter classrooms (Mortkowitz, 2010). Some have banned the use of Google, Wikipedia and social media applications in classrooms (Chiles, 2008), while other professors have achieved momentary notoriety by dismantling wireless hubs during lectures, as they can no longer contend with the distractions laptops pose. Whereas faculty often argue that banning laptops makes students more attentive in content-based classes, students at the University of Memphis Law School reacted by signing a petition protesting to the American Bar Association, claiming that they had been denied the technology for an "up-to-date education" (Young, 2006). For these students attending a western university in the first decade of the new millennium, digital technologies and the Internet have become a "normalized" and expected part of their daily learning experience (Thomas, 2011). This is far from an expectation or reality elsewhere, however.

While young people attend school and university in the west, often lamenting the weight of their laptops in their rucksacks or the slow speed of their micro-processors, at the same time some children in Asia and South America peer at the Internet through a hole in the wall of their shanty town (Mitra, 2006), use a networked $100 laptop designed by MIT, or, more probably, have never seen such technologies, never mind used them.

The conflicts and contrasts noted above are nothing new. In fact, the history of technology has often been characterized by a debate between uncritical romantics and dismissive skeptics. Neither position, however, is an effective response to the opportunities and challenges new technologies present; both in turn often exaggerate or downplay the impact of technology, and this leads to entrenched positions and polarization. In the sphere of education in particular, such entrenched positions can be harmful and produce simplistic forms of analysis, their popularity due to the fact that they are often more exciting, easily digestible, and media-friendly than the highly differentiated analysis produced by careful, longitudinal research. In the field of educational technology, driven as it is by rapid changes in hardware and software, it is difficult to get excited about a research report that takes two years to write, especially as the technology in question may have changed dramatically in the intervening time. Advocates of technology integration in education must therefore attempt to understand the discourses that drive it and, in some cases, harm its acceptance, and find a balance between the technological innovations that can be sustained by sound pedagogy and those driven more by commercial interests.

Beginning with an entry in 2005, Wikipedia contains a definition of "technology evangelist," a term that appropriately perhaps conjures up images of the almost religious intensity displayed sometimes by technology vendors bringing a new product to market, supported more recently in the age of Web 2.0 digital applications by an army of bloggers, podcasters, and, latterly, tweeters. Witness in this respect the reception of the iPhone as well as the educational debate about the wisdom of investing in interactive whiteboards before there has been sufficient time for teachers to teach with them or researchers to research them. A techno-evangelist, then, can be regarded as

> a person who attempts to build a critical mass of support for a given technology in order to establish it as a technical standard in a market . . . Professional technology evangelists are often employed by firms which seek to establish their proprietary technologies as *de facto* standards or to participate in setting non-proprietary open standards. Non-professional

> technology evangelists may act out of altruism or self-interest (e.g., to gain the benefits of early adoption or the network effect).
>
> (Wikipedia, 2010, n.p.)

This striking definition has a particular resonance in the age of the "network society" and the "knowledge economy," where technology evangelists have become particularly prominent in many areas of education, promising to "transform" and "revolutionize" pedagogy using a variety of devices, all the way from digital television to the Nintendo DS and the Apple iPad.

One of the most important terms used by technoevangelists to promote digital technologies and the so-called "transformation of learning"—the digital native—is the subject of this book. Over the last decade the "Digital Native," a description now typically identified by marketers with a young person who has grown up with digital technologies and the Internet as ever-present parts of their lives, has been the subject of a number of popular books including *Growing up Digital* (Tapscott, 1998), *Born Digital* (Palfrey & Gasser, 2008), *Grown up Digital* (Tapscott, 2009), and *Teaching Digital Natives* (Prensky, 2010), to name but a few high profile examples. Like it or not—and increasingly many academics who emphasize the need for a research-led approach to technology integration in education do not—"Digital Natives" has retained a powerful and enduring if, albeit, problematical resonance since Prensky popularized it in his essay, "Digital Natives/Digital Immigrants" (2001a, 2001b), following Barlow's (1996) earlier usage.

One decade later the term causes disdain as well as fervent acceptance. Some researchers have been asked to remove all trace of the term from academic papers submitted to conferences in order to be seriously considered for inclusion. At the same time in other parts of the world, whole conferences are still being organized in which the assumptions about digital natives are an integral part—witness for example the New England Regional Association for Language Learning Technology (NERALLT) Fall 2010 Conference in the United States entitled, "The Digital Native Language Learners are Here: How Do We Effectively Teach Language to the Digital Native?"

While disputed in academia, the term has become common parlance in the media as well as other areas of business where it is an easy handle for a potentially lucrative demographic trend. A Demos report from 2007, is emblematic of such claims:

> The current generation of young people will reinvent the workplace, and the society they live in. They will do it along the progressive lines that are built into the technology they use everyday—of networks, collaboration, co-production and participation. The change in behavior has already happened. We have to get used to it, accept that the flow of knowledge moves both ways and do our best to make sure that no one is left behind.
>
> (Green & Hannon, 2007, n.p.)

Moreover, a Gartner conference from a year later entitled, "The Attack of the Digital Natives," captures the evangelistic mood, as well as the fact that the "new generation" is no longer spoken of in the *future* but rather the *present* tense:

> Digital natives are working in your organization today. They are solving business problems, building social networks and creating new processes—with or without your help and support. They have new expectations about what information and technologies they should be able to access. They use defined processes in new ways, and invent new processes of their own. And they have a different expectation about how they want to work and play. Come visit with some of these digital natives and learn how to leverage their knowledge, enthusiasm and skills.
>
> (Gartner, 2008, n.p.)

Bennett, Maton, & Kervin (2008; see Chapter 11, this volume) have rightly described the mood of such passages as increasingly akin to a form of "moral panic," in which the *differences* between young people have been eradicated and they *all* appear to have been born with the same potentially transformative powers: digital natives are problem-solvers; they have new expectations; they invent new processes; they don't only work for an organization, they think of work as play; they are enthusiastic and skillful.

Derived from publications by Prensky (2001a, 2001b) and Tapscott (1998, 1999, 2009) and supported by a range of other popular appropriations of the term, then, the discourse of the digital natives in this simplified form can be considered as a type of technoevangelism, helping to make straight the roads of the global knowledge economy (Solomon & Schrum, 2007). This discourse takes a number of forms in different contexts but is popularly based on three main assumptions in which young people—those typically born after 1980—are said to:

1. constitute a largely homogenous generation and speak a different language vis-à-vis digital technologies, as opposed to their parents, the "Digital Immigrants";
2. learn differently from preceding generations of students;
3. demand a new way of teaching and learning involving technology.

This book is an attempt to examine these arguments from a range of international and disciplinary perspectives and to understand both the temptations and dangers of technoevangelism, which often drive them, as well as the technoskepticism that may too easily dismiss them.

In adopting an international perspective the limitations of the generational argument are immediately apparent. While the Internet celebrates its fortieth anniversary in 2010, it is only in the two last decades that larger numbers of the world's population have begun to use the World Wide Web, and only in the last five that the so-called "read/write web" has appeared. From a world population of almost 7 billion, however, approximately 2 billion have access to the Internet. While the percentage of people using the Internet in North America, Europe and Oceania/Australia lies between 58 percent and 77 percent, it is less than 35 percent for the populations of Africa (10.9 percent), Asia (21.5 percent), the Middle East (29.8 percent), and Latin America/Caribbean (34.5 percent) (Internet World Stats, 2010). To this international perspective we can also add a highly differentiated picture of access within nations. None of the contributors to this volume accept this undifferentiated "generational" viewpoint based on age alone.

The inclusion of the word "deconstruction" in the title of the volume provides an immediate clue as to one of its key aspects, then, in that I understand deconstruction to be a form of close reading in which the foundational assumptions of "naturalized" or "taken-for-granted" concepts are interrogated, thereby "dismantl[ing] the logic by which a particular system of thought . . . maintains its force" (Eagleton, 1983, p. 148; Thomas, 2006). As we turn to consider points two and three of the argument, deconstruction has an important resonance in the book in that a number of other potentially fascinating associations exist.

Both terms have been attacked as leading to damaging implications for education, the assumption being that they are concerned with the attempt to dismantle decades of tradition without having anything to replace it with. In the case of the discourse of digital natives, when viewed productively it derives from a deep suspicion of the way formal education has developed since the industrial revolution, in that the industrial model of education is failing learners by not keeping pace with the way students today are experiencing learning mediated by technology, particularly in non-formal or home environments (Ito, 2009; Ito et al., 2010). Interpreted in this light the discourse of digital natives springs from this wider critique of an educational system in which institutions are portrayed as a site of struggle between tendencies to centralize pedagogical and teacher control and decentralize learner autonomy by encouraging situated, authentic, and collaborative learning (Gee, 2007; Weller, 2009).

Deriving from this context the chapters in the book examine the arguments associated with a "generation" of digital natives through the lens of a number of different studies conducted in Europe, North America, and Asia. Some of the most prominent labels associated with digital natives—"cyberkids" (Holloway & Valentine, 2003) or the "Net Generation" (Tapscott, 1998, 2009)—are discussed alongside others such as the "digital divide" and "digital literacy."

In this respect the discourse of the digital natives is intimately related to the emergence of new forms of literacy based on a pluralization of the concept that moves it beyond the narrower sense of merely reading and writing to encapsulate an understanding of different "semiotic domains" or "multimodality" (Gee, 2007). Tapscott (1998), for example, develops these connections, suggesting that the net generation bring with them a truly transformative power to supplant the existing "linear" model of pedagogy with one based more on interactivity and collaboration. A major focus of criticism in this respect is the so-called "transmission model" of learning, which predicated on a one-size-fits-all mentality, assumes that knowledge can be disseminated to all learners regardless of individual differences or learning styles.

Drawing on social constructivism, Tapscott (1998, 1999) outlined the principle of an interactionist pedagogy closely aligned with what he views as the requirements and opportunities of the digital age, in which he identifies a movement from:

1. linear to hypermedia learning
2. instruction to construction and discovery
3. teacher-centered to learner-centered education
4. absorbing material to learning how to navigate and how to learn
5. school to lifelong learning
6. one-size-fits-all to customized learning
7. learning as torture to learning as fun
8. the teacher as transmitter to the teacher as facilitator.

(Tapscott, 1999, pp. 6–11)

Based on these principles of learning, according to Tapscott, the net generation exhibits ten clear criteria. They demonstrate a strong propensity for independence, being able to search for and access information that is required by them. Through the use of blogs and other communication tools, they demonstrate an emotional and intellectual openness to others. This spirit of openness is reflected in the net generation's focus on social inclusion evident in their interest in online communities. In addition they demonstrate "free expression and strong views," "innovation," and, in contrast to the "baby boomer" generation, net generation members emphasize their mature attitude to life and learning. Unlike their predecessors, they are "investigators" by nature and enjoy exploring the myriad of opportunities available on the Web. An investigative spirit is coupled with a great sense of "immediacy," and the need to do everything at a high speed. While being open to the excessive levels of information available on today's Web, the net generation are sensitive to information being peddled for unseen corporate interests. Similarly, although surrounded by more information, they are sensitive to the continuous need to verify and authenticate the information that surrounds them. It is clear from this that Web 2.0, with its emphasis on user-generated content and sharing, has become a "key framing device" for work on digital literacies (Lankshear & Knobel, 2008, p. 1).

Research on learners' actual digital literacy skills, however, reveals glaring contradictions within the so-called "Google generation" (Brabazon, 2007; see Kennedy and Judd, Chapter 8 of this volume). Many undergraduates have only a basic familiarity with the commonly used information and communication technology (ICT) functions, and many fewer are concerned with *creating* multimedia content rather than merely searching for it, usually in unsophisticated ways. Though numerous arguments have established a connection between digital natives and their ability to use Web 2.0 technologies, only a limited number have familiarity with the most commonly cited emerging technologies, and even fewer use them frequently. Where students do use them, it is most often in their social lives for communication purposes and rarely in educational contexts. Moreover, in certain cases, students see a conflict between the use of Web 2.0 technologies in their social and educational lives, and would like to see them remain separate rather than intertwined.

The availability of new digital technologies and the changing assumptions about the nature of learners and styles of learning have to be read against the background of the dramatic increase in the number of students entering higher education around the world and the need to discover new ways of both communicating with them and instructing them. Discussions about the nature and effectiveness of digital technologies are inevitably associated with a complex range of other factors, thereby giving the whole debate a wider sociopolitical significance (Warschauer, 1999). These contributing contextual factors include, "the globalization and commercialization of education, the quality of education, the merits of distance versus campus based learning, and the very nature of learning institutions themselves" (Weller, 2002, p. 19) within a global economy.

It is necessary to engage with these discourses, evangelical and dissenting, and as Bennett and Maton suggest in Chapter 11, to resist the all too frequent association between educational technology and its "transformative" potential. Such a discourse cheapens research on educational technology and does little to advance it as a discipline. In deconstructing these implicit assumptions, this book establishes a number of research directions for future studies shown in the concerns of the contributors.

An Overview of this Book

The book is divided into three parts. In Part I, "Reflecting on the Myth," the first section of Marc Prensky's contribution provides a fascinating reflection on the origins, use, and abuse of the term "Digital Natives," arguing that it was intended to be little more than a "metaphor" that described a widely observable phenomenon rather than a literal or scientific concept. These reflections function as a preface to his 2009 essay, "Digital Wisdom and Homo Sapiens Digital: From Digital Immigrants and Digital Natives to the Digitally Wise," which, reprinted here, represents his own attempt to move the debate forward through his concept of "digital wisdom." In Chapter 3, "Students, the Net Generation and Digital Natives: Accounting for Educational Change," Chris Jones presents a critique of the arguments identifying digital natives as a distinct generation, while suggesting that research on digital technologies is merited and should engage in more sophisticated ways with the differences research has actually found to exist between digital-age learners.

The seven chapters contained in Part II, "Perspectives," continue Jones's arguments by addressing a number of different national and disciplinary contexts in order to explore a more finely nuanced view of young peoples' engagement with digital technologies. Chapter 4, "Disempowering by Assumption: Digital Natives and the EU Civic Web Project," discusses research findings from a seven-country, three-year European Union sponsored research project about the use of digital technologies to aid young peoples' participation in contemporary society. Casting further afield, Chapter 5 provides a unique perspective on young peoples' use of Internet communities in Japan, discussing in particular the types of "techno-orientalism" that have been used by westerners to describe the Japanese context. Focusing in particular on current trends in mobile Internet usage, Toshie Takahashi draws on ethnographic studies involving young people over the decade since 2001 in the Tokyo Metropolitan Area, to investigate the diversity among young Japanese people and their experience of online communities in Asia. Chapter 6, "Analyzing Students' Multimodal Texts: The Product and the Process," discusses two case studies exploring learners at an Australian high school and their use of digital technologies and multimodal skills. Based on a longitudinal study conducted by Griffith University between 2003 and 2008, the case study data suggests significant variation in technological skills and abilities, as well as traditional skills, among learners. In Chapter 7, "Citizens Navigating in Literate Worlds: The Case of Digital Literacy," Ola Erstad examines the idea of "digital literacy" from a Nordic perspective, describing how young people explore creativity in digital culture and as a consequence, how literacy practices need to be rearticulated.

In Chapter 8, "Beyond Google and the 'Satisficing' Searching of Digital Natives," Gregor Kennedy and Terry Judd discuss the findings of their research on medical students in Australia, exploring how students seek and gather information using digital technologies. Identifying that learners have developed rather superficial approaches to information retrieval, they conclude that in opposition to the typical image of the highly skilled digital natives, today's learners require *support* and *guidance* about how to best develop their digital literacy skills in educational contexts.

In Chapter 9, "Actual and Perceived Online Participation among Young People in Sweden," Sheila Zimic and Rolf Dalin discuss what is meant by participation in the digital age among Swedish youth and their use of Web 2.0 technologies such as blogs to engage with political activities. In Chapter 10, "Young Children, Digital Technology and Interaction with Text," Rachael Levy questions the assumptions behind the "Digital Natives" hypothesis with reference to case study data collected from three young children at the time of their entry into the formal education system in the UK. This chapter argues that the children not only experienced technology in different ways, but demonstrates how this experience had a unique impact on their literacy development.

Finally, Part III, "Beyond Digital Natives," contains two chapters that look to the future of research in this area, examining what parts should be abandoned and what can meaningfully be retained. Chapter 11, "Intellectual Field or Faith-based Religion: Moving on from the Idea of 'Digital Natives'," argues that both "Digital Natives" and recent articulations such as "Digital Wisdom" are representative of "unevidenced" ideas that have been harmful for the field of educational technology in general. Moreover, it is time to move beyond both this style of analysis and these concepts in order to engage with the diversity rather than the conformity suggested by young peoples' use of digital technologies. In contrast to Bennett and Maton, in Chapter 11, "Reclaiming an Awkward Term: What We Might Learn from 'Digital Natives'," John Palfrey and Urs Gasser explore the continued use of "Digital Natives" as a distinctive "population" among young people, rather than as a blanket generational term, using it to identify and examine how it can be used in a constructive way to help move research forward.

Three points are worth underlining in conclusion. First, the way many people use technology to find, interact with, and process information is changing. Second, the nature of global networks is altering the way communities are formed and developed. Third, digital technologies bring with them both the potential for great opportunities in connecting people and communities as never before, as well as significant challenges in the form of a myriad of issues from cyber-crime to information overload. In emphasizing the potential of the former, it is a responsibility not to neglect the latter, and to adopt a critical perspective that, in being sensitive to differences, is not easily swept along by either evangelistic advocacy or skepticism.

The discourse of the digital natives is, as Palfrey and Gasser recognize, best conceived of as a

> metaphor, as a hermeneutic tool, to invite readers to join us on this journey and engage in a debate about the promises and limitations, opportunities and challenges, potential benefits and possible downsides of the evolving global network that we call cyberspace.
>
> (2008, p. 290)

In addressing the digital literacy skills of learners and the evolution of new forms of pedagogy, educators have to be wary of adopting conveniently dichotomized modes of thinking—building on the binary logic of "natives" and "immigrants," other structuring oppositions include the "transmission" mode of delivery and that of "collaborative" learning. In this vein, it is hoped that as one of the first books to engage critically with the debate about how digital technologies are being used in a series of different contexts, this book will encourage wider national and international discussion and collaboration on the subject in the future.

References

Barlow, J. P. (1996). *A declaration of the independence of cyberspace*. Retrieved September 10, 2010, from http://homes.eff.org/~barlow/Declaration-Final.html

Bennett, S., Maton, K., & Kervin, L. (2008). The "Digital Natives" debate: A critical review of the evidence. *British Journal of Educational Technology*, *39*(5), 775–786.

Brabazon, T. (2007). *The university of Google: Education in the (post) information age*. Aldershot: Ashgate.

Chiles, A. (2008). Lecturer bans students from using Google and Wikipedia. *The Argus*, January 13, 2008. Retrieved September 10, 2010, from www.theargus.co.uk/news/1961862.lecturer_bans_students_from_using_google_and_wikipedia

Eagleton, T. (1983). *Literary theory: An introduction*. Oxford: Blackwell.

Gartner. (2008). Panel: The attack of the digital natives. Retrieved September 10, 2010, from http://agendabuilder.gartner.com/ea8/webpages/SessionDetail.aspx?EventSessionId=821

Gee, J. P. (2007). *What video games have to teach us about learning and literacy*. London & New York: Palgrave Macmillan.

Green, H., & Hannon, C. (2007). *Their space: Education for a digital generation*. Retrieved June 20, 2009, from www.demos.co.uk/files/Their%20space%20-%20web.pdf

Holloway, S. L., & Valentine, G. (2003). *Cyberkids: Children in the information age*. London: Routledge.

Internet World Stats (2010). World internet usage and population statistics. Retrieved September 15, 2010, from www.internetworldstats.com/stats.htm

Ito, M. (2009). *Engineering play: A cultural history of children's software*. Cambridge, MA: The MIT Press.

Ito, M. et al. (2010). *Hanging out, messing around, and geeking out*. Cambridge, MA & London: The MIT Press.

Lankshear, C., & Knobel, M. (Eds.) (2008). *Digital literacies: Concepts, policies and practices*. New York: Peter Lang.

Mitra, S. (2006). *The hole in the wall: Self-organising systems in education*. New Delhi: Tata McGraw Hill.

Mortkowitz, L. (2010). More colleges, professors shutting down laptops and other digital distractions. *The Washington Post*, April 25, 2010. Retrieved September 10, 2010, from www.washingtonpost.com/wp-dyn/content/article/2010/04/24/AR2010042402830.html

Palfrey, J., & Gasser, U. (2008). *Born digital: Understanding the first generation of digital natives*. New York: Basic Books.

Prensky, M. (2001a). Digital natives, digital immigrants. *On the Horizon*, *9*(5), 1–6.

Prensky, M. (2001b). Digital natives, digital immigrants, Part II: Do they really think differently? *On the Horizon*, *9*(6), 1–6.

Prensky, M. (2010). *Teaching digital natives: Preparing for real learning*. Thousand Oaks, CA: Corwin.

Solomon, G., & Shrum, L. (2007). *Web 2.0: New tools, new schools*. Eugene, OR, & Washington, DC: International Society for Technology in Education.

Tapscott, D. (1998). *Growing up digital: The rise of the net generation*. New York: McGraw-Hill.

Tapscott, D. (1999). Educating the net generation. *Educational Leadership, 56*(5), 6–11.

Tapscott, D. (2009) *Grown up digital: How the net generation is changing your world*. New York: McGraw-Hill.

Thomas, M. (2006). *The reception of Derrida: Translation and transformation*. London & New York: Palgrave Macmillan.

Thomas, M. (Ed.) (2011). *Digital education: Opportunities for social collaboration*. London & New York: Palgrave Macmillan.

Young, J. R. (2006). The fight for classroom attention: Professor vs Laptop. *Chronicle of Higher Education, 52*(39), A27–A29.

Young, J. R. (2010). College 2.0: Teachers without technology strike back. *The Chronicle of Higher Education*, August 15, 2010. Retrieved September 10, 2010, from http://chronicle.com/article/College-20-Teachers-Without/123891

Warschauer, M. (1999). *Electronic literacies: Language culture and power in online education*. Mahwah, NJ: Lawrence Erlbaum Associates.

Warschauer, M. (2006). *Laptops and literacy: Learning in the wireless classroom*. New York: Teacher College Press.

Weller, M. (2002). *Delivering learning on the net: The why, what & how of online education*. London: Kogan Page.

Weller, M. (2009). The centralisation dilemma in educational IT. *International Journal of Virtual and Personal Learning Environments, 1*(1), 1–9.

Wikipedia. (2010). Technology evangelist. Retrieved September 10, 2010, from http://en.wikipedia.org/wiki/Technology_evangelist

PART I

Reflecting on the Myth

2

DIGITAL WISDOM AND HOMO SAPIENS DIGITAL

Marc Prensky

Reflections on Digital Natives/Digital Immigrants, One Decade Later

Exactly ten years separates the original publication of my paper "Digital Natives/ Digital Immigrants" in 2001 and the publication of this book, *Deconstructing Digital Natives*, in 2011. One decade later it is fitting to reflect on these terms, on how they have entered the popular imagination, and on how, arising from a conversation I once had, they have been used by people all around the world in ways I could neither have imagined nor foreseen. I can more or less remember the conversation in which, having already established the notion of Digital Natives, the interesting idea of extending the metaphor to Immigrants, who would speak of digital technologies with a different "accent," arose. The distinction was intended to be a *metaphor* for describing the differences that many people observed, around the turn of the twenty-first century, between the attitudes of younger and older people regarding digital technology (Prensky, 2006). In the eyes of many, it was a very useful metaphor, because it finally gave a shorthand "name" to a phenomenon they were all struggling to classify.

Many praised the metaphor as adding to our understanding of the phenomenon and situation. For example, John Seely Brown called the metaphor "evocative" (as opposed to "provocative") (personal conversation, n.d.), as it invited further discussion. Rupert Murdoch and Bill Gates used the terms in speeches. A Digital Natives Institute was created at Harvard. And, as expected, there were some who disagreed.

What has surprised me the most is the violence and vitriol of some of the disagreements. I am shocked at how many supposedly well-educated, thinking people just "can't take a metaphor." Rather than see it as a way of looking at and naming a phenomenon that was clearly taking place (i.e., young people often knowing more about digital technology than their parents or teachers), some denied the whole thing (e.g., "The Myth of the Digital Native") or took issue with various points such as its universality, start date, or meaning. Some of the things people wrote really took me aback, not because they disagreed (I like that) but because of the lack of sense of proportion, and even sense, sometimes, in their reactions.

For example, many took huge issue with the fact that the metaphor was a broad generalization, when that was, in fact, precisely what made it useful. *Of course* dividing all human beings into only two groups is a huge generalization. Even dividing people into "men" and "women" leaves out all sorts of categories. But we do it, often, to make, or highlight, useful points.

In the case of the Digital Natives/Digital Immigrants metaphor, the point is about why so many adults in developed countries felt, around the turn of the century (and still feel today) "at sea" when confronted by new digital technologies, whereas their children didn't or don't. The answer, the metaphor implied, was because their children were born into the age when these technologies were around from their birth, whereas their parents were not. This made instant, intuitive sense to a great many people. That is why the metaphor was picked up so quickly and spread so widely: for those people, it put into words something they had felt intuitively, but had been previously unable to articulate in any other way. As soon as they heard the terms there was an immediate "aha!" This is, I am sure, because there can be no doubt that—within some limits—the Digital Natives/Digital Immigrants metaphor and distinction contains some real truth. The issue, of course—and the reason for this book—is what those limits are. The authors of the chapters in this volume almost all—to their credit—take the position of "let us accept the overall premise and intentions, and then go on to make some useful distinctions." I think this is the right way to go, and appreciate it.

The second great surprise (and disappointment) for me was how many people began interpreting very literally—rather than *metaphorically*—what a "Digital Native" was. This was done principally, it seemed, so that those people could disagree. Some people argued over the starting birth date or year, as if the Digital Native had magically appeared in the world on some given day. Other people groused about the word "native," as if the designation "demeaned" those to whom it was given. Still others argued that the term "immigrants" was demeaning.

Many critics just ignored words they may not have wanted to see—that is, modifiers, such as brains "may be" different, or "the evidence for this is in Part II" of the Digital Natives paper. One even made a mountain out of a typo.

But the worst, in my view, were those who thought I was making the absurd claim (or who themselves made the patently absurd assumption) that if someone was born after a certain date, and was therefore included as a Digital Native, that person *automatically knew everything there was to know* about digital technology. It was as if these critics (call them the "literalists" if you will) thought the metaphor meant that Digital Natives were born knowing everything about Microsoft

Windows, Word, file systems, and all other computer systems. And of course, as soon as these literalists came across young people who—never having been taught or shown by their peers how to find a saved file (or do something else)—failed at a technology task, they concluded—and ran out to shout to the world—that the idea of a Digital Native is a "myth."

As I listened to all these critics, nice and not-so-nice (and as my own views evolved), it seemed clearer and clearer to me that being a Digital Native is *not*, at its core, about capabilities, or even knowledge, regarding all things digital. No matter who you are, all those things have to be learned in some way.

The distinction is, I think, much more about culture. It is about younger people's *comfort* with digital technology, their belief in its ease, its usefulness, and its being generally benign, and about their seeing technology as a fun "partner" that they can master, without much effort, if they are shown or choose to. (They don't, of course, always choose to.)

Having grown up with digital technology as toys, Digital Natives are much more at ease with its use than the generation that did not. But this surely doesn't mean they know everything, or even want to. A non-intuitive file system that dates back to the earliest days of computing may be of little interest to them—even though it may be of great interest to their teachers, and even though it could be important for getting certain things done.

So to me, being a Digital Native is about growing up in a digital country or culture, as opposed to coming to it as an adult. In WWII, one of the ways they tried to ferret out non-native Americans who were possible spies was to ask them about cultural things that any kid who grew up in America would almost certainly know, but that foreigners, no matter how much they studied, would probably not. Digital Natives have that same kind of "growing up with it" knowledge. It is not so much of "facts" about hardware or software as of having experienced so much of digital devices and interfaces that their use comes naturally and intuitively. For example, I know far more about digital technology than my five-year-old son does (I hope), but I often find myself being shown tricks or shortcuts by him that he has figured out and that I had not.

Obviously, not every kid in America, or the world, has grown up in the same digital culture. But more and more of the world's kids have game consoles (their penetration in US households with children is more than 90 percent), cell phones, and other devices, or at least have friends who let them try them. In the developed world, the "digital culture" (as opposed to knowledge of specific hardware and software) is close to universal, and with the rapid spread of cell phones and game machines, it is growing quickly in the rest of the world.

Still, there is one criticism of the Digital Native/Digital Immigrant metaphor that I think has some validity. This is that the Digital Native/Digital Immigrant distinction and categorization can be used (and has been used by some people) to justify continuous division, and their own inaction, rather than the coming together and mutual learning that I want the distinction to support. When an adult uses the metaphor to assert "I'm an immigrant, I'll never speak your language or understand you, so why should I even try" or a young person says "I'm a native, so you'll never understand me," that is a dangerous misuse, I would say, of the metaphor, a use I would firmly oppose and discourage.

Of course, given demographics, the concept of Digital Natives and Digital Immigrants does have a "limited shelf life." Very soon there will come a time, even in the less developed countries of the world, when digital technology will be almost universal and taken as much for granted as, say, electricity is today (although, sad to say, even that, in the twenty-first century, is not yet completely universal). That is why it is so important not to dwell too much on the Digital Native/Digital Immigrant distinction, but to think ahead to the concept of "Digital Wisdom."

Beyond Digital Immigrants and Digital Natives to the Digitally Wise

I believe digital technology can be used to make us not just smarter but truly wiser. Digital wisdom is a twofold concept, referring both to wisdom arising *from* the use of digital technology to access cognitive power beyond our innate capacity and to wisdom *in* the prudent use of technology to enhance our capabilities. Because of technology, wisdom seekers in the future will benefit from unprecedented, instant access to ongoing worldwide discussions, all of recorded history, everything ever written, massive libraries of case studies and collected data, and highly realistic simulated experiences equivalent to years or even centuries of actual experience. How and how much they make use of these resources, how they filter through them to find what they need, and how technology aids them will certainly play an important role in determining the wisdom of their decisions and judgments. Technology alone will not replace intuition, good judgment, problem-solving abilities, and a clear moral compass. But in an unimaginably complex future, the digitally unenhanced person, however wise, will not be able to access the tools of wisdom that will be available to even the least wise digitally enhanced human.

Moreover, given that the brain is now generally understood to be highly plastic, continually adapting to the input it receives, it is possible that the brains of those who interact with technology frequently will be restructured by that interaction. The brains of wisdom seekers of the future will be fundamentally different, in organization and in structure, than our brains are today. Future wisdom-seekers will be able to achieve today's level of wisdom without the cognitive enhancements offered by increasingly sophisticated digital technology, but that wisdom will not be sufficient, either in quality or in nature, to navigate a complex, technologically advanced world.

Digital Extensions and Enhancements

We are all moving, by fits and starts and each at our own speed, toward digital enhancement. In many ways, we are already there; digital enhancement is or will soon be available for just about everything we do. This includes—and here is the important part—cognition. Digital tools already extend and enhance our cognitive capabilities in a number of ways. Digital technology enhances memory, for example, via data input/output tools and electronic storage. Digital data-gathering and decision-making tools enhance judgment by allowing us to gather more data than we could on our own, helping us perform more complex analyses than we could unaided, and increasing our power to ask "what if?" and pursue all the implications of that question. Digital cognitive enhancement, provided by laptop computers, online databases, three-dimensional virtual simulations, online collaboration tools, personal digital assistants (PDAs), and a range of other, context-specific tools, is a reality in every profession, even in nontechnical fields such as law and the humanities.[1]

We are already becoming dependent on these enhancements. As philosophers Andy Clark and David Chalmers (1998) argue, "extended cognition is a core cognitive process, not an add-on extra," as "the brain develops in a way that complements the external structures and learns to play its role within a unified, densely coupled system" ("Active Externalism," ¶17). As I recently heard a teenager say, expressing this idea more colloquially, "If I lose my cell phone, I lose half my brain." Many would express the same sentiment in regard to a PDA or a laptop computer; we are already embracing a basic level of digital enhancement, and we will accept ever more sophisticated enhancements as technology continues to develop.

These developing technologies, which will connect us more directly to their power by linking to our brains directly, are already here or on the horizon. Two recently released devices, one produced by Smart Brain Technologies and another by Emotive Systems, allow players to control the action in video games using their minds; NeuroSky is working on another version of the technology. The US Air Force is experimenting with using similar technology to train pilots in hands-off flying (*Satnews Daily*, 2008). Other emerging digital tools promise to facilitate communication and enhance understanding; for example, voice-stress analysis tools will allow users to perceive deception and automated translation utilities will help create translations free of human bias. As these tools become widely available, digital enhancement will become even more vital for everyone.

Home Sapiens Digital

What should we call this emerging digitally enhanced person? Homo sapiens digital, or digital human, perhaps. The key to understanding this development is to recognize that it includes both the digital and the wise. As digital enhancements develop, so too will the concept and practice of wisdom.

Wisdom, as any search will quickly show, is a universal but ill-defined concept. Definitions of wisdom fill entire volumes. The *Oxford English Dictionary* suggests that wisdom's main component is judgment, referring to the "Capacity of judging rightly in matters relating to life and conduct, soundness of judgment in the choice of means and ends" (OED, 1989). Philosopher Robert Nozick (1990) suggests that wisdom lies in knowing what is important; other definitions see wisdom as the ability to solve problems—what Aristotle called "practical wisdom." Some definitions—although not all—attribute to wisdom a moral component, locating wisdom in the ability to discern the "right" or "healthy" thing to do. This is, of course, problematic since agreement on moral issues is frequently difficult to come by. So wisdom cannot be conclusively defined without a consideration of context. One interesting definition of wisdom that is particularly useful in this discussion comes from Howard Gardner (2000), who suggests that wisdom may be seen in the breadth of issues considered in arriving at a judgment or decision. Combining these sources, we can define wisdom as the ability to find practical, creative, contextually appropriate, and emotionally satisfying solutions to complicated human problems (as Solomon famously did with the baby problem). Many see it as a more complex kind of problem solving.

As technology becomes more sophisticated, developing the capacity to help us make moral and ethical choices as well as more pragmatic decisions, what we call "human wisdom" will reach new levels. Some of that evolution will arise from the breadth of resources available to the wisdom seeker. More development will emerge from wider access to more experience, provided by hours of exposure to realistic simulation, similar to that required for today's airline pilots and astronauts. It is also possible that reflective capabilities will themselves be enhanced; we are already seeing some evidence of this possibility in the speed with which video game players review previous games, searching for ways to improve before beginning the next game. Future technological tools will allow people engaged in making judgments and decisions to evaluate their decisions very quickly in light of collective past experience, just as today financial strategies can be back-tested on the historical market. And given the enhanced communications possibilities, wisdom will certainly involve a lot more sharing and testing of ideas while they are in formation than is possible today.

Homo sapiens digital, then, differs from today's human in two key aspects: He or she accepts digital enhancement as an integral fact of human existence, and he or she is digitally wise, both in the considered way he or she accesses the power of digital enhancements to complement innate abilities and in the way in which he or she uses enhancements to facilitate wiser decision making. Digital wisdom transcends the generational divide defined by the immigrant/native distinction. Many digital immigrants exhibit digital wisdom. Barack Obama, who grew up in the pre-digital era, showed his digital wisdom in enlisting the power of the Internet to enhance both his fundraising ability and his connection with the American people. Understanding that his judgment is enhanced by his ability to get instant feedback from his closest friends and advisors, he has refused to give up his BlackBerry. Rupert Murdoch, a self-confessed digital immigrant (Murdoch, 2005), has also shown digital wisdom in recognizing the need to add digital newsgathering and dissemination tools to his media empire.

The point is that while the need for wise people to discuss, define, compare, and evaluate perspectives is not changing, the means by which they do so and the quality of their efforts are growing more sophisticated because of digital technology. As a result, the unenhanced brain is well on its way to becoming insufficient for truly wise decision making. When we are all enhanced by implanted lie detectors, logic evaluators, and executive function and memory enhancements—all of which will likely arrive in our children's lifetimes—who among us will be considered wise? The advantage will go, almost certainly, to those who intelligently combine their innate capacities with their digital enhancements.

Wisdom Enhancement

So how can digital technology enhance our minds and lead to greater wisdom? One way to answer this question is to consider where our unenhanced wisdom fails us and explore how technology can enhance our capabilities in those arenas.

As unenhanced humans, we are limited in our perceptions and constrained by the processing power and functioning of the human brain. As a result, we tend to go astray in our thinking in ways that limit our wisdom; for example:

- We make decisions based on only a portion of the available data.
- We make assumptions, often inaccurate, about the thoughts or intentions of others.
- We depend on educated guessing and verification (the traditional scientific method) to find new answers.
- We are limited in our ability to predict the future and construct what-if scenarios.
- We cannot deal well with complexity beyond a certain point.
- We cannot see, hear, touch, feel, or smell beyond the range of our senses.
- We find it difficult to hold multiple perspectives simultaneously.
- We have difficulty separating emotional responses from rational conclusions.
- We forget.

Some of these failures arise because we do not have access to necessary data, while others stem from our inability to conduct complex analyses, derive full understanding from the ever-increasing volumes of data available to us, understand others fully, or access alternative perspectives. All of these factors reduce our capacity to judge situations, evaluate outcomes, and make practical decisions wisely. Fortunately, available and emerging digital tools can allow us to overcome these deficiencies and attain true digital wisdom.

Enhancing Our Access to Data

The human mind cannot remember everything; detailed, voluminous data are quickly lost. In some ways, this is good in that it forces us to be selective, but it also limits our analytical capacity. Digital technology can help by providing databases and algorithms that gather and process vast amounts of data far more efficiently and thoroughly than the human brain can. Expert systems are one example of sophisticated digital tools that can help humans access a wider array of data. These systems gather the expertise of hundreds of human experts in one program in order to provide a more thorough assessment of a given situation than even a highly trained and experienced professional might be able to offer. One example of such a system is the Acute Physiology & Chronic Health Evaluation (APACHE) system, which helps doctors allocate scarce intensive care resources to those patients most in need.[2]

Few would consider it wise to use an expert system such as APACHE as the only decision maker; expert system technology is both imperfect and still in development. But would it be wise for a human to make the decision without at least consulting it? Wise decisions often involve not just ethical considerations but also tradeoffs; in the context of a complex, delicate decision, such as the one to remove a patient from intensive care, those tradeoffs can be difficult to assess. Expert systems and other sophisticated analytical tools allow for a fuller understanding of the risks and benefits inherent in such a decision.

Enhancing our Ability to Conduct Deeper Analyses

In an article provocatively titled "The End of Theory," writer Chris Anderson (2008) describes how the massive amounts of data now being collected and stored by Google and others is allowing a new type of scientific analysis. In many cases, scientists no longer have to make educated guesses, construct hypotheses and models, and test them with data-based experiments and examples. Instead, they can mine the complete set of data for patterns that reveal effects, producing scientific conclusions *without* further experimentation because they can rely on analysis of a complete, digitally stored dataset. In a similar way, Google's advertising tools draw valid and useful conclusions about what works in advertising without actually knowing anything either about what is advertised or about the projected consumers of the advertising. The software draws conclusions based purely on sophisticated analyses of available data; the analyses improve as the amount of data increases (as it does exponentially), and the analysis tools improve as well. This is the same principle, according to Anderson, that allows Google to "translate languages without actually 'knowing' them (given equal corpus data, Google can translate Klingon into Farsi as easily as it can translate French into German)" (2008, p. 5). Here, too, the tools will improve as more data becomes available. Imagine what will happen when the entire universe of everything ever written is available for analysis.

This approach reverses the generally accepted nature of the human/machine coupling. Rather than the mind imagining possibilities that the data confirm or deny, the data announce facts and relationships and the human looks for explanations or—as Google does with advertising—simply uses the relationships to achieve a goal without knowing or caring why they exist. Surely, such ability should lead us to question what wisdom is in such situations and to consider the relationship between mind and machine in producing wisdom in a digital future. Future wisdom will involve as much skill in eliciting relationships as in imagining them.

On the other hand, there are areas where a human mind's ability to imagine relationships will be crucial to attaining digital wisdom. From warfare to architecture to politics, asking "what if?" has always been critical to understanding complex systems, and human wisdom has always included the ability to what-if well. While simulation, practiced for thousands of years in sandbox, mechanical, and thought experiments, is a sophisticated way to explore possible interpretations of data, unenhanced humans are limited in the number of options and end states that they can explore in this way. Pairing human intelligence with digital simulation allows the mind to progress further and faster. A person's ability to create, interpret, and evaluate the models underlying the simulations plays a large role in his or her ability to use them wisely. In the future, more sophisticated simulation algorithms will allow humans to exercise their imaginative capacity in ever-more complex what-if constructions, allowing for more thorough exploration of possibilities and, in turn, wiser decisions. With the introduction of modern simulation games such as *Sim City*, *Roller Coaster Tycoon*, and *Spore*, this kind of digital wisdom enhancement already begins at a very early age.

Enhancing Our Ability to Plan and Prioritize

As the world becomes more complex, planning and prioritization skills far beyond the capability of the unenhanced human brain will be required; digital enhancements will be needed to help us to anticipate second- and third-order effects to which the unaided mind may be blind. The full implications of massive undertakings such as human space travel, the construction of artificial cities in the Arabian Sea, the building of huge machines such as large Hadron colliders, and complex financial dealings such as those that have recently wrought havoc on the economy cannot be fully perceived or assessed by even the wisest unaided minds. Alan Greenspan, for example, is widely considered one of our wisest financial gurus, and yet his assessment of the fundamental workings of our economy was mistaken: "You know," he admitted in a Congressional hearing in October 2008, "that's precisely the reason I was shocked [by the economic downturn], because I have been going more than 40 years or more with very considerable evidence that it was working considerably well" (Leonhardt, 2008). Humans will require digital enhancement in order to achieve a full understanding of these increasingly complex issues and a full sense of the practical wisdom of pursuing them. We currently do not have, in many areas, either the databases of past successes and failures, or the tools to analyze them, that are required to enhance our wisdom and collective memory—but we will going forward.

Enhancing Our Insight into Others

One of the greatest barriers to human understanding and communication is that we cannot see inside another person's mind. This limitation gives rise to unintended misunderstandings and allows people to employ all sorts of deceptive strategies, both consciously and unconsciously. Some of the ways digital technology is helping us overcome this barrier include various means of truth (or lie) detection, multimodal communications, and digital readouts of our own and others' brain waves. Already, researchers at Carnegie Mellon University (CMU), using digital computer analyses of brain patterns captured by functional magnetic resonance imaging (fMRI) scans, are able to tell what a person is thinking about (Mitchell et al., 2008). It is likely, according to these researchers, that our children will, in their lifetimes, be able to read people's thoughts and even have access to direct brain-to-brain communication. While these developments will clearly raise ethical issues and privacy questions that will have to be addressed, there can be little doubt that as people gain access to and learn to take into account others' unspoken motives, thoughts, needs, and judgments in their own thinking, their wisdom will increase.

Enhancing Our Access to Alternate Perspectives

The world is full of things we cannot perceive with our unenhanced senses, things that are too small, too large, too fast, too abstract, too dangerous, or too far away. Exploring these things through digital enhancements will certainly help expand both our understanding of these things and our knowledge of how they can help or hurt us. It will also expand our ability to assume multiple perspectives —to see things from more than one point of view—and, hence, our wisdom. The perception of things outside our normal sensory range can be enhanced digitally in numerous ways, from manipulable three-dimensional simulations to digitally monitored biofeedback controls that enhance mental and sensory states, which may also enhance memory and emotional control. Access to alternative perspectives can also be attained through increasingly sophisticated digital role playing, using simulations in which people can experience difficult and critical situations from various points of view.

There are undoubtedly other ways in which digital technology will enhance our understanding and wisdom. None of these tools will replace the human mind; rather, they will enhance our quest for knowledge and our development of wisdom.

Objections to Digital Enhancement

Not everyone accepts the power of digital enhancement to make us both smarter and wiser. On its July/August 2008 cover, *The Atlantic* magazine asks "Is Google Making Us Stupid?" Google serves as a stand-in for the Internet and digital technology more generally; the author's concern is that digital enhancements such as the Internet make our natural minds lazier and less able (Carr, 2008a). While that is certainly something we should guard against, we must also bear in mind that new technologies have always raised similar objections; as Carr points out, in Plato's *The Phaedrus,* Socrates objects to writing on the basis that it undermines the memory.

In fact, what's happening now is very much the opposite: digital technology is making us smarter. Steven Johnson has documented this in *Everything Bad is Good For You* (2005), in which he argues that the new technologies associated with contemporary popular culture, from video games to the Internet to television and film, make far more cognitive demands on us than did past forms, thus increasing our capabilities in a wide variety of cognitive tasks. As Johnson puts it, "Today's popular culture may not be showing us the righteous path. But it is making us smarter" (p. 14). Socrates was correct in his fear that writing would diminish our memories but was shortsighted in that concern. While we may remember less and memorize less readily than humans in Socrates' day, the addition of writing has made us considerably wiser by expanding our collective memory and increasing our ability to share information across time and distance.

Worries that ubiquitous global positioning system (GPS) devices might diminish our map-reading ability or that spell checkers and calculators will result in a generation that cannot spell or do mental math are similarly shortsighted. Every enhancement comes with a tradeoff: We gave up huge mental memory banks when we started writing things down; we gave up the ability to tell time by the sun when we began carrying pocket watches. But we gained a set of shared cultural memories and a more precise notion of time that fueled the Industrial Revolution. Digital wisdom arises from the combination of the mind and digital tools; what the unenhanced mind loses by outsourcing mundane tasks will be more than made up for by the wisdom gained. Wisdom, and particularly practical wisdom, must be understood in light of the digital enhancements that make it stronger.

Being Digitally Wise

So what constitutes digital wisdom? What habits do the digitally wise use to advance their capabilities and the capabilities of those around them? Can digital wisdom be taught?

Examples of digital wisdom are all around us. Leaders are digitally wise when they use available techniques to connect with their constituents for polling and to solicit contributions and encourage participation, as Barack Obama did so well in the 2008 US presidential campaign. Journalists are digitally wise when they take advantage of participative technologies such as blogs and wikis to enlarge their perspectives and those of their audience. Nicolas Carr exhibited digital wisdom in posting his notes and sources for his *Atlantic* article on his blog in response to reader requests for more information (Carr, 2008b). Digital wisdom can be, and must be, learned and taught. As we offer more courses in digital literacy, we should also offer students guidance in developing digital wisdom. Parents and educators are digitally wise when they recognize this imperative and prepare the children in their care for the future—educators by letting students learn by using new technologies, putting themselves in the role of guides, context providers, and quality controllers, and parents by recognizing the extent to which the future will be mediated by technology and encouraging their children to use digital technology wisely.

The digitally wise distinguish between digital wisdom and mere digital cleverness, and they do their best to eradicate digital dumbness when it arises.[3] They know that just knowing how to use particular technologies makes one no wiser than just knowing how to read words does. Digital wisdom means not just manipulating technology easily or even creatively; it means making wiser decisions because one is enhanced by technology. Therefore, the digitally wise look for the cases where technology enhances thinking and understanding. No digitally wise leader would make any major decision, no digitally wise scientist would come to any conclusion without digital tools enhancing their own thinking. They may rely on intuition, but that intuition is informed, inspired, and supported by digital enhancements and by the additional data digital tools provide. Those who are truly digitally wise do not resist their digitally enhanced selves but accept them gladly, even as they make careful judgments about what digital enhancements are appropriate and when.

Being digitally wise involves not only enhancing our natural capabilities with existing technologies but also continuously identifying additional areas where our natural human tools—even when they are developed to a very high level—cannot do the job unaided. As new digital tools appear, especially ones that take hold in a strong way, the digitally wise seek them out actively. They investigate and evaluate the positives as well as the negatives of new tools and figure out how to strike the balance that turns tools into wisdom enhancers.

The digitally wise also realize that the ability to control digital technology, to bend it to their needs, is a key skill in the digital age. As a result, they are interested in programming, in the broadest sense of the word—that is, in making machines do what people want them to do.

Conclusion

Within the lifetimes of our children, more powerful digital mental enhancements —the embedded chips and brain manipulations of science fiction—will become a reality, just as gene manipulation, long considered a far-off dream, is with us now. Just as we have begun to confront the ethical, moral, and scientific challenges presented by genetic medicine, we will have to confront the issue of digital wisdom sooner or later, and we will be better off doing it sooner. Many of these enhancements will bring ethical dilemmas, but the digitally wise will distinguish between true ethical issues (is the enhancement safe? is it available equally to all?) and mere preferences and prejudices.

Nobody suggests that people should stop using and improving their unaided minds, but I am opposed to those who claim the unenhanced mind and unaided thinking are somehow superior to the enhanced mind. To claim this is to deny all of human progress, from the advent of writing to the printing press to the Internet. Thinking and wisdom have become, in our age, a symbiosis of the human brain and its digital enhancements.

I do not think technology is wise in itself (although some day it may be) or that human thinking is no longer necessary or important. It is through the interaction of the human mind and digital technology that the digitally wise person is coming to be. I believe it is time for the emerging digitally wise among us, youth and adults alike, to embrace digital enhancement and to encourage others to do so. With our eyes wide open to enhancement's potential harm as well as its benefits, let us bring our colleagues, students, teachers, parents, and peers to the digital wisdom of the twenty-first century.

Acknowledgments

A version of this article was originally published in *Innovate* (www.innovateonline.info) in 2009 as "H. sapiens digital: From digital immigrants and digital natives to digital wisdom." It is reprinted here with permission of the author.

Notes

1 A somewhat different type of mind extension, which I will touch on here only in passing, is the use of cognition-enhancing drugs by healthy people, particularly by college students. Greeley et al. (2008) report that more and more students are routinely taking drugs such as Ritalin and Adderal that "increase executive functions" and "improve their abilities to focus their attention, manipulate information in working memory and flexibly control their responses" (Greeley et al., 2008, "Paths to Enhancement," ¶1). The authors, a group of respected scientists and ethicists, support this practice, encouraging the responsible use of "cognitive enhancement tools—including the pharmacological," by healthy people, claiming the drugs "will be increasingly useful for improved quality of life and extended work productivity, as well as to stave off normal and pathological age related cognitive declines" (Greeley et al., 2008, "Conclusion," ¶1). Even pharmacological cognitive enhancement can be seen as an outgrowth of digital enhancements: modern synthesized cognition-enhancing drugs would not be possible without the digital tools for creating them.

2 The APACHE system was created by medical researchers and doctors seeking a better way to determine which patients should be retained in a hospital's intensive care unit

when beds became scarce. The system worked by comparing key statistics for a particular patient with millions of cases with similar characteristics in order to project likely outcomes. The system capsulized its analysis into a number for each patient, called the APACHE score. A higher score meant that the patient stayed in intensive care; a lower score meant the patient left.

It seems startling that a single, computer-generated number could even be considered useful in making such a potentially life-or-death decision, and even more so that it could carry as much weight as a doctor's personal evaluation. The reasoning behind the APACHE score is that, while there are some things the human brain is very good at, it tends to focus too much attention on two types of occurrences: the recent and the unusual. While that sometimes serves us very well, it is much better, for decisions like this, to take into account every relevant case. That is something that, in an unaided state, the human mind is just not capable of doing.

And the system works. APACHE III:

> has been shown to be predictive of in-hospital mortality rate. It has performed equally well in community based and academic settings. [But] the APACHE, like other scoring systems presents some limitations. It is dependent on an operator and requires a long period of training to be used efficiently.
>
> (Murabito, Rubulotta, & Gullo, 2008, p. 349)

The point is not that machines are better than the human mind; the point is that the mind and the machine together produce the wisest decisions.

3 Does digitally wise imply digitally dumb as well? It most certainly does, and we already see a lot of digitally dumb behavior. Although the term is demeaning, it is an apt description of behavior that misuses technology to escape unpleasantness or cause harm rather than using it to enhance wisdom.

Digital dumbness includes acts of digital plagiarism, such as deliberately appropriating online materials without regard for copyright or proper attribution. The new sin here is not the cheating—that's happened forever—rather, it's the digital stupidity of not understanding the consequences of one's digital acts and of using technology not to acquire wisdom but to avoid an onerous task.

Being digitally dumb goes even further. It includes having access to digital technologies that are potentially enhancing yet refusing to consider the advantages they may offer. It includes summarily dismissing, based on old thinking, tradition, or unconsidered prejudice, the potential benefits of technology for thinking or wisdom enhancement. And it includes using technology in a thoughtless rather than a wisdom-enhancing way.

Just as digital wisdom may transcend age or other categories, people of any age or profession can be digitally dumb. People of all ages leave sensitive data on accessible computers, misuse email in incriminating ways, or forget to back up critical files. But as a description, "digitally dumb" applies to behavior, not people; even the most unaware can certainly move toward digital wisdom by becoming aware of the repercussions of their behavior and of the potential of behaving in a way that is digitally wise.

References

Anderson, C. (2008). The end of theory: The data deluge makes the scientific method obsolete. *Wired Magazine, 16*(7). Retrieved January 28, 2009, from www.wired.com/science/discoveries/magazine/16–07/pb_theory

Carr, N. (2008a). Is Google making us stupid? What the internet is doing to our brains. *The Atlantic, 301*(6), 56–63. Retrieved January 28, 2010, from www.theatlantic.com/doc/200807/google

Carr, N. (2008b). "Is Google making us stupid?": Sources and notes. [Weblog entry, August 7.] *Rough Type*. Retrieved January 29, 2010, from www.roughtype.com/archives/2008/08/is_google_makin.php

Clark, A., & Chalmers, D. J. (1998). The extended mind. *Analysis, 58*, 7–19. Retrieved January 28, 2010, from http://consc.net/papers/extended.html

Gardner, H. (2000). *Intelligence reframed: Multiple intelligences for the 21st century*. New York: Basic Books.

Greeley, H., Sahakian, B., Harris, J., Kessler, R. C., Gazzaniga, M., Campbell, P., & Farah, M. J. (2008). Toward responsible use of cognitive-enhancing drugs by the healthy. *Nature, 456*, 702–705. Retrieved January 28, 2009, from www.nature.com/nature/journal/vaop/ncurrent/full/456702a.html

Johnson, S. B. (2005). *Everything bad is good for you*. New York: Riverhead Books.

Leonhardt, D. (2008). Greenspan's mea culpa. [Weblog entry, October 23.] *Economix*. Retrieved January 28, 2009, from http://economix.blogs.nytimes.com/2008/10/23/greenspans-mea-culpa

Mitchell, T. M., Shinkareva, S. V., Carlson, A., Chang, K., Malave, V. L., Mason, R. A., & Just, M. A. (2008). Predicting human brain activity associated with the meanings of nouns. *Science, 320*, 1191–1195.

Murabito, P., Rubulotta, F., & Gullo, A. (2008). Quality management in the ICU: Understanding the process and improving the art. In A. Gullo (Ed.), *Anesthesia, pain, intensive care, and emergency: Proceedings of the 22nd postgraduate course in critical care medicine, Venice-Mestre, Italy, November 9–11, 2007* (pp. 345–404). Milan, Italy: Springer-Verlag Italia.

Murdoch, R. (2005). Speech to the American society of newspaper editors, April 13. Retrieved January 26, 2009, from www.newscorp.com/news/news_247.html

Nozick, R. (1990). *The examined life: Philosophical meditations*. New York: Simon & Schuster-Touchstone.

Oxford English Dictonary (2nd ed.). (1989). "Wisdom," definition 1a. Oxford: Oxford University Press.

Prensky, M. (2001a). Digital natives, digital immigrants. *On the Horizon, 9*(5), 1–6. Retrieved January 28, 2009, from www.scribd.com/doc/9799/Prensky-Digital-Natives-Digital-Immigrants-Part1

Prensky, M. (2001b). Digital natives, digital immigrants, Part II: Do they really think differently? *On the Horizon, 9*(6), 1–6. Retrieved January 28, 2009, from www.twitchspeed.com/site/Prensky%20-%20Digital%20Natives,%20Digital%20Immigrants%20-%20Part2.htm

Prensky, M. (2006). Digital natives, digital immigrants: Origins of terms. Retrieved June 10, 2010, from www.marcprensky.com/blog/archives/2006_06.html

Prensky, M. (2009). H. sapiens digital: From digital immigrants and digital natives to digital wisdom. *Innovate, 5*(3). Retrieved February 4, 2009, from www.innovateonline.info/index.php?view=article&id=705

Satnews Daily (2008). Hands off F-16 lands using Lockheed Martin computer control technology. December 11. Retrieved January 28, 2009 www.satnews.com/cgi-bin/story.cgi?number=1057554591

3

STUDENTS, THE NET GENERATION, AND DIGITAL NATIVES

Accounting for Educational Change

Chris Jones

Introduction

This chapter examines a number of different terms and popularized accounts of young people who are now at the stage in their lives of engaging in university education across the world. Students are an interesting group because they remove a significant demographic factor that often differentiates groups in society—that is, educational background (Hargittai, 2010). University students also have a generally high level of network connectivity and access to resources. If a digitally aware generation is emerging then this is a social arena in which it has been generally assumed the effects of change will be most in evidence (Oblinger & Oblinger, 2005). Three of the more common terms that have been used to describe this cohort of young people are the "Net Generation" (Tapscott, 1998, 2009), "Digital Natives" (Prensky, 2001a; 2001b, 2009), and "Millennials" (Howe & Strauss, 2000; Oblinger & Oblinger, 2005).

While there are many common strands linking these descriptions, each term carries with it some particular features. For example, there is no agreed point at which the new generation is said to arise. Tapscott starts the new generation with extreme precision in January 1977 and ends it with a further generational shift into Generation Next in December 1997 (Tapscott, 2009, p. 16). Prensky, however, does not specify any particular year, while other authors using the term "Digital Native" have been more precise and argued that digital natives appear after 1980 (Palfrey & Gasser, 2008, p. 1). Oblinger and Oblinger (2005) following Howe and Strauss (2000) put a precise date on the Millennials, suggesting that they were born "in or after 1982" (Oblinger, 2003, p. 38). Unlike Howe and Strauss, Oblinger and Oblinger also provide an end date for the Millennial grouping in 1991 (Oblinger & Oblinger, 2005). All these authors suggest that the generational boundary is sharp and that a short period of time would make a significant difference to young people's attitudes. Indeed, Prensky writes about a "discontinuity" or "singularity" marking out this new generation (Prensky, 2001a).

The literature concerning the Net Generation and digital natives provides very little theoretical argument about how this generational effect arises. The argument for a Millennial generation, by contrast, rests on a sweeping historical analysis, which covers most if not all of American history. In *Grown Up Digital* (2009) Tapscott has reported a $4 million dollar research project, but in his writing he draws on no strong theoretical account to explain how an entire generation has developed a distinct and novel set of ideas and approaches to new technology and life more generally (2009, pp. 1–3). Rather Tapscott tells us that he "noticed" that his children and their friends were all "talented" in relation to new technology and that the reason for their talents was that: "they were the first to grow up surrounded by digital technology" (2009, p. 2). At a more general level Tapscott provides the following account for generational change: "Each generation is exposed to a unique set of events that defines their place in history and shapes their outlook" (2009, p. 16). An alternative account can be found in the writings of Prensky, who developed the idea of the digital native, a group he described by drawing an extended contrast with older "Digital Immigrants" to identify a similar generational change (2001a, 2001b, 2009). The arguments found in both the Net Generation and digital natives literature is that the existence of an environment infused with digital and networked technologies and the interaction of young people with that environment on a significant scale leads directly to a generational break between young people and all previous generations.

This chapter critically examines the argument, common to writers using both terms: that the existence of an environment infused with digital and networked technologies, combined with an active engagement in these new technologies, leads directly to a sharp generational break. The chapter goes on to examine the determinist nature of the argument and the way this has been related to one particular pedagogical approach: collaborative learning. It examines the wider social and technological context and in particular the ideas of networked individualism and networked sociality. Finally, the chapter concludes by examining which aspects of the digital native and Net Generation arguments are worth taking forward and identifying those aspects of the arguments that need to be abandoned.

Technological Determinism

A striking feature of Net Generation and digital native discourses is a particular understanding of the relationship between technologies and change. Tapscott (1998, 2009) has argued that an entire generation of young people is different to previous generational cohorts because of its experience of networked and digital technologies. For over ten years Tapscott has claimed to identify a generational shift that includes significant changes in attitudes and approaches to learning. Tapscott has suggested that it is because of changes in technology that there have been some "inevitable" consequences for learning. In particular, Tapscott has argued that the ultimate interactive environment is the Internet itself and that education needs to follow those young people who grew up with the new technologies and move from what he describes as a teacher-centered approach to learning to learner-centered approaches: "But as we make this inevitable transition we may best turn to the generation raised on and immersed in new technologies" (Tapscott, 1999, p. 11). By teacher-centered Tapscott means a transmission model of education in which the teacher or lecturer imparts knowledge to the student. Learner-centered in Tapscott's view places the focus on the individual student's activity.

Prensky, using the term "Digital Natives" (Prensky, 2001a, 2001b), has also argued that there has been a generational step change in attitudes and styles and that the emergence of digital natives leads to a significant change:

> A really big discontinuity has taken place. One might even call it a "singularity"—an event which changes things so fundamentally that there is absolutely no going back.
>
> (Prensky, 2001a, p. 1)

Prensky's comments were not limited to students in universities, and like Tapscott he identifies an entire generation. Prensky suggests the new generation thinks differently and he goes on to make the claim that the brains of the new generation are different from previous generations (Prensky, 2001b). Fundamentally, both authors suggest that there has been a generational change caused by a process of technological change.

Technological change is often seen as arising independently and then having an impact on other dependent domains in society. Even when technological change is not seen as independent, it is often described as an inevitable outcome of social development. Writing about the discourses that surround children's use of technology in 2003, Selwyn noted that:

> The six different discourses presented in this article also ultimately conform to one of the two dominant paradigms that characterize societal discussion of technology in general. All the stories are underpinned by either a technological or a social determinism, where information technologies are presented as an inevitable consequence of either technological development or the technological needs and requirements of society.
>
> (Selwyn, 2003, p. 367)

Selwyn goes on to note that the problem with such discourses is that they fundamentally fail to reflect the diversity and complexity to be found in real lives.

This weakness in the discourses can have real impacts on the way these views are taken up and embedded in policy. It also leads to the position whereby "the framing of children, adults and technology within these determinist discourses tends to hide the key shaping actors, the values and power relations behind the increasing use of ICT in society" (Selwyn, 2003, p. 368).

A similar problem can be seen in relation to the older population entering university. Students are described as different from their teachers in generational terms and the university as an institution is portrayed as threatened by new Internet-based technologies. Change is not an option or a choice, it is "inexorable," an "imperative":

> Universities are losing their grip on higher learning as the Internet is, inexorably, becoming the dominant infrastructure for knowledge—both as a container and as a global platform for knowledge exchange between people—and as a new generation of students requires a very different model of higher education. Many people have written about this topic, in EDUCAUSE Review and other publications. The transformation of the university is not just a good idea. It is an imperative, and evidence is mounting that the consequences of further delay may be dire.
>
> (Tapscott & Williams, 2010, p. 18)

This rhetoric about the kind of changes required in universities has led Bennett et al. (2008) to argue, in relation to digital natives, that the discourse resembles an academic "moral panic" by restricting critical and rational debate. Moral panic is a term that has arisen to describe conditions in which an identified group in society is portrayed as a threat to social values and norms. The identified group is placed in a media spotlight and often described in sensational terms as a threat to the status quo. Digital natives and the Net Generation can perform this role in relation to universities and university teaching. Compare the idea of a moral panic with Tapscott and Williams' account of the necessity for radical change:

> Change is required in two vast and interwoven domains that permeate the deep structures and operating model of the university: (1) the value created for the main customers of the university (the students); and (2) the model of production for how that value is created. First we need to toss out the old industrial model of pedagogy (how learning is accomplished) and replace it with a new model called collaborative learning. Second we need an entirely new *modus operandi* for how the subject matter, course materials, texts, written and spoken word, and other media (the content of higher education) are created.
>
> (Tapscott & Williams, 2010, p. 10)

The changes they advocate are not minor or superficial; they permeate the "deep structures and operating model" of the university. Fundamental change in the university is predicated on changes taking place in an identified subgroup in the population, young people identified as a Net Generation of digital natives: "A powerful force to change the university is the students. And sparks are flying today. A huge generational clash is emerging in our institutions" (Tapscott & Williams, 2010, p. 29). The determinism is complete—not only are young people determined by their technological environment to become a Net Generation, but that generation then becomes the motor for change in universities. According to Tapscott and Williams a generational clash is a major force for university transformation. The criticism of technological determinism in this context is not new (e.g., Buckingham & Willett, 2006; Herring, 2008) and the interests that might influence the popularity of this outlook are not hard to find. Bayne and Ross (2007) identify the role of the market, commercial interests, and a one-way determinism concerning change in institutions that leads to a deficit model of professional development (see also Jones & Healing, forthcoming).

Tapscott and Williams offer two solutions to universities, first, the adoption of collaborative learning and, second, collaborative knowledge building. The first of these has been a longstanding part of the argument that Tapscott has developed around the Net Generation and appeared in his earlier writings (1998). It is in line with arguments that arose with the first introduction of the Internet in university teaching, which stressed cooperation and collaboration as the best means of making use of the asynchronous text-based media, such as computer conferencing (Kaye, 1992; McConnell, 1994). The second solution takes things further by arguing for an entirely new *modus operandi* for universities involving the opening up of the institution to allow collaboration among institutions and between institutions and the wider world. It would be mistaken to believe that this argument is itself entirely new. The suggestion that students could select from among the world's best professors and assemble their own program of study predated the Internet (Illich, 1970) and became a powerful argument in the earliest days of Internet-enabled higher education (Harasim, 1990). In the hands of Tapscott and Williams this argument takes a free-market neo-liberal turn, suggesting that private initiative and the market should replace existing models. They only retain a role for government in the building of the digital infrastructure, such as broadband networks, that would allow such private commercial approaches to succeed.

Bates (2010) argues that Tapscott and Williams miss the main point because: "The interesting question is not what universities should be doing, but why it isn't happening" (Bates, 2010, n.p.). Bates goes on to question the underlying presumption of Tapscott and Williams, which asserts that the problem in universities is the "obstructive, non-market-based business models" (Tapscott & Williams, 2010, p. 29). Bates' criticism focuses on three main points:

- That the "new" constructivism identified by Tapscott and Williams is not in fact new.

- That constructivist methods require staff/student ratios that have been eroded in cost-cutting drives for efficiency in universities.
- That privatization would harm some of the most basic and essential functions of university (e.g., knowledge creation and autonomy).

Bates argues that the future of university provision is a choice not a technological requirement, and that while technological change can help in the reform of university teaching and learning, resistance to change arises more from issues of funding, organization, and vision than it does from a non-market form of organization. The key question for the purposes of this chapter is in relation to the determinism inherent in Net Generation and digital natives arguments and it is the issue of choice. To what degree do the technological and age-related changes affecting young people leave universities with little or no choice about their future?

Collaborative Learning

Technological changes consequent on the development of the Internet have been linked to cooperative and collaborative forms of learning for many years. Computer conferencing was identified in the late 1980s and early 1990s as a technology that inclined users towards cooperative or collaborative learning techniques (Kaye, 1992; McConnell, 1994; O'Malley, 1995). In two complementary texts issued as part of the NATO ASI series, computer conferencing was identified as a key area for research into collaborative methods with its own specific design issues based on the textual and asynchronous nature of the medium (Kaye, 1992; O'Malley, 1995). In this debate about collaborative learning the contrast was often drawn with the transmission model:

> Learning based on a transmissive or information-processing model of education, where the main learning activity is the individual reception and organisation of information and books, lectures, videos or computer based training materials is not collaborative.
>
> (Kaye, 1992, p. 2)

The traditional method of teaching suggested in this contrast with collaboration was the direct transfer of knowledge from the tutor or lecturer by a largely one-way transmission. A common phrase used to describe the changes taking place in teaching and tutoring was, from the "sage on the stage" to the "guide on the side." We might note in passing that the transmission model was always something of a gloss. As Macbeth has pointed out, education even in its most traditional form, contains many elements of cooperation and collaboration enabling the transmission of knowledge (Macbeth, 1990).

Tapscott and Williams make similar claims in their recent article, suggesting that the traditional model is a broadcast model and that: "A broadcast is, by definition, the transmission of information from transmitter to receiver in a one-way, linear fashion" (Tapscott & Williams, 2010, p. 20). This claim ignores an entire literature that has grown up over many years concerning media consumption that emphasizes the active role of the audience in any broadcast medium:

> At one pole there have been models of media consumption which stress the power of the media (or Cultural industries) and correspondingly treat media audiences as relatively passive and powerless, "victims" of various kinds of media effects. Against this, especially in recent years a variety of approaches have been developed, which lay more or less stress on media consumption, on the active process, in which audience members are understood not only actively to select from the range of media materials available to them but also to be active in the different uses, interpretations and "decoding" of the material which they consume.
>
> (Morley, 1995, p. 296)

Tapscott and Williams are taking a very crude media-effects position in which the student audience has a largely passive role.

The audience, in general terms, is by no means passive and co-constructs meaning with the resource transmitted and the sender of that resource. Equally, the sender of a message always has an audience in mind, and there is a dialogic component to any broadcast (Bakhtin, 1986). Let us take this further. Any communication is in some sense a broadcast. When I speak to someone, whether they are present or not, I construct a message and transmit it to a prospective receiver. Collaboration rests on this essentially broadcast base. There can be no common understanding without communication and no communication without the mechanism that Tapscott and Williams define as broadcast. Furthermore, Tapscott and Williams appear to endorse aspects of broadcast in their collaborative model for universities. Students access video lectures of key professors; faculty share resources and make use of open resources. All these features are adaptations of a broadcast model. Overall, this reminds me of the false polarization between metaphors that Sfard criticized using the terms "acquisition" and "participation" (Sfard, 1998). Sfard argued that:

> When a theory is translated into an instructional prescription, exclusivity becomes the worst enemy of success. Educational practices have an over-powering propensity for extreme, one-for-all practical recipes. A trendy mixture of constructivist, social-interactionist, and situationist approaches—which has much to do with the *participation metaphor*—is often translated into a total banishment of "teaching by telling," an imperative to make

> "cooperative learning" mandatory to all, and a complete delegitimatization of instruction that is not "problem-based" or not situated in a real-life context. But this means putting too much of a good thing into one pot.
>
> (Sfard, 1998, p. 10)

The deterministic argument about the Net Generation has taken a further step with the argument that universities must change in a radical pro-market and neo-liberal fashion in order to meet the challenges posed by the new generation of students. The arguments that Tapscott and Williams (2010) advance are not new, as Bates has already noted (2010). Indeed, they reprise arguments that pre-date the emergence of a Net Generation age group and they take the form of a deterministic claim that collaborative learning is an outcome of technological change.

Digital Wisdom

Writing in Chapter 2 and previously about the terms "Digital Native" and "Digital Immigrant" Marc Prensky has commented that:

> Although many have found the terms useful, as we move further into the 21st century when all will have grown up in the era of digital technology, the distinction between digital natives and digital immigrants will become less relevant. Clearly, as we work to create and improve the future, we need to imagine a new set of distinctions. I suggest we think in terms of digital wisdom.
>
> (Prensky, 2009, p. 1)

Leaving aside the assumption that all will have grown up in an undifferentiated way in the era of digital technologies, Prensky retains many of his previous arguments. He retains a modified form of the claim that use of digital technologies changes the brain of the user: "The brains of wisdom seekers of the future will be fundamentally different, in organization and in structure, than our brains are today" (Prensky, 2009, p. 1). Furthermore, he continues to claim that the use of digital technologies is essential: "in an unimaginably complex future, the digitally unenhanced person, however wise, will not be able to access the tools of wisdom that will be available to even the least wise digitally enhanced human" (Prensky, 2009, p. 1). The significant shift Prensky makes is that he now views everyone as moving towards digital enhancement, and he has abandoned or, more accurately, reduced the divide he previously identified between Natives and Immigrants. Prensky defines wisdom, the key term in this turn in his argument: "as the ability to find practical, creative, contextually appropriate, and emotionally satisfying solutions to complicated human problems" (Prensky, 2009, p. 2). Prensky sums up this revised position in this way:

> Homo sapiens digital, then, differs from today's human in two key aspects: He or she accepts digital enhancement as an integral fact of human existence, and he or she is digitally wise, both in the considered way he or she accesses the power of digital enhancements to complement innate abilities and in the way in which he or she uses enhancements to facilitate wiser decision making. Digital wisdom transcends the generational divide defined by the immigrant/native distinction.
>
> (Prensky, 2009, p. 3)

Prensky's revised position is still deterministic; it suggests that digital enhancement is essential, and even though it moves beyond a straightforward divide between immigrants and natives, the argument retains a simple moral imperative: digital enhancement has to be accepted in order to succeed. The move that Prensky makes is from a hard form of technological determinism, claiming that technology has created the divide between natives and immigrants, to a soft form of determinism in which digital enhancement is necessary for everyone if they are to succeed in the new digital world. This determinism links to wider arguments, for example about education and Web 2.0, that encourage panic and a competitive logic focused on social change and the way the demands for a new workforce affect students:

> As society and the world of work change, the skills that students need to live and thrive in it also change. The competition will be fierce and can come from anywhere in this flat world. In some ways, students today are ahead of their elders. Technology is second nature to them and they accept and use it without question. Schools lag behind.
>
> (Solomon & Schrum, 2007, p. 17)

While Prensky has softened the edges of the immigrant–native divide, he retains a deterministic argument that relies on a technology driven imperative for educational change.

Generations

Howe and Strauss wrote the book *Millennials Rising* (2000) several years after the book they co-authored arguing a general case about generations in the United States. The earlier book *Generations: The History of America's Future and The Fourth Turning: An American Prophecy* (1991) articulated a cyclical view of history that suggested that the history of the United States had followed a regular and predictable pattern since the sixteenth century. They argue that there are four turnings in a ninety-year-long cycle, with each turning having a length of approximately twenty-two years. In this context, the "Millennials" are simply a recent outcrop of a long historical process and the fusion of the idea of the Net Generation with the idea of Millennials in the work of Oblinger and Oblinger (2005) can be seen as cementing this cyclical generational view into the idea of a Net Generation in education. In Howe and Strauss the length of the period of a saeculum is between eighty and a hundred years, and it corresponds to a full human lifespan. The four turnings that occur within a saeculum are periods of just over twenty years and they contain generational cohorts—groups of people who share the same defining experiences. In this context, it could be argued that the Net Generation was a purely US phenomenon, corresponding to the final generation prior to a new crisis occurring somewhere between 2010 and 2025. Millennials, although described by their digital and networked technological context, are part of a much more long-term process rooted in human history, biology, and culture. In this scheme they are just the most recent form of the civic generation, who are said to be heroic, collegial, and rationalistic. Interestingly they are also said to have core values that include community, technology, and affluence.

Although it would be farfetched to say that those who use the term Net Generation adhere to this strong generational stance, it has had a clear influence on thinking about young people. Oblinger and Oblinger, for example, clearly build on Howe and Strauss in their book *Educating the Net Generation* (2005). While Oblinger and Oblinger are careful to state their claims cautiously, they roughly associate the new generation, drawn directly from Howe and Strauss, with the Net Generation defined in terms of its exposure to technology. The generational argument does not have any real academic support and a review of relevant literature from a human resources perspective draws attention to a series of weaknesses, both in the sources of support and the practical implications drawn from the generational argument (Giancola, 2006). Empirical work examining the nature of young university students has found that young students entering university are a more complex group than the literature would lead observers to expect (Czerniewicz et al., 2009; Hargittai, 2010; Jones et al., 2010; Kennedy et al., 2008). Kennedy et al. (2008) found that in terms of use of technologies, among first-year Australian students, there was significant diversity when looking beyond the basic and entrenched technologies. They found that the patterns of access to, use of, and preference for a range of other technologies varied considerably. In a similar vein, Jones et al. (2010) report that English first-year students show significant age-related variations, but these are not generational in character and the Net Generation age group is itself divided internally. Both studies suggest that while age is a factor there is no single Net Generation or digital native group and that first-year university students show a diversity that is inconsistent with a generational hypothesis.

Networked Individualism and Networked Sociality

Castells, drawing on work by Wellman, has described the social form taken by the network society as networked individualism (Castells, 2001; Wellman, 2001;

Wellman et al., 2003). Wellman has characterized this kind of relationship in relation to community, stressing that community can be found in networks rather than groups:

> In networked societies: boundaries are permeable, interactions are with diverse others, connections switch between multiple networks, and hierarchies can be flatter and recursive.
>
> (Wellman, 2001, p. 17)

The term "networked individualism" suggests a move away from place-to-place interaction towards interactions that are person-to-person in character. The pattern of social life enabled by networked digital technologies is one that allows for a sociability based on the person, connecting people through geographically dispersed social networks. Rather than classic notions of community and collaboration, networked individualism allows for a new network sociality (Wettel, 2001). The new networks rely as much on weak ties as they do on the strong ties of traditional groups and communities (Jones, 2008).

A related move in education is away from the institutional provision of learning systems, variously called learning management systems (LMSs), course management systems (CMSs), and virtual learning environments (VLEs)—such as Blackboard, WebCT, and their open source competitors Moodle and Sakai—and towards personal learning environments (PLEs) (Weller, 2007). This is not a simple move determined by technology, and there are significant institutional constraints on how far and how fast such a move can take place (see, for example, the blog posting from my own university, linking to a course-related podcast, Weller, 2009). As one might expect in an era of digital scholarship, much of the discussion of this topic has taken place in blog postings, and so it is difficult to find a peer-reviewed reference to stand as a permanent record of the debate. However, a recent article by Weller (2010) provides an accessible introduction. A significant aspect of the blog debate is that for all the technological advances referenced in it, it is fundamentally about choice. Choices made about what kind of education we wish to provide and about what kinds of social environments we think are most conducive to teaching and learning. Networked societies may tend in a certain direction but we can choose how to work with these tendencies, we can go along with them or stand in some form of opposition to them.

The emphasis on choice, in terms of the discussion about networked individualism, stands in sharp contrast to the deterministic form that the Net Generation and digital natives debate has taken. Bennett and Maton (2010) suggest that networked individualism places the focus on the individual who navigates through their own personal networks. This focus on choice is welcome, but it may be insufficient as the choices people make are in conditions that they themselves are not able to control. In a related article, Jones and Healing (2010) argue that choice cannot be confined to the individual and that choices are made at various levels of social scale, including in universities, departments, and whole institutions. Decisions about what kind of infrastructure to provide for students has an impact on the range of choices that students are faced with. Universities may decide to pursue one version or another of a PLE, or they may decide that institutional requirements make it important for the university to retain strong institutional boundaries and to resist the pressures that lead to the adoption of personal learning environments in the university (Weller, 2010).

Discussion—Digital Natives as Digital Phrenology?

In the mid-nineteenth century the idea that the shape of a person's skull could be related to the development of localized brain functions and character traits related to the mind became popular. The pseudo-science of phrenology has entered the popular consciousness as an example of an outlandish idea that can become highly popular and resistant to refutation. Indeed, it is still possible today to find phrenology-influenced websites, despite the idea having been systematically undermined for over a century (see, for example, www.phrenology.org). Phrenology is interesting because, although a flawed approach to a topic, it did point towards a significant approach to the brain, the idea that there were localized functions in different parts of the brain. It is also interesting because of its resistance to refutation. For the purposes of this chapter it offers a parallel to the idea of a new Net Generation of digital natives. These approaches both point towards potentially significant age-related changes in the activities of young people who have grown up in environments that are heavily interpenetrated by digital and networked technologies. The approach they take has, however, been shown to be a poor predictor of the actual changes taking place as, although they have an age-related component and that is perhaps the most important one of several, it does not follow generational lines nor is it universal, applying in all states or regional areas in the same way. As with phrenology, it is also highly resistant to refutation. Many of those who are critical of the theories have had the experience of making a presentation that identifies the weaknesses and draws on detailed empirical work only to hear someone who has just endorsed the speaker's comments revert almost immediately to a way of thinking that is deeply ingrained with the idea of a Net Generation being composed of digital natives.

There are some good reasons for this persistence. First, there is a general need to stereotype in order to reduce complexity and to apply simplified rules of thumb. Perhaps because of this, some work has tried to replace the idea of a Net Generation and digital natives with a new replacement metaphor such as "visitors" and "residents" (see, for example, the Tall Blog: Online Education with the University of Oxford 2008). In this revised metaphor the generational terms "immigrants" and "natives" are replaced by an experiential divide between "residents" and "visitors." A resident spends a proportion of their life online whereas a visitor uses the Web as a tool to address their specific needs. My own view is that this resort to alternative metaphors is a mistake, and when I am asked whether there is a better metaphor I always reply that we are best advised to remove the use of metaphors, in this topic area, because they have been so pervasive and misleading. As noted above, others have described the terms as part of a "moral panic" (Bennett et al., 2008) and as with all moral panics the idea is that the Net Generation and digital native descriptions are part of a disproportionate response by academics to a perceived threat contained in the new digital and networked technologies that are having an impact on education and society. Most importantly, the debate about the ideas contained in the digital native and Net Generation arguments is closed down, or narrowed, allowing the continued circulation of ideas without supporting evidence. As noted above, Buckingham and Willett (2006), Herring (2008), and Bayne and Ross (2007) have all pointed to the commercial and market interest in perpetuating the idea of a new generation that requires certain kinds of technological change. Selwyn noted that the persistence of the six discourses he identified in relation to children's use of computers had a relationship to the market:

> Thus it can be argued that the six discursive constructions of child computer users identified in this article are all predominantly attempts to "sell" information technology to the adult population.
>
> (Selwyn, 2003, p. 368)

There is no doubt that commercial and market interests play a part in the persistence of the Net Generation and digital native arguments.

Conclusion

The argument that there is a sharp generational break between a group of young people who are immersed in new technologies—however they are defined and described—and older generational groups who are less familiar with technology, has persisted despite repeated reports of empirical work that undermine the basic case (Czerniewicz et al., 2009; Hargittai, 2010; Jones et al., 2010; Kennedy et al., 2008). There are potentially two different arguments about the changes taking place among young people. The first argument, and the one that is most associated with the idea of the Net Generation and digital natives, is that:

- The ubiquitous nature of certain technologies, specifically gaming and the Web, *has affected the outlook of an entire age cohort* in advanced economies.

A second, related but distinct argument is that:

- The new technologies emerging with this generation have particular characteristics that *afford certain types of social engagement.*

It is the first of these arguments that we may need to abandon in the face of the empirical evidence. The second argument, like the idea of localized functions of the brain in phrenology, is the rational kernel at the heart of the argument. A good reason why the Net Generation and digital native arguments persist is because they draw attention to the way new technologies are changing the approaches that young people take, not in generational ways, but in ways that are significant and require careful observation and assessment.

The idea that technologies simply determine the outlook of an entire generation is one that should be discarded. However, the idea that the area of choice in education has been expanded by new technologies is one that still needs to be explored. One of the problems that has arisen out of the Net Generation and digital native debate has been a narrowing of the area for debate. Teachers have been identified as being part of a generational group that is distinct from their young students, and it has been argued that the characteristics of the two generational groups are fixed and already known. By shifting our attention to the ways in which technologies open up the potential for new kinds of social engagement, the argument moves towards choice and the ways in which technologies might allow for new kinds of educational engagement. Research is showing a more complex set of changes among young people than either the Net Generation or digital native arguments suggest (Czerniewicz et al., 2009; Jones et al., 2010; Kennedy et al., 2008). This variety among young people and the patterns that arise in relation to their use of technologies needs to be explored. As new technologies arise we can expect adoption patterns to vary by age but they may also vary in relation to the time that each technology was first introduced. Adoption patterns are also likely to be affected by other factors such as gender and the different technological infrastructures found in a variety of national and regional contexts. Educational change is not fixed into generational patterns, which themselves are determined by technology, even though the affordances of technology still set the limits to what is possible.

References

Bakhtin, M. (1986). *Speech genres and other late essays*. C. Emerson & M. Holquist (Eds.). (V. W. McGee, Trans.). Austin, TX: University of Texas Press.

Bates, T. (2010). A critique of Tapscott and William's views on university reform. Retrieved May 10, 2010, from www.tonybates.ca/2010/02/14/a-critique-of-tapscott-and-williams-views-on-university-reform

Bayne, S., & Ross, J. (2007). The "Digital Native" and "Digital Immigrant": A dangerous opposition. Paper presented at the Annual Conference of the Society for Research into Higher Education. Brighton, UK, December 11–13, 2007. Retrieved May 10, 2010, from www.malts.ed.ac.uk/staff/sian/natives_final.pdf

Bennett, S., & Maton, K. (2010). Beyond the "digital natives" debate: Towards a more nuanced understanding of students' technology experiences. *Journal of Computer Assisted Learning*, *26*(5), 321–331.

Bennett, S., Maton, K., & Kervin, L. (2008). The "Digital Natives" debate: A critical review of the evidence. *British Journal of Educational Technology, 39*(5), 775–786.

Buckingham, D., & Willett, R. (Eds.). (2006). *Digital generations: Children, young people and new media.* Mahwah, NJ: Erlbaum.

Castells, M. (2000). *The rise of the network society* (2nd ed.). Oxford: Blackwell Publishers.

Castells, M. (2001). *The internet galaxy: Reflections on the internet, business, and society.* Oxford: Oxford University Press.

Czerniewicz, L., Williams, K., & Brown, C. (2009). Students make a plan: Understanding student agency in constraining conditions. *The Association for Learning Technology Journal, 17*(2), 75–88.

Giancola, F. (2006). The generation gap: More myth than reality. *Human Resource Planning, 29*(4), 32–37.

Harasim, L. (Ed.). (1990). *Online education: Perspectives on a new environment.* New York: Praeger.

Hargittai, E. (2010). Digital na(t)ives? Variation in internet skills and uses among members of the "Net Generation." *Sociological Inquiry, 80*(1), 92–113.

Herring, S. (2008). Questioning the generational divide: Technological exoticism and adult construction of online youth identity. In D. Buckingham (Ed.), *Youth, identity and digital media* (pp. 71–92). Cambridge, MA: The MIT Press.

Howe, N., & Strauss, W. (1991). *Generations: The history of America's future and the fourth turning: An American prophecy.* Oxford: Oxford University Press.

Howe, N., & Strauss, W. (2000). *Millennials rising: The next greatest generation.* New York: Vintage Books.

Illich, I. (1970). *Deschooling society.* New York: Harper & Row. Retrieved May 10, 2010, from www.preservenet.com/theory/Illich/Deschooling/intro.html

Jones, C. (2008). Networked learning: Weak links and boundaries (special section editorial). *Journal of Computer Assisted Learning, 24*(2), 87–89.

Jones, C. (forthcoming). Networked learning, the net generation and digital natives. In L. Dirckinck-Holmfeld, V. Hodgson & D. McConnell (Eds.), *Exploring the theory, pedagogy and practice of networked learning.* New York: Springer.

Jones, C., & Healing, G. (2010). Net generation students: Agency and choice and the new technologies. *Journal of Computer Assisted Learning, 26*(5), 344–356.

Jones, C., Ramanau, R., Cross, S., & Healing, G. (2010). Net generation or digital natives: Is there a distinct new generation entering university? *Computers and Education, 24*(3), 722–732.

Kaye, A. R. (Ed.). (1992). *Collaborative learning through computer conferencing: The Najdeen Papers.* Berlin: Springer-Verlag.

Kennedy, G., Judd, T. S., Churchward, A., Gray, K., & Krause, K. (2008). First year students' experiences with technology: Are they really digital natives? Questioning the net generation: A collaborative project in Australian higher education. *Australasian Journal of Educational Technology, 24*(1), 108–122. Retrieved May 10, 2010, from www.ascilite.org.au/ajet/ajet24/kennedy.html

Macbeth, D. H. (1990). Classroom order as practical action: The making and un-making of a quiet reproach. *British Journal of Sociology of Education, 11*(2), 189–214.

McConnell, D. (1994). *Implementing computer supported cooperative learning.* London: Kogan Page.

Morley, D. (1995). Theories of consumption in Media Studies. In D. Miller (Ed.), *Acknowledging consumption: A review of new studies.* London: Routledge.

Oblinger, D. G., & Oblinger, J. L. (2005). *Educating the net generation: An Educause e-book publication*. Retrieved January 15, 2011, from www.educause.edu/educatingthenetgen

O'Malley, C. (Ed.). (1995). *Computer supported collaborative learning*. Berlin: Springer-Verlag.

Palfrey, J., & Gasser, U. (2008). *Born digital: Understanding the first generation of digital natives*. New York: Basic Books.

Prensky, M. (2001a). Digital natives, digital immigrants. *On the Horizon*, *9*(5), 1–6.

Prensky, M. (2001b). Digital natives, digital immigrants, Part II: Do they really think differently? *On the Horizon*, *9*(6), 1–6.

Prensky, M. (2009). H. sapiens digital: From digital immigrants and digital natives to digital wisdom. *Innovate*, *6*(3). Retrieved May 10, 2010, from www.innovateonline.info/index.php?view=article&id=705

Selwyn, N. (2003). "Doing IT for the kids": Re-examining children, computers and the "Information Society." *Media, Culture and Society*, *25*(3), 351–378.

Sfard, A. (1998). On two metaphors for learning and the dangers of only choosing one. *Educational Researcher*, *27*, 4–13.

Solomon, G., & Schrum, L. (2007). *Web 2.0: New tools, new schools*. Washington DC: ISTE.

Tall Blog: Online Education with the University of Oxford (2008, July 23). Not "Natives" & "Immigrants" but "Visitors" & "Residents." Retrieved May 10, 2010, from http://tallblog.conted.ox.ac.uk/index.php/2008/07/23/not-natives-immigrants-but-visitors-residents

Tapscott, D. (1998). *Growing up digital: The rise of the net generation*. New York: McGraw-Hill.

Tapscott, D. (2009). *Grown up digital: How the net generation is changing your world*. New York: McGraw-Hill.

Tapscott, D., & Williams, A. (2010). Innovating the 21st century university: It's time. *EDUCAUSE Review*, *45*(1), 17–29.

Weller, M. (2007). *Virtual learning environments: Using choosing and developing your VLE*. London: Routledge.

Weller, M. (2009, April 21). VLE vs PLE Fight Club. Weblog posting. Retrieved May 10, 2010, from http://nogoodreason.typepad.co.uk/.m/no_good_reason/2009/04/vle-vs-ple-fight-club.html

Weller, M. (2010). The centralisation dilemma in educational IT. *International Journal of Virtual and Personal Learning Environments*, *1*(1), 1–9.

Wellman, B. (2001). Physical place and cyberplace: The rise of the networked individual. In L. Keeble & B. Loader (Eds.), *Community informatics: Shaping computer-mediated social relations*. London: Routledge.

Wellman, B., Quan-Haase, A., Boase, J., Chen, W., Hampton, K., Isla de Diaz, I. et al. (2003). The social affordances of the internet for networked individualism. *JCMC*, *8*(3). Retrieved May 10, 2010, from http://jcmc.indiana.edu/vol8/issue3/wellman.html

PART II

Perspectives

4

DISEMPOWERING BY ASSUMPTION

"Digital Natives" and the EU Civic Web Project

Shakuntala Banaji

New Technologies, Young People, and Civic Participation

Notwithstanding a number of sophisticated critiques emerging in relation to some of the homogenizing rhetoric of the "Digital Natives" debate (Bennett, Manton & Kervin, 2008; Buckingham, 2007; Livingstone, 2007; Livingstone, Bober & Helsper, 2005; Selwyn 2003, 2009; Stoerger, 2009), the idea that civic action in online environments will appeal to young people more naturally than offline action has now become a commonplace suggestion. In addressing this subject, this chapter effectively connects two differing sets of problematic assumptions about young people and new technologies—those following the writings of Tapscott (1998, 2009) and Prensky (2001a, 2001b), which characterize all young people as having particular affinities with new technologies, and those who argue that this affinity can be molded and transferred to the arena of politics and civic action by involving new technologies as a sweetener or bait. But what effects do such assumptions about young citizens have in real civic contexts? How do conceptualizations of youth as "Digital Natives" and older generations as "Digital Immigrants" inflect the ways in which all age groups of civic and political producers attempt to appeal to young people in on- and offline environments? And what do young people have to say about their feelings towards digital technologies, politics, and civic action? To shed light on these questions, this chapter draws on key findings and data from an extensive seven-country, three-year European project *CivicWeb: Young People, the Internet and Civic Participation* (Banaji & Buckingham, 2010). All examples aim to deconstruct rhetoric around the digital generation doing politics online and point to the ways in which further civic exclusions and disadvantage might accrue to certain groups of youth if all are perceived as equally free, skilled, and active online.

Arguments suggesting that (new) technologies fundamentally alter social relationships and political landscapes are not new. As Norris (2001) and Warschauer (2004) discuss, from radio, television, and the telephone to mobile phones and the Internet, each technology, which was new in its time, has been hailed by techno-optimists as the potential solution to a wide array of social problems and decried by techno-pessimists as potentially implicated in new social travails or political challenges. During the last decade increasing attention in both the academic and policy spheres has been devoted to the possibilities offered by the Internet and digital communications technologies for involving young people in political deliberation and civic action. Of the features most stressed in studies of the Internet, "interactivity" (Newhagen, 1997) appears most often as the characteristic that distinguishes it from "old" media and disrupts the "one-to-many" communication model of mass media (Lievrouw, 2002; Murray, 2003) in a revolutionary manner. With its apparent potential for increasing vertical as well as horizontal communication, it is also the main feature of the Internet considered by cyber-optimists to have a significant democratizing effect (Benkler, 2006). In tandem, commentators such as Bentivegna (2002) and Tapscott (1998, 2008) have enthused about the connections between young people's skills and predilections and the role of new technologies of communication in their lives. Tapscott's work focused attention on the idea of fundamental properties that differentiate various media from each other and the abilities and predispositions that dissociate generations from each other. Television, which in his account has shaped (or rather distorted) the consciousness of the generation termed "baby boomers," is an irredeemably *authoritarian* and *passive* medium. The "Net Generation," by contrast, he describes as having an affinity for the Internet in democratic, creative, and active ways. Tapscott moves through the net's apparent propensity to encourage playful learning and its interactivity, to the conclusion that it is engendering new collective, non-hierarchical forms of politics and participation that appeal to the Net Generation particularly.

Arising from legitimate critiques of formal education's negotiation of young people's technological knowledge, Prensky's work over the past decade has popularized the notion of a universal generational divide in relation to digital technology. For instance:

> Digital Natives are used to receiving information really fast. They like to parallel process and multi-task. They prefer their graphics before their text rather than the opposite. They prefer random access (like hypertext). They function best when networked. They thrive on instant gratification and frequent rewards. They prefer games to "serious" work.
>
> (2001a, p. 2)

Recently, Prensky has introduced a notion that appears less generationally deterministic, that of "Digital Wisdom" and "homo sapiens digital" (2009). He notes, for instance, that "leaders are digitally wise when they use available technologies to connect with their constituents for polling and to solicit contributions and encourage participation" (2009, n.p.). More widely, however, there appears to have been little fundamental shift in the acceptance of the idea that human brains are "plastic" and "mutate" in response to technology, thus allowing those who use technology most heavily (still mainly considered to be young people) to process, access, and use information in fundamentally different ways from other generations and non-technology users. Ideas take time to diffuse across disciplinary and professional borders, but once they do, their effects can be felt sometimes long after their originators have moved on or their critics have proved flaws in their logic. As Selwyn contends, "the commonsensical notion of the digital native is foregrounded increasingly in the thoughts and pronouncements of policy-makers, technology vendors and opinion formers throughout the world" (2009, p. 366). In this vein, a number of studies have attempted to suggest that the comfort and confidence (some) young people display around new media can be employed to better young people's relationship with traditional political processes and their participation in civil society. But, how problematic is it, exactly, that technological issues begin to overshadow questions about democracy and ideology in civic organizations and networks?

Macintosh et al. examine action taken to address what they call "young people's apathy to the democratic process and politics in general, by considering possibilities for using information and communication technology to engage young people" (2003, p. 43). While the bulk of this article is devoted to an examination of two Scottish e-democracy initiatives with young people, the theorizing of these initiatives is based on a barely explored link between politics and new media. As in the commonsense notion that two dissimilar things or people placed side by side will automatically influence each other, statements quoted imply that some (magic) transfer is likely to occur between the motivation (and opportunity) to "play," "chat," or "shop" online and the motivation (and opportunity) to debate, deliberate, protest, or vote online. This analysis does end, however, with the warning that young people care about being *listened to* as much as they do about technological tools—which leads to the sensible suggestion that young people must be included in e-design processes and that technology by itself is not the answer to participation gaps.

Other research in this field reviews an increasingly rich and organic online sphere for youth civic participation, but argues the need for the further use of interactive and socially oriented technological tools to engage young people specifically. In other words, digital natives need a different kind of civic experience online than other generations. Montgomery and Gottlieb-Robles are optimistic that the Internet is already inspiring and will continue to generate new forms and venues for young people to learn about and participate in local, national, and global society (2006, p. 146). They see its potential for developing *civic literacy* as one of its most hopeful outcomes. However, they appear to link the use of certain new digital tools and applications to the potential outcome of the process of developing such engagement when they caution that "much of the information available online is non-interactive in form" (2006, p. 143). But the question remains: does the fact that some young people may use the Internet and its Web 2.0 tools such as wikis, podcasts, blogs, file sharing sites and social software more than other generations for socializing, information gathering, or leisure purposes (boyd, 2007) necessarily mean that they will all be *motivated* to use it for equal volumes of civic or political deliberation and intervention? Our research for CivicWeb, discussed in the following sections, suggests not.

Without challenging the model of youth as a digital generation, others argue for attention to be paid not only to technological and interactive features but also to the civic and democratic models to which youth civic initiatives subscribe (Albrect, 2006; Bennet, 2008; Dahlberg, 2001). A major proponent of the Internet as a space where young people are creatively appropriating and "remixing" aspects of cultural content from the digital to the social, Stephen Coleman (2008, pp. 203–204) emphasizes the need for the following characteristics of online youth civic spaces: non-interference from government; total freedom of expression; horizontal as well as vertical channels of communication; dialogic links with those in authority; clear agreements about what involvement will achieve; an openness to opposing points of view; a commitment to mobilizing against social injustice; the valuing of emotion and everyday political experience; enthusiasm about technological innovation; and a desire to challenge existing stereotypes about youth identities. Coleman's argument usefully complicates the apparently clear-cut distinction between (young people's) use of commercialized/individualized media cultural models and efficacy at rational debate in the civic sphere (Dahlberg, 2001, p. 628). Nevertheless, there are aspects of his argument with regard to what he calls the "analog and digital models of e-citizenship" (Coleman, 2008, pp. 202–204) that make claims for young people, technologies, and politics that could essentialize young people and other generations. In an attempt to understand the practical implications of such suggestions, however, the following sections engage with a broad sweep of findings from CivicWeb.

Civic Websites for Youth: Textual, Producer, and Youth Perspectives

CivicWeb is the largest existing cross-national study of young people, the Internet, and civic participation. The project had a strong mixed-methods ethos, with a cross-sectional multi-country user survey examining connections between variables such as gender and class, Internet use and young people's on- and offline civic participation; qualitative content surveys of 560 civic websites; in-depth interviews with new media producers of civic content; focus groups with users in towns, villages, and cities across six different European nations and Turkey;

and in-depth qualitative textual analyses of websites. These methods were used to inform the analysis of key research questions about, for instance, the existence or otherwise of a democratic deficit; the role of the Internet in young people's civic and social cultures; their attitudes to politics and the public sphere and the contexts and conditions of the production of online civic content for young people. In the UK and across the European Union, the promotion of civic participation among young people has become a priority for a number of governmental, political, charitable, and other non-governmental organizations led by, with, and/or apparently for young people. Some ensuing projects have both on- and offline incarnations, whereas others operate primarily online and were set up with the objective of reaching young people who might not have been reachable in the offline realm. But are young people taking up the invitations to use the online spaces in question? Quantitative surveys of youth carried out by the UK Children Go Online project in 2004 found that:

> . . . girls, middle-class and older teenagers tend to visit a broader range of civic sites. On average, however, only one of these kinds of sites (out of a possible five) is visited by each individual, suggesting that, overall, visiting civic websites is low on young people's priorities.
>
> (Livingstone et al., 2005, p. 295)

These findings are replicated with slight differences of emphasis in the CivicWeb survey of 3,300 young people's online and offline participation. Here, the civic and political potential of the Web pertains to social justice, new social movements and spirituality, and electoral politics. Over half the respondents expressed most interest in entertainment (music, movies, news, and shopping) sites, and little interest in explicitly civic sites, with the interest in electoral politics lowest. However, some 10–20 percent of our respondents expressed some interest, especially in environmental, new social movement, and spirituality-related sites. About 15 percent demonstrated strong interest in all three kinds of civic and political sites mentioned (CivicWeb deliverable 8, 2008). It is interesting therefore to look more specifically at some of the civic sites that are available to—if unused by—many such young people.

Here, I draw on a qualitative content analysis of a range of youth civic websites, covering issues of content, design, and interactivity for the CivicWeb project (deliverable 6, 2007). The British websites in the sample pertained to various causes, such as anti-suicide support for young men, help for the young homeless, improving childhood, disability, or supporting the environment, as well as both mainstream and radical political and activist civic participation. Some sites were not especially aimed at young people but contained sections for young people. Many contained possibilities to make online donations or requests for offline information. Other common features were links to officials and authorities to protest a policy or promote a cause and agendas for offline events, protests, lobbies, and demonstrations. In terms of participation, these sites promote offline participation in the form of volunteering or direct action much more than they enable online participation.

Sitting firmly within a paradigm that views young people as having an affinity for new technologies, some of these websites and networks aim to tap the potential of digital media and especially of Web 2.0 features such as video uploads, file sharing, podcasts, and forums as new means for civic engagement (CivicWeb deliverable 6, 2007). *MediaSnackers*, for instance, has a whole array of new digital tools both for the use of young people and for training young people and adults in new media communication skills, pleasures, and uses. It is the view of this site's producers that new media communication is not a given for everyone and that skills can and need to be taught in order to foster participation of all sorts online. Other UK sites rely on what might be termed new forms of political participation, such as "ethical consumerism," to invite their young audiences. *Generation Why*, for instance, which used to be the youth site of the large global charity Oxfam, was explicit in linking pleasurable consumption to ethical and political issues in its online shopping section and on other areas of the site. Similarly, sites such as *Ethics Girls* and *Adilli* offer possibilities for online civic engagement through consumption (Banaji & Buckingham, 2009), while in the Netherlands the website *Spunk* offers some young people opportunities for online journalism (Duits, Van Zoonen & Hirzalla, 2010). As pointed out in the studies cited, these opportunities are not, however, equally available to all, but require vast amounts or social, cultural, or material capital on the part of sustained participants.

Further, the meaning of civic communication and active participation are themselves not clearly defined on websites and need to be interpreted in relation to civic web-producers' intentions, pedagogy, the ideological content of the sites, and users' experiences. While some rhetoric about young people and new technologies see connections between the use of Web 2.0 technological tools and young people's willingness to return and contribute to civic websites or networks, what is actually happening in online civic spaces for young people reflects a more complex picture. Bachen et al.'s content analysis of a sample of 73 US-based civic websites for youth found that "[f]ewer than 40% of sites . . . developed young people's skills with interactive communication features such as listservs, chat rooms, message boards, and online games, and . . . most sites offered a passive experience to youth" (2008, p. 134). CivicWeb's in-depth survey of 560 websites found that out of an average of ten potential interactive tools for civic participation online (such as photographic and video content, audio content, podcasts, wikis, blogs, file sharing, forums, share-it function, chat-rooms, and vodcasts), most civic websites for young people seem to use an average of 2.5 such tools, with a very small proportion using as many as four and many more using none at all. Needless to say, the most common one was pictorial content, which is not necessarily viewed by many people as interactive at all (CivicWeb deliverable 13, 2009). It is therefore a fact that the websites in question often do not make use of the range of interactive digital tools potentially available, or under-utilize ones they do include, and this leaves the producers open to a number of the criticisms framed in previous sections by those who feel that young people are innately attuned or socialized to expect interactive options. Also, given that a number of the least interactive websites are made by people from older generations and aimed at young people, this might seem to support claims that older generations are frightened of using new digital technologies, or simply unable to do so. But are these assumptions justified? And should expectations of civic websites' success or lack of success in engaging young people be based, to any significant extent, on their use of new digital and Web 2.0 technologies?

In the great majority of cases in the UK sample, on the evidence of the producers, the absence of forums, video-upload facility, and podcasting is due to the limitations in budgets and funding, not to an unwillingness on their part to use the latest digital tools; in others it does represent a lack of interest in cutting edge technology and a focus on pedagogy or communicating a specific ideology—but here sites run by young people for young people are equally implicated; in yet other cases it is a conscious choice that relates to civic producers' understanding of the factors that motivate participation in the offline civic sphere, which is a primary area of interest. UNICEF *Youth Voice* (now *Tagd*) for instance, used lots of pictorial content, a few online polls, and a few games, while *MuslimYouth.Net* contains user-moderated forum discussion boards, images, podcasts, occasional polls, and the possibility of commenting on content. Both British and Dutch *Young Socialists*' websites contain fewer than three interactive options. Hungary's *Helpi*, meanwhile, saves most of its funding for offline civic and social work with young people. danah boyd notes that there are "four properties that fundamentally separate unmediated publics from networked publics": "persistence," "searchability," "replicability," and "invisible audiences" (2007, p. 126). But the fact that these possibilities exist online and not offline does not mean that all users rely equally on all of them for their motivation to become part of an online public space. This is equally true of young people and older adults. Focus group interviews suggest that the motivations for young people joining social networking sites such as Bebo and Facebook when they first started were primarily social and psychological (to do with friendship, peer group issues, and boredom) rather than related to the technology or to civic motivation. And, now, these same group interviews as well as related evidence from other sources (Wray & Jones, 2009) point towards the fact that, for some, boredom and frustration has set in with social networking sites and applications and, while such sites are still used by the 15–20 year-old age group, they are not used as heavily or with as much excitement and commitment as hype about them would suggest (Banaji, 2009). Such findings may change, but they should alert us to the perils of generalizing from behavior to motivation in relation to young people and digital technologies.

CivicWeb Youth: Technology, Social Class, and Civic Change

While interviews with a range of civic website producers from different generations showed that the rhetoric about young people as a "digital generation" who are "net-savvy" and "born to surf" are espoused by many and questioned by some, we were told repeatedly about the problems encountered in relation to online spaces for participation such as comments' sections, content upload facilities, and forums. Some producers have even been reduced to faking comments in their forums to stimulate debate from "real" young people, which, sadly, failed to materialize. Others told tales of flaming and trolling, ethnic slurs, and sexist comments posted by opposing groups of youth or random strangers. Yet others mentioned that they were not being paid to maintain forums because all the funding had gone into constructing a high-tech website, but they were still expected to moderate them on a daily basis, thus effectively removing time for any more creative civic activity on their part. There were success stories too, of course, involving interactive applications, but these were related to organizational ethos and civic purpose rather than to the technology *per se* (CivicWeb deliverable 13, 2009). Following these interesting revelations, our fifty focus groups with diverse populations of young people across Europe attempted to unpick from the bottom up some of the presuppositions so evident on both Web 2.0-savvy and fairly static civic websites and networks. Space constraints notwithstanding, it is worth examining more closely some of the findings.

In Turkey, while there exist a number of highly engaged groups of young volunteers and activists engaging in political and civic work online, the Turkish researchers report that:

> Generally speaking, except for the few common websites used among young people in Turkey, the sites in our sample for the CivicWeb project were not visited often by the interviewees. They had heard of and visited most of the websites mentioned during the interviews, but they did not seem to use all their functions such as writing in forums or making comments. Uploading sources and looking for specific information were the two main reasons for logging on to these civic/political websites.
>
> (Aydemir, 2009)

And at the younger end of the spectrum most had not even heard of any civic or political websites.

In Spain, on the whole across the range of focus groups, civic and/or political activities in the family seemed to be the basis for the interest of young people in these activities. Many of the participants in the Spanish groups mentioned that interest in politics could not be arrived at through use of the Internet. Spanish youth activists and those in political groups were particularly skeptical of the idea that new digital tools or the Internet without other influences might have a motivating effect on young people from non-political families and backgrounds. Many youth cited the language used on civic websites as a barrier to engagement —the fact that these sites are addressed to "the usual suspects" and offer an overload of information was pointed out to the Spanish researchers (Albero-Andres & Bastardas, 2009) as a possible reason for this situation. In Slovenia (Turnšek-Hančič & Slaček Brlek, 2009), researchers found a fascinating mix of skepticism and concern in relation to the way the Internet and digital tools might aid or hinder young people in civic initiatives.

Interviews by the Slovenian research team with the producers of youth civic web spaces and focus groups with young people more broadly found that young people expressed no differences between themselves and their parents' generation in terms of Internet use; especially those who were under eighteen perceived their parents as having the same levels of Internet skills as they had. One girl, aged sixteen, said that her mother's friends are starting to use Facebook and that it is completely normal for her mother to do so. Concomitantly, the Internet was seen by most participants as an "information gathering tool" or a "tool for personal communication." Many of the young participants from all different demographic and political groups in Slovenia saw civic participation as mostly an offline activity. They did not talk about civic action online unless specifically provoked by the interviewers, and even on these occasions the young civic activists were not particularly enthusiastic about online civic action. In several cases the metaphor for passiveness was employed when talking about online activities— this metaphor specifically envisions online activity as something passive: "you just sit at home behind the computer"—in some cases they added "playing video games all day." Sitting behind the computer was thus associated by some participants as an activity of having too much spare time and as passive in relation to offline activity such as sports or spending time with friends. These examples highlight a number of salient points in relation to generational patterns, youth motivating, technology, and civic participation across different regions of Europe and Turkey. Family and local political and civic actions and affiliations still play a key role in young people's participation—there has not been a widespread disconnect in this regard between the generations. Similarly, media such as television and film continue to be the centre of many cross-generational youth and leisure activities. Nor are young people as uniformly confident with and enthused about the arrival of the Internet and digital technologies as one would imagine, given the literature on their generation's predisposition reviewed at the outset of this chapter. Quite ironically, many of the young people interviewed have absorbed and recount some of the more negative rhetoric in relation to the Internet, viewing it as a problematically passive medium or as one that serves those already civically active: to those that have, more shall be given. In other cases, young people in these focus groups challenge the idea that their parents' generation is not as digitally literate as they are. Culture, location, and region play a huge role in inflecting young people's attitudes to and experiences of technology and civic participation.

In the UK, a significant minority of young people in focus groups of both civically engaged and disengaged young people from all demographics mentioned the fact that websites aimed at civic and political participation need to be "fit to purpose" rather than full of digital interactive tools in order to grab their attention and persuade them to return. Thus, a group of young British farmers, several of whom did not use the Internet on a regular basis, showed us the website they visit and engage with on a regular basis. It was rich with local information of a cross-generational nature, of information about offline rural activities for youth, but used few interactive tools and had virtually no opportunities for online interaction. Exemplifying a sense that ubiquitous technologist rhetoric and increases in digital access among educated and/or middle class people are forcing a different pace and style of youth politics that suits some but disadvantages others, one UK activist youth group expressed the opinion that young people with anti-authoritarian politics have more elaborated and extended arguments to make about democratic processes and hence do not come off well online in the quick "sound-bite" world of social network sites. However, it was their feeling, and there was some debate between them about this, that ultimately they would *have to engage* with social networking in their campaigning over students' rights and union democracy. They would need to campaign online, despite their preference for face-to-face contact, leafleting, meetings, and debates, which they feel reaches people—particularly working class people—that the Internet does not:

> **Mark**: This referendum has been a really good eye opener for me about how the internet works because yeah, the [rightwing students'] campaign was based on the internet, they mobilised from the internet and have a look, there were people making comments at 4 in the morning to debate. As a person who's busy out campaigning doing . . . a job, I've got things to do . . . you can't keep [doing that] . . . we're going to have to discuss . . . how we're going to deal with [the internet] because we can't be sitting on a computer all night, constantly debating all these people online, you know what I mean . . .
>
> **Moderator**: What would your strategy be then?
>
> **Mark**: . . . I always feel like blogs are not real in a sense because they're not accountable and . . . you need to define social relations a bit in the *real world*, so it's very easy to sit in front of a computer, get a screen come up with an argument and you can look at it, try and debate it, try and skewer it, quickly go online, check a couple of facts, whereas I always feel like *real democracy in real life is* based on being up there debating like what a student meeting was, you have to combat an argument quickly, face-to-face.

Katie: Yeah but we know there's so many people that would like go to the ballot box and they'd be like "oh, do you know how you're voting?" and they'd be like "yeah I'm voting 'no' to student rights, I saw it on Facebook." Because [leftwing and rightwing activists are] the only ones who engage with the Union, this is what this system does, only we know how it works and get anything out of it, everyone else does just sit and the way they relate to their union is through the shitty Facebook page and so when they see these things . . . so we can't just rely on (face-to-face) because no longer is that the playing field, it's been pushed away and marginalised.

Moderator: And yet you're saying that people like to have the real community, people like to have the real communication, but they obviously . . .

Aneesa: I think the reality is people want both . . . having the internet at home, having a computer at home, having the facilities and the experience and the knowledge to be able to make videos and stuff like they did, you have to be quite middle class.

(Activist Students' Focus Group, London, 2009)

It becomes evident that these young activists' motivation for using the Internet for political purposes is related to the ways in which it is being used by others who oppose their ideals rather than by their own feeling that it is a hugely democratic medium. Meanwhile, their sense that by moving to an entirely online arena for activist campaigning they are failing to connect with a whole swathe of young people whose concerns are intimately bound up with issues of rights and access is borne out in other studies. Lisa Lee's data based on a survey "on internet access and use, carried out in four schools in the Brighton and Hove area, England, as well as a small number of in-depth interviews with heavier internet users, and participant observation to contextualize the schools" between 2000 and 2001 emphasizes that

socio-economic groups still matter in the internet age, since at a basic level imbalances between groups are found in terms of access, level of support and training, types of uses and use cultures, reflecting the impact and interrelationship between economic, cultural and social capital.

(2008, p. 150)

Cathy Edwards' study of young people and the civic sphere in Australia makes similar points in relation to the difficulties faced by some groups in relation to institutional civic participation:

The political marginalisation of young people, legislation that renders it hard for young people to enrol to vote, and housing policies that make it harder

> for all low-income earners, including young people, and especially marginalised young people, to gain access to public housing are all state-induced barriers that result in disenfranchisement.
>
> (2007, p. 55)

Her poignant case studies of homeless young people such as Mia and Alfie (Edwards, 2007, p. 546) and their struggles to find some way of interacting with a political system that demands but blocks their active participation at almost every level stand as a sobering counterpoint to anecdotal evidence about young people's scorn for their teachers' technology use (Prensky, 2007).

Undeniably in an era when it has become *de rigueur* to suggest that technology use enhances learning, teachers do place PowerPoint slides in front of their classes and expect students to think "wow"! Indeed, like the students quoted by Prensky (2007, pp. 40–42), it is also the case that in the institutional dynamic of compulsory school, many students do feel underwhelmed by the ways in which technology and pedagogy are thrust at them. By focusing on the tensions in formal schooling around the uses of new technologies as if these arise from a biological generational divide rather than a complex and constrained institutional and political context, we lose sight of the groups of young people who have never had access to the skills, hardware, and cultural environments that make people into digital natives (Bayne & Ross, 2007; Kennedy et al., 2008; Helsper & Eynon, 2009). Equally problematically, by doing so in relation to civic web producers and political organizations operating online, we risk removing attention from the political power structures that curtail the participation of groups from all generations, but perhaps particularly the young, and refocusing attention on the form of communication rather than its ends and content. This is not to say that form never matters. Digital form, and available digital tools, both in civic online spaces and in classrooms are clearly important and worthy of attention for the different potentials they embody, the different pedagogies they can support, and the different connotations of their ownership.

Cautious Conclusions

In an environment where moral panics in relation to youth apathy and the dangers of new technologies are rife (Fearn, 2008; Keen, 2007), it is tempting to counter them with optimistic rhetoric about young people's capabilities and actions. Additionally, research evidence from Europe and North America suggests that in socio-economically stable, urban contexts, a greater proportion of younger people than other generations use the Internet, and in particular its newest features, for sociable, creative, and leisure purposes (boyd, 2007; Lee 2008; Raynes-Goldie & Walker, 2008). Again, new digital Internet tools do enable new forms of creativity, communication, and participation, but not necessarily for all young people, or for the groups who are most excluded historically in the offline sphere by socio-economic factors. What started out as a conceptual predilection within academic circles takes on a widespread afterlife in policy, economy, business, and politics.

But how have these now ubiquitous notions of a "digital generation," of "Digital Natives" and "homo sapiens digital" inflected the ways in which social, political, and civic organizations are using or are urged to use digital technology to address and engage young people? The rhetoric of digital flexibility and individualization serves to create a wider perception of all young people as free to choose among many aspects of their lives such as education, work, and civic action, however much the reality is context-specific, politically determined, and linked to culture or economic class. The notion that all young people are free to "volunteer" their labor for the good of communities and civic organizations has become entrenched, alongside the notion that older adults have more responsibilities and less time, because young people "save time" by multitasking digitally. Overt social prejudices—about the "fecklessness" of the young or about their automatic grasp of everything digital sans training—find willing partners in crime when it comes to the exigencies of many civic organizations' ideological and funding structures. Within cross-generational civic organizations, this can take the form of anything from a hierarchy in which people under thirty are assigned mundane "techie" tasks (while those over thirty are given control of organizational philosophy and ideology) to an automatic assumption that young volunteers do not need training in the use of the technologies or payment for running forums and editing content (while older members are guaranteed financial remuneration). Everywhere, of course, we found exceptions to these rules—but they were few and far between.

Further, the assumption that young people are "Digital Natives" can have profound impacts on the ways in which they are addressed by civic organizations and on the expectations displayed in the deployment of technological tools on websites. In some cases, again, this assumption leads to a more playful, creative interaction between politics and technology on youth civic sites—the idea of "jamming" a local fascist website, posting Google-earth images of SUVs that have had their tires slashed, "speed dating your MP" online, or blogging the successes of a young mayor are informative and exciting for some and not inherently problematic. But again, these cases are the exception rather than the rule, and pro-democratic youth groups have no monopoly on them. What usually happens in more institutional online settings is that a "one size fits all" model of language and technology is applied in the design features of a website. RSS feeds, wikis, and podcasting tools are offered but not explained; high-speed broadband and/or mobile connectivity is assumed. This model is generally consonant with a range of beliefs about young people, either as inherently tech-savvy, as content creators, or as interested more in fun and entertainment than in policies and politics.

CivicWeb findings from both content analysis and qualitative research among civic producers and young people across Europe and Turkey suggest that the myth, thoughtfully contested by Hargittai and Walejko (2008) of *most* young people as ever-ready, avid creators of online content bursting with new strategies that they want a forum to express has resulted in probably the largest number of under-utilized and spam-filled spaces in history—expensive digital dustbins. Civic forums are labor-intensive and costly to run well precisely because young people do not spring forward in droves to contribute content; forums require skills, motivation, encouragement, and feedback. And, more problematically, if one is interested in persuading disenfranchised, homeless, socioeconomically excluded, or other hard-to-reach young people to contribute ideas and experiences to civic websites and social networks, the amount of work and commitment needed offline is phenomenal and, frequently, glaringly absent. As Lance Bennet reminds us, "[t]here is need for caution and considerable creativity in thinking about implementing more creative approaches to engage young people in communication with each other about real political concerns" (2008, p. 17). His own project, in which students were "invited to participate in chats and to design other networked communication applications to develop a public voice," showed that while to some this was an ongoing reality "the poorest of the public schools presented infrastructure obstacles for even getting a single computer in some classrooms." Assuming that all the students were already digitally skilled and informationally literate because of out-of-school experiences (with mobile phones) proved an obstacle to their learning skills that would enable them to debate social and civic issues online in a creative manner. Equally, the supposition that the motivations of diverse adults using technology to communicate with young people spring from some kind of altruistic "Digital Wisdom" sidesteps issues of power, ideology, and privilege.

Useful and problematic, democratic and authoritarian, civic and non-civic content often jostles for attention on entertainment and social forums or networks used by a cross-section of generations. Just as with offline discussions, these can be self-serving or socially altruistic or they can embody a cacophony of individual prejudices and alignments. CivicWeb's findings suggest that policy-makers, educators, and civic practitioners in this area should certainly recognize the considerable potential of the Internet and related digital technologies in terms of connecting with new forms of civic and political culture and orientation that are emerging among some strata of young people. However, they need to beware of an over-optimistic or utopian approach: the use of networked technologies is not inherently democratic, nor does it automatically have democratic consequences. Our research suggests that the Internet can be a valuable tool for young people who are *already* engaged in civic and political activity. However, policy-makers and practitioners should beware of assuming that the Internet will be the most effective means of engaging all young people who are currently disengaged and/or excluded: different means are required for different young people. There is a danger that the fetishization of cutting-edge technologies by civic organizations may reinforce inequalities. Consequently, funding for offline projects in this area must be balanced against that for online ventures.

People integrate new media and technologies into the ensemble of their existing media practices, and into the processes and relationships of daily life. While media do possess particular potentialities or affordances, these will be realized (or not realized) in different ways by different people in different social contexts. Many of those combining media, politics, and technology in the most fluent, effective ways turn out to be not young people in particular, but people of all ages with a sense of context and purpose suited to new media and particular political projects. Indeed, far from having a monopoly on online civic content, a significant number of young people, including homeless youth, those who practice alternative or non-mainstream politics, or are answerable to parents who have discouraged media use, risk being silenced by other generations and by normative discourses on youth and technology (even in supposedly youth-oriented online spaces). Surely, in order to reduce the danger of perpetuating a double exclusion, we need to continue to show how in what could be a "digital melting pot" (Stoerger, 2009), cultural contexts, socioeconomic conditions, elite political interests, and essentialist presuppositions are barriers when it comes to young people, civic life, and new technology? And if, in order to do so, we have to moderate, nuance, or even dispense entirely with entrenched but contradictory notions that *all* young people are more creative, more at risk, more individualistic, more flexible and fun-loving, more apathetic, or even more digitally confident than *all* members of other generations, then let's get started.

References

Albero-Andres, M., & Bastardas, A. (2009). Young people, the internet and the civic sphere in Spain. *Report on the young users of civic websites in Europe: CivicWeb deliverable 16*, 74–105.

Albrect, S. (2006). Whose voice is heard in online deliberation?: A study of participation and representation in political debates on the Internet. *Information, Communication and Society*, *9*(1), 62–82.

Aydemir, A. T. (2009). Young people, the internet and the civic sphere in Turkey. *Report on the young users of civic websites in Europe: CivicWeb deliverable 16*, 127–145.

Bachen, C., Raphael, C., Lynn, K-M., McKee, K., & Philippi, J. (2008). Civic engagement, pedagogy, and information technology on web sites for youth. *Political Communication*, *25*(3), 290–310.

Banaji, S. (2009). Young people, the internet and the civic sphere in the UK. *Report on the young users of civic websites in Europe: CivicWeb deliverable 16*, 146–181.

Banaji, S., & Buckingham, D. (2009). The civic sell: Young people, the internet, and ethical consumption. *Information, Communication and Society*, *12*(8), 1197–1223.

Banaji, S., & Buckingham, D. (2010). Young people, the internet, and civic participation: An overview of key findings from the CivicWeb project. *International Journal of Learning and Media*, *2*(1), 1–11.

Bayne, S., & Ross, J. (2007). The "Digital Native" and "Digital Immigrant": A dangerous opposition. Paper presented at the Annual Conference of the Society for Research into Higher Education (SRHE), December 2007.

Benkler, Y. (2006). *The wealth of networks: How social production transforms markets and freedom*. New Haven and London: Yale University Press. Retrieved April 12, 2010, from www.benkler.org/wealth_of_networks/index.php?title=Download_PDFs_of_the_book

Bennet, L. (Ed.). (2008). *Civic life online: Learning how digital media can engage youth*. Cambridge, MA: The MIT Press. Retrieved January 12, 2010, from http://mitpress.mit.edu/catalog/item/default.asp?ttype=2&tid=11388

Bennett, S., Maton, K., & Kervin, L. (2008). The "Digital Natives" debate: A critical review of the evidence. *British Journal of Educational Technology*, *39*(5), 775–786.

Bentivegna, S. (2002). Politics and new media. In L. A. Lievrouw & S. Livingstone (Eds.), *Handbook of new media: Social shaping and consequences of ICTs* (pp. 50–61). London & Thousand Oaks: Sage.

boyd, d. (2007). Why youth [*heart*] social network sites: The role of networked publics in teenage social life. In D. Buckingham (Ed.), *Youth, identity and digital media* (pp. 119–142). Cambridge, MA: The MIT Press.

Buckingham, D. (2007) *Beyond technology: Children's learning in the age of digital culture*. Cambridge, UK: Polity Press.

CivicWeb deliverable 6 (2007). *Websites and civic participation: A European overview*. Retrieved May 29, 2010, from www.civicweb.eu

CivicWeb deliverable 8 (2008). *Uses of the web for civic participation in Europe and Turkey: A survey of young users*. Retrieved May, 29, 2010, from www.civicweb.eu

CivicWeb deliverable 13 (2009). *The producers of civic websites in Europe and Turkey*. Retrieved May 29, 2010, from www.civicweb.eu

Coleman, S. (2008). Doing it for themselves: Management versus autonomy in youth e-citizenship. In L. W. Bennett (Ed.), *Civic life online: Learning how digital media can engage youth* (pp. 189–206). Cambridge, MA: The MIT Press.

Dahlberg, L. (2001). The internet and democratic discourse: Exploring the prospects of online deliberation forums extending the public sphere. *Information, Communication and Society*, *4*(4), 615–633.

Duits, L., van Zoonen, L., & Hirzalla, F. (2010). As the world Spunks: Does the internet help to transform youth journalism? In P. Dahlgren & T. Olsson (Eds.), *Young citizens, ICTs and democracy*. Gothenburg: Nordicom.

Edwards, K. (2007). From deficit to disenfranchisement: Reframing youth electoral participation. *Journal of Youth Studies*, *10*(5), 539–555.

Fearn, H. (2008). Grappling with the digital divide. *The Times Higher Education Supplement*, 14 August, 37–40.

Hargittai, E., & Walejko, G. (2008). The participation divide: Content creation and sharing in the digital age. *Information, Communication and Society*, *11*(2), 239–256.

Helsper, E., & Eynon, R. (2009). Digital natives: Where is the evidence? *British Educational Research Journal*, *36*(3), 503–520.

Keen, A. (2007). *The cult of the amateur*. London: Nicholas Brealey.

Kennedy, G., Judd, T. S., Churchward, A., Gray, K., & Krause, K. (2008). First year students' experiences with technology: Are they really digital natives? Questioning the net generation: A collaborative project in Australian higher education. *Australasian Journal of Educational Technology*, *24*(1), 108–122. Retrieved April 30, 2010, from www.ascilite.org.au/ajet/ajet24/kennedy.html

Lee, L. (2008). The impact of young people's internet use on class boundaries and life trajectories. *Sociology, 42*(1), 137–153.
Lievrouw, L. A. (2002). Introduction to Part Two: Technology design and development. In L. A. Lievrouw & S. Livingstone (Eds.), *Handbook of new media: Social shaping and consequences of ICTs* (pp. 131–135). London and Thousand Oaks: Sage.
Livingstone, S. (2007). Interactivity and participation on the internet: Young people's response to the civic sphere. In P. Dahlgren (Ed.), *Young citizens and new media: Learning for democratic participation* (pp. 103–124). London & New York: Routledge.
Livingstone, S., Bober, M., & Helsper, E. (2005). Active participation or just more information? *Information, Communication & Society, 8*(3), 287–314.
Macintosh, A., Robson, E. Smith, E., & Whyte, A. (2003). Electronic democracy and young people. *Social Science Computer Review, 21*(1), 43–54.
Margolis, M., & Resnick, D. (2000). *Politics as usual: The cyberspace "revolution."* Thousand Oaks, CA.: Sage Publications.
Montgomery, K., & Gottlieb-Robbles, B. (2006). Youth as e-citizens: The internet's contribution to civic engagement. In D. Buckingham & R. Willett (Eds.), *Digital generations: Children, young people and new media* (pp. 131–148). Mahwah, NJ & London: Lawrence Erlbaum Associates.
Murray, J. H. (2003). Inventing the medium. In N. Wardrip-Fruin & N. Montfort (Eds.), *The new media reader* (pp. 3–11). Cambridge, MA & London: The MIT Press.
Newhagen, J. E. (1997). On hitting the agenda reset button for net research, and getting it right this time. Paper presented to The Association for Education in Journalism and Mass Communication, July–August. Retrieved May 24, 2008, from http://jnews.umd.edu/johnen/research/agenda.htm
Norris, P. (2001) *Digital divide: Civic engagement, information poverty, and the internet worldwide.* Cambridge, UK & New York: Cambridge University Press.
Prensky, M. (2001a). Digital natives, digital immigrants. *On the Horizon, 9*(5), 1–6.
Prensky, M. (2001b). Digital natives, digital immigrants, Part II: Do they really think differently? *On the Horizon, 9*(6), 1–6.
Prensky, M. (2007). *How to teach with technology: Keeping both teachers and students comfortable in an era of exponential change.* Coventry, UK: BECTA.
Prensky, M. (2009). H. sapiens digital: From digital immigrants and digital natives to digital wisdom. *Innovate, 5*(3). Retrieved May 6, 2009, from www.innovateonline.info/index.php?view=article&id=705
Raynes-Goldie, K., & Walker, L. (2008). Our space: Online civic engagement tools for youth. In L. Bennet (Ed.), *Civic life online: Learning how digital media can engage youth* (pp. 161–188). Cambridge, MA: The MIT Press.
Selwyn, N. (2003). Doing IT for the kids: Re-examining children, computers and the "Information Society." *Media, Culture and Society, 25*(3), 351–378.
Selwyn, N. (2009). The digital native—myth and reality. *Aslib Proceedings: New Information Perspectives, 61*(4), 364–379.
Stoerger, S. (2009). The digital melting pot: Bridging the digital native-immigrant divide. *First Monday, 14*(7), 1–10. Retrieved July 10, 2010, from http://firstmonday.org/htbin/cgiwrap/bin/ojs/index.php/fm/article/view/2474/22
Tapscott, D. (1998). *Growing up digital: The rise of the net generation.* New York: McGraw-Hill.
Tapscott, D. (2009). *Grown up digital: How the net generation is changing your world,* New York: McGraw-Hill.

Tapscott, D., & Williams, A. (2010). Innovating the 21st century university: It's time. *EDUCAUSE Review*, *45*(1).

Turnšek-Hančič, M., & Slaček Brlek, S. (2009). Young people, the internet and the civic sphere in Turkey. In *Report on the young users of civic websites in Europe: CivicWeb deliverable 16*, 55–73.

Warschauer, M. (2004). *Technology and social inclusion: Rethinking the digital divide*. Cambridge, MA, & London, UK: The MIT Press.

Wray, R., & Jones, S. (2009). It's SO over: Cool cyberkids abandon social networking sites. *The Guardian*, Thursday, August 6, 2009. Received July 10, 2010, from www.guardian.co.uk/media/2009/aug/06/young-abandon-social-networking-sites

5

JAPANESE YOUTH AND MOBILE MEDIA

Toshie Takahashi

Introduction

Digital media are becoming increasingly embedded in young people's everyday lives, producing new time-spaces for their self-expression, connectivity, and "self-creation" (Takahashi, 2003, 2009, 2010). In *Born Digital*, young people are described as "Digital Natives" and are shown to share a common global culture, demonstrating certain attributes and experiences in the ways they interact with media and ICT, information itself, with each other, and with other people and institutions (Palfrey & Gasser, 2008). It is a commonly held assumption that the diffusion of new communication technologies has led, along with other developments, to a "downsizing" of the world. An example of this phenomenon can be seen in the way in which young people in the global age share a common culture on YouTube and digital satellite television transnationally. They constantly use mobile phones for immediate communication with their peer group and family and connect with each other beyond time-space via Internet sites such as Facebook and Twitter. However, while we can observe similar uses and experiences of engagement with mobile phones and the Internet in different places in the world, digital media have also reinforced social norms and cultural tendencies within their specific regions or nations.

In this chapter, I will begin by introducing an overview of the discourse of digital natives within the social, cultural, economical, and political contexts of Japan. Second, I will outline the history and current trends of mobile Internet use among youth in Japan. Third, I will investigate Japanese young people and mobile media in everyday life using data from my ethnographic studies in the media-rich Tokyo Metropolitan Area, conducted between 2000 and 2010. I will discuss freedom and control, opportunities and risks, and de-traditionalization and reflexive traditionalization in the context of my fieldwork. Finally, I will examine the implications for young people, digital media, and education in our contemporary mobile-saturated society. It is my intention for this chapter to reveal the diversity of Japanese young people as well as their commonality and cultural specificity in relation to the wider picture of youth's engagement with digital media in the globalized world.

The Discourse of Digital Natives in Japan

The discourse of digital natives has looked at complex emotional perceptions of hopes and fears of youth in Japan as well as debated utopian and dystopian views of youth in the West (Buckingham, 1998). In this section, I will look at the social, cultural, economic, and political contexts of digital natives in Japan.

Utopian and Dystopian Views of Youth

Hope

Yoshiki, a twenty-five-year-old web designer said, "Digital natives are like characters from the novel *Kibō no Kuni no Exodus* [*Exodus of the Country of Hope*]." In 2000, one year before Marc Prensky (2001a, 2001b) wrote his essay "Digital Natives, Digital Immigrants" in the USA, a Japanese popular novelist, Ryu Murakami, wrote a story *Kibō no Kuni no Exodus* about junior high school students who lose their ability to conform socially at school and in Japanese society. In this novel, while Japanese society is collapsing due to the failure of politics and a serious economic recession, these young people create a new country united by the Internet. They achieve great success and influence the world economy through their Internet investments. The teenage heroine's words have become popular among Japanese people: "We have everything in Japan. But there is one thing we don't have. That is Hope." At the beginning of the twenty-first century, the Japanese government, companies, and people are seeking a type of "exodus," or escape from the perceived collapse of Japanese society. As a countermeasure, the Japanese government announced a new policy for the digital age, the so called, "e-Japan strategy" (where "e" means electronic) in 2000. This policy was redeveloped as the "u-Japan Promotion Program" in 2006 (where "u" refers to the "ubiquitous" nature of digital technologies) and is purported to be the key to Japan's survival in the global economy. Japanese companies are currently experimenting with new business models, shifting from the traditional seniority and hierarchical structure with its promise of lifelong employment, which underpinned Japan's economic success after World War II.

The term "Digital Natives" was first introduced and disseminated in Japan by NHK, the national broadcasting company. NHK broadcast the sensational documentary program entitled, "Digital Natives: Portrait of the Young People Who Will Shape the Next Age" in 2008. This program featured teenagers both in the USA and Japan who achieved great business success via the Internet without face-to-face communication. Tapscott's book, *Grown up Digital: How the Net Generation is Changing Your World* was translated into Japanese and given an even more sensational Japanese title, *Digital Natives ARE Changing the World* (the word "ARE" being highlighted), in 2009.

The term embodies a powerful conception of young people as being the hope for the future, and has become a buzzword among government bodies, industry, academia, and the population in general. Educationists and media scholars sponsored by computer and education industries such as Microsoft and the Benesse Corporation have developed new educational tools and software for mobile phones and ICT, including games with a serious academic purpose.

Fear

On the one hand, the idea of digital natives has been willingly accepted by idealists with a utopian view, but on the other hand, the term has given rise to a sort of "moral panic" (Cohen, 1972) in concordance with a dystopian view. By emphasizing the discontinuity of generations and "singularity" (Prensky, 2001a, p. 1), parents and teachers fear that they can no longer fully understand or control children and young people. People talk about the collapse of home, school, and society. Juvenile crimes have been given considerable media attention, with some critics blaming new media such as violent videos and video games, mobile phones, and the Internet. Television news frequently reports young people's suicides caused by cyber-bullying. Daytime and night-time "wide shows" (popular Japanese tabloid shows) sensationally cover these news items and stories by following and interviewing their friends, families, neighbors, and schools for several hours everyday on most commercial channels. For example, twenty-five-year-old Tomohiro Kato killed seven people and injured ten people in Akihabara, the centre of youth subculture such as *manga* (anime), Internet, and *otaku* (geek) culture in Tokyo. He had posted thirty messages from his mobile phone on a mobile Internet site before the killings. Under the title, "I will kill people in Akihabara," he gave notice of his intended crime with the following message at 5:21 am on June 8, 2008, "I'll crash my vehicle into people and if the vehicle breaks down, I'll get out a knife. Goodbye everyone!" (translated by BBC News, 2008). This event was broadcast not only via mass media but also on YouTube and *Niko-niko Douga* (Japanese video sharing sites). Clips were recorded and uploaded via mobile phone by other passengers who were witnesses to this event on the street in Akihabara. Many photos of the events were also uploaded by bystanders. These appeared on blogs or were exchanged on social networking sites (SNSs) via their mobile phones. Thus it was not only the actions of Kato but also those of witnesses that caused widespread shock and criticism both inside and outside of Japan. This event reinforced the notion of "techno-orientalism" (Morley & Robbins, 1995) vis-à-vis Japan, and this describes the stereotypical image of Japan as a "strange high-tech other" to the West, as exemplified in many Hollywood movies. Similarly, the exoticism of young people in digital native discourses can be regarded as a type of "techno-youthism." Thus, the discourse of the digital native has developed into a complex combination of hope and fear.

The Discourse of Digital Natives and Mobile Phones

In Japan, since 1999, people have been buying mobile phones with i-mode service (allowing access to the Internet via mobile phones for the purposes of sending email, getting news and information, and doing banking). Over the past ten years, young people have been able to watch television and video, listen to music, play games, take photographs, and access the Internet entirely by means of their mobile phones. To describe people in their late twenties who have grown up adept at manipulating their mobile phones (without looking at them), the Japanese term often used is *oyayubibunka* (literally, thumb culture).

Because of the rapid diffusion of mobile Internet and the unique youth culture that has developed as a result of mobile phones (Ito et al., 2005), the idea of "Digital Natives" has been uncritically accepted as a means of highlighting the distinction between generations in Japan. However, the term itself has been replaced, in order to adapt to the specific Japanese context, by "cyber natives" (Kimura, 2010), "neo-digital natives" (Hashimoto et al., 2010), and "keitai [mobile] natives" (Harada, 2010). These replacement terms emphasize the uniqueness of Japan as well as that of the young generation. They distinguish digital natives not only from digital immigrants but also from Western digital natives.

Hashimoto et al. (2010) divide young people into three generation groups: both the 76 generation (people who were born after 1976 and are now in their thirties) and the 86 generation (people who were born after 1986 and are now in their twenties) are called "Digital Natives." The 96 generation (people who were born after 1996 and are now teenagers) are called "neo-digital natives." While digital natives communicate with each other by text and voice using the Internet on PCs, neo-digital natives communicate with each other by video or movies using mobile phones. They emphasize the shift from PCs to mobiles and from text and voice to video and movies as the principal communication tools among Japanese youth.

Harada (2010) replaced the term "Digital Natives" with "keitai [mobile] natives." Referring to the *kuuki* or climate of opinion theory (Ito, 2002; Littlejohn & Foss, 2009; Watson & Hill, 2000; Yamamoto, 1977), he claims that mobile phones have revived traditional village society in Japan. As young people constantly connect with each other via mobile phones, they feel the same kind of commitments and obligations as Japanese people used to have when they lived in small villages in the pre-modern era. A significant minority of young people become targets of cyber-bullying, as is anyone who cannot understand *kuuki* contextually in their online and offline communication. In Japanese history, in small villages if someone did something wrong she or he was ostracized by the community except in the case of a house fire or a funeral. However, in the digital age, Harada (2010) suggests that there are no exceptions in terms of ostracism via mobile phones. There are strict implicit rules among young people such as immediate responses to emails and constant comments on others' blogs on SNSs within their *uchi* (a Japanese term meaning inside, us, or social group) (Nakane, 1967; Takahashi, 2003, 2008, 2009).

Youth and Mobile Internet

Historically, the mobile Internet has been developed by including the creative input of junior high and high school girls in Japan. In this section, I will summarize the history and recent trends of mobile Internet use among young people in Japan.

Pagers were first introduced in 1968 in Japan and were used principally by business people and professionals. Teenagers appropriated pagers in the 1990s, and they started to attach meanings to various numbers—for example, 86 (*Hachi Roku*) means "Hello." At this time, long queues of teenagers holding Hello Kitty pagers formed in front of public telephones. The i-mode service (mobile phones with access to the Internet) began to be developed in 1999 and benefited from users' creativity with pagers.

Mobile phone novels became popular among teenage girls and women in their early twenties in 2002. The stories are written and read via mobile phones by those girls. When they read the novels, they feel as if they have received personal emails from their close friends. This personal feeling is reinforced by the informal writing style and the themes are very personal, dealing with issues such as drugs, sex, pregnancy, abortion, rape, and disease. Writers can interact with their readers via mobile phones and sometimes change their stories in response to readers' feedback. Therefore, they feel they are creating those novels together via their mobile phones. Moreover, these days, new types of mobile phone novels have emerged. These include "wiki novels," which enable the readers to change the story, and "relay novels," whereby multiple authors write the story in turn. These are emerging examples of so-called "participatory culture" (Jenkins, 2006). When novels achieve popularity among those young girls, they are sometimes published as books, broadcast on TV, or made into films, and they have become extremely popular.

As for SNSs, Mixi was established in Japan and has become the most popular social networking site in Japan. Since the introduction of Mixi Mobile in 2006, there has been a huge increase in young people's use of Mixi, frequently while on the train or during their spare time, to check the news, messages, and their friends' blogs. Prof (Profile page) and Real (Real-time Diary/Blog), which were originally based on the mobile Internet, have become popular among children and young people who are under eighteen years old and cannot officially register with Mixi. From the time they wake up until the time they go to bed, they frequently check their friends' blogs and photos, which they upload via mobile phones. It is expected among *uchi* members that blogs are read and commented on quickly.

According to a *Naikakuhu* (Cabinet office) survey (2009), 21.8 percent of children of elementary school, 45.6 percent in junior high school, and 96.0 percent in high school have their own mobile phones. Further, 16.4 percent, 45.6 percent, and 95.4 percent (respectively) of children access the Internet via mobile phones. This means 80 percent of elementary school users and almost 100 percent of both junior high and high school mobile users have access to the Internet via their mobile phones. There are vast mobile Internet sites whose services and interfaces are different from PC Internet sites. They have been uniquely developed inside Japan through teenagers' creative use of mobile phones.

Youth Engagement with Digital Media in Everyday Life in Japan

How do children and young people engage with media and ICT in their everyday life in Japan? In this section, I will first give a short description based on my fieldwork in Japan. Then I will discuss the following three issues with reference to my fieldwork: freedom and control, opportunities and risks, and de-traditionalization and reflexive traditionalization.

Rui: A Sixteen-Year-Old Girl's Typical Day

Rui, a sixteen-year-old high school student, lives with her father, mother, and elder brother in Tokyo. Each room has a television set—therefore the family has four television sets and three personal computers in the household. Each family member has his/her own mobile phone and father has two mobile phones—one is for business and the other for private use.

Rui has never switched off her mobile phone. While she sleeps, she puts her mobile next to her pillow on her bed while the battery is charging. She sets her alarm on her mobile. The first thing she does when she wakes up at 6:30 in the morning is to switch off the alarm of her mobile phone and then check her emails, text messages, and SNSs.

As soon as she closes the front door of the house to leave for school, she starts to listen to music on her iPod. As she shuffles all kinds of music on her iPod, she listens to music, from newly released Japanese popular music such as Mr. Children and L'Arc~en~Ciel (both are popular Japanese boy bands) to the Beatles and Queen, whose CDs she found in her parents' collection. On the bus, she responds to all her emails (she normally exchanges 200 emails a day via her mobile), reads blogs and SNSs (whenever someone updates their own blogs she receives messages via her mobile phone), and watches video clips on YouTube via mobile.

At 7:50 am, she puts her mobile in her bag when she gets off the bus at the bus station. Although her school does not allow students to use mobile phones, she still finds ways to use her phone even during class. At lunchtime, she reads blogs, watches videos on YouTube, talks about television and YouTube with her friends, and shows videos she finds interesting on her mobile phone via face-to-face interaction in the classroom.

After school, she comes home and has dinner with her family, watching the television in the living room. Then she goes to her bedroom at about 8 pm and starts to chat on Skype with her best friend. She does her homework with her friend together via Skype, while chatting and talking or playing video games, until midnight. She always leaves Skype on when she is in her bedroom. This interaction continues sometimes until 4 am, although they sometimes fall asleep in the middle of their chats or conversations via Skype.

Freedom and Control

Mobile phones give children and young people freedom from the constraints of time-space and control of teachers and parents. In this section, I will discuss connectivity freedom in public, at school, and at home.

Connectivity: Freedom from Time-Space

The mobile phone and SNS mobile allow children and young people to connect with their friends beyond time-space. Not only Rui but also most of my informants have never switched off their mobile phones. Nakajima et al. (1999) conducted surveys on the use of mobile phones by young people and concluded that the mobile phone promotes the creation of a "full-time intimate community" with their close friends. Young people use their phones to maintain and reinforce their friend *uchi*, which is sometimes referred to as telecocooning.

As Rui's case shows, mobile media are used during the commute from home to school. The use of iPods and mobile phones make it possible for young people to connect with people and culture beyond time-space and also to create their own private time-space in public. As Bull (2000) noted when discussing the Walkman, the "locale" in which individuals are physically situated becomes invisible for them:

> [Personal stereo] users appear to achieve, at least subjectively, a sense of public invisibility . . . public spaces are void of meaning and are represented as "dead" spaces to be traversed as easily and as pleasurably as possible . . . Public space in this instance is not merely transformed into a private space but rather negated so as to prioritize the private.
>
> (p. 79)

Music via iPod always provides a personalized time-space in public and on journeys —users thus experience trans-age and trans-culture on the streets of contemporary Tokyo. Mobile media momentarily and situationally connect individuals, time, places, and cultures together, beyond clear boundaries between the public and private.

Tactics: Freedom from Teachers' Control

By appropriating the new form of mobile technology, children and young people have freedom from the control of teachers and parents. Let's listen to Rui discuss the use of mobile phones at school:

> **Rui:** Some kids break the speaker of their mobile phones and take photos during the class.
>
> **Researcher**: Really? Can you do that? . . . Actually it makes quite a loud sound when we take photos via mobile phone.
>
> **Rui**: Yeah. So if I look at my friends' Real, she writes, "Now in classics literature class" and uploads a photo.
>
> **Researcher**: When did she take photos?
>
> **Rui**: It said 10:46 am. It was in the class.
>
> **Researcher**: What did she take?
>
> **Rui**: She took her friend with a peace sign under the desk [she showed her Real with a gesture of taking a photo].

Although Japanese mobile phones are designed to make loud sounds when people take photos, in order to avoid problems such as strangers taking covert photos in crowds, young people intentionally break their phone's loudspeaker so they can use it during class. They exchange many emails as well as write their blogs and upload photos during class on Real sites. Through Real, they communicate with people both inside and outside the classroom. Mobile phones are used tactically (de Certeau, 1984) for escape from control but also to form emotional relationships among peers at school.

Personalization of Media: Freedom from Parents' Control

While parents have been giving mobile phones to their children to help protect them in case of emergencies, Shimoda (2004) suggests that, "what is the most attractive feature of the mobile phone for children is perhaps 'its power to offer escape from parents' control'." When the home telephone was situated at the entrance hall or living room at home, and before mobile phones became popular, parents could control the people who tried to enter their domestic space from outside. However, now family members have their own PCs and mobile phones, so the home has become open to the outside world. They can easily access any information from outside and communicate with friends and strangers whom parents have never met or known beyond their domestic time-spaces.

In Rui's home, we can witness the personalization of television and ICT in the domestic space. While television has in the past served as a "hearth" bringing families together, in the contemporary world, because of the personalization of television and ICT, the domestic space or "home" is opened up to the outside, thereby contributing to the fragmentation of family life (Flichy, 1995; Van Rompaey & Roe, 2001). Rui continually switches between on- and offline spaces, between personal time and sharing time-space with family or friends at home.

Time-shift, Place-shift, and Platform-shift: Freedom from the National Audience

Scannell (1988) discusses the idea that the formation of "the national audience," watching the same program at the same time, is the role of public broadcasting bodies such as the BBC. However, these days, the so-called national audience does not always watch the same program at the same time because satellite television provides the same show at different time slots throughout the day. People watch the same shows but at times that better suit their personal schedules. Technological developments since DVDs and the recent convergences between television and the Internet such as BBC iPlayer, ITV Player, and E4 in the UK have given the audience some opportunities to shift the time of viewing. Moreover, young people watch television dramas and sports events via mobile phones outside of their homes in real time. Mobile phones give audiences opportunities to shift the location used for viewing.

In addition to these time- and place-shifts, young people shift the platform of viewing. They watch television programs, movies, and video clips at any time and in any place via portable media. An eighteen-year-old girl called Yumi registers the title of her favorite drama in her Sony Blu-ray recorder, which automatically records the drama every week. She clicks it into her Sony Walkman, which has the same Blu-ray, and watches it in her class with her friends. She shifts not only national television dramas from terrestrial television but also American dramas from cable television into her portable media, beyond its original platform. Thus audiences are not necessarily structured by the television producers in terms of time-space. They shift its time and space from the hitherto domesticized viewing context into their everyday context while also selecting people for co-viewing.

Opportunities and Risks

Children and young people participate in various online communities via mobile phone and PC beyond the clear distinction between online and offline and public and private. The Internet offers many opportunities as well as risks (e.g., Livingstone, 2009; Livingstone & Haddon, 2009). These will now be discussed.

PCs and the mobile Internet provide opportunities such as connectivity, communication, creativity, self-expression, entertainment, and popularity. While older teenagers use Mixi via both PC and mobile phones, younger teenagers create their profiles on sites such as Prof and Real, which are based on mobile phone Internet. These social media give young people opportunities to communicate with a number of people who are outside school via mobile phones, and also to demonstrate their popularity among their friends.

However, the PC and mobile Internet also entail risks such as dating sites, pornography, violence, targeted marketing, direct emails, and cyber-bullying. Recently, Prof has become popular among younger teenagers and 44.3 percent of sophomore high school students create their own Prof via mobile phone (*Naikakuhu* [Cabinet office] survey, 2009). However, the popularity of Prof has a darker side. Prof has also become a powerful tool for cyber-bullying among young people. People who are aware of its risks tend to move from Prof to Real, whose sites are more closed, in order to express themselves while avoiding these risks.

As Prof has been designed for teenagers, is available through mobile Internet applications, and has a friendly interface and "cute" design, young people feel as if they are protected and can communicate with each other within a closed personal and private time-space. They believe they can express themselves freely on Prof solely with their own *uchi* members. They share their private information and personal issues and upload their photos via mobile phones. However, sometimes others expose their friends' profiles from Prof to the major Internet sites based on the PC Internet with unpleasant comments, a practice that can be regarded as a form of cyber-bullying, known as *sarasu*. Once their profile on Prof has been exposed, anyone can look at children's profiles via the PC Internet. This is potentially more harmful because it is more open to the world and people normally write their comments anonymously. Thus, sometimes these sites are subject to critical and radical comments. Children may feel as if they have suddenly been thrown into a battlefield where they are attacked by strangers. A case of cyber-bullying, for example, was reported by my informant Rui when I asked her about Prof:

> **Researcher**: How about Prof?
>
> **Rui**: Prof is . . . well . . . there was a problem. Someone sometimes exposes it to 2 chan [2 channel sites in the PC Internet; see Sekiguchi, 2001]. It is easy to find and be searched for . . . This has become a serious problem. We show our faces because we upload our *purikura* [print club stickers] . . . we normally upload our photos . . .
>
> [*Later*]

Researcher: Are you afraid of exposing your privacy?

Rui: I am, because when I was a junior of my junior high school, my friends exposed her close friends to 2 chan. It became a serious problem and teachers gathered all parents at school. I have become very scared of it since then.

Researcher: Did she intentionally expose her friend?

Rui: Yes, she did.

Researcher: Did she write any bad comments on it?

Rui: Yes, she did. So now I use Real and we only tell our close friends the address [of Real].

Although Prof is still popular, these days young people tend to use Real, which is more of a closed community. Real has become the most recent trend among children and young people. However, some use Real with links to their Prof, so again they could have the same trouble with Prof. While they have opportunities to receive comments and get to know people from outside their *uchi*, they are at risk of exposing their photos and privacy to the public. In order to minimize the risk, they share their Real address only with their *uchi* members without linking to any other websites in the Internet. They sometimes share the password among a limited number of friends. They feel more secure and have a social space where they can express themselves freely among their close friends in a closed Real space. While they reinforce their social intimacy in their *uchi*, they lose opportunities to meet others outside of school and communicate freely with each other, which is one of the benefits of the Internet. Thus, they are faced with both opportunities and risks.

De-traditionalization and Reflexive Traditionalization

In the process of globalization, the force of de-traditionalization has been accelerated. Young people access information and images via the Internet and digital satellite television outside Japan. They communicate with non-Japanese people via American social media sites such as MySpace and Facebook in everyday life transnationally. They also participate in these American SNSs to disembed themselves from their Japanese *uchi* and have a chance to express themselves free from Japanese cultural norms. At the same time they communicate with their *uchi* members via Japanese-oriented platforms such as Mixi and reinforce their intimacy and social norms in Japan. As Harada (2010) suggests, the mobile Internet reinforces reflexive traditionalization in Japan. In this section, I will focus on reflexive traditionalization in terms of youth engagement with mobile SNSs, using data from my fieldwork in Japan.

Recently, young people have developed a psychological problem: the so-called Mixi *tsukare* (fatigue). As they come to register too many *maimiku* (e.g., friends on Facebook) from a different *uchi*, they can only write inoffensive things in the compound *uchi*, of a kind that anyone can accept. Mixi has the same time-space as real social interaction, therefore it is not a time-space for many informants where they can express their opinions anonymously and freely. They are too sensitive to the *kuuki* (climate of opinion) among *maimiku* who are from different backgrounds with different identities to write anything important, or even stop writing their diaries because they are afraid that someone might be offended or feel they cannot share their experiences or feelings. Within the traditional *uchi,* opinions, beliefs, values, and philosophies must be shared to create internal homogeneity. As people belong to multiple *uchi* in contemporary society, they show their different faces and play different roles within each *uchi* in real life in order to keep its internal homogeneity. By opening up the closedness of each *uchi* and melting into a "Mixi *uchi*" all together, they face the problems posed by a virtual Japanese *uchi*. People have to accommodate to the traditional social norm of feeling unwilling to express themselves within a Japanese *uchi* (see Takahashi, 2009). Therefore, young people tend to write their own blogs about daily activity (for example, what they ate and what they did during the day) or their feelings (for example, loneliness, happiness, and boredom) with a desire to connect with others, rather than express their political opinions or criticisms:

> **Yusaku**: I write nothing important, for example, "cherry blossoms are in full bloom today!" and I put some photos of cherry blossoms in my diaries these days . . . To tell the truth, I want to quit Mixi. But if I quit, I'm afraid of isolation because everyone does it [uses Mixi]. If everyone quits at the same time, I can quit, too. But everyone is on Mixi.
>
> **Researcher**: Oh, I see.
>
> **Yusaku**: If no-one had mobile phones, then it would be OK. But everyone has their own mobile phone so I must have one and email them frequently, too. Mixi is the same.
>
> **Researcher**: Are you afraid of isolation if you quit Mixi?
>
> **Yusaku**: Yes. I'm not brave enough.

They are afraid of the isolation and estrangement that could result if they express their opinion too freely within a Japanese *uchi* that is constructed through people's online interaction on Mixi. They reinforce their connectivity and closeness to each other in order to keep security and stability, by reflexively adapting the traditional ways of interpersonal relationships to ongoing social processes. Even though Mixi is open to the public, they still believe Mixi is a closed space: therefore they say "I can trust Mixi." Acquisti and Gross (2006) find the same misconceptions concerning Facebook. As "trust" and interdependency are the preconditions for ontological security, people feel secure in being together through their everyday SNS interaction and affirm their sameness through their social actions. Thus they participate in Mixi to gain a sense of "ontological security" (Giddens, 1990, 1991).

Conclusion

Children and young people, defined as digital natives, have become an attractive target for marketing. They have led the technological development of mobile media largely due to the creative ways they use this technology, especially in Japan. However, the widespread dissemination of the idea of digital natives has led to many criticisms of the term, on both theoretical and empirical grounds (Bennett, Maton & Kervin, 2008; Helsper & Eynon, 2010; Livingstone, 2009; Selwyn, 2009). These criticisms concern determinism, especially in terms of technological determinism (e.g., Selwyn, 2003), as well as generational determinism and the notion of an homogenous generation. The criticism centers around the idea that this term overemphasizes differences between generations and undermines diversity within the generation in question (e.g., Buckingham, 2006; Facer & Furlong, 2001; Livingstone, 2008). As stated at the outset, the intention behind this chapter has been to reveal the diversity of Japanese young people as well as their commonality and cultural specificity in relation to the wider picture of youth's engagement with digital media in the globalized world. Children and young people appropriate such information and communication technologies in their everyday life and tactically use mobile phones and the Internet to become free from the control of teachers, parents, and institutions. They connect with images and people nationally and transnationally via social media. While some express themselves freely via non-Japanese social media, others gain a sense of "ontological security" by participating in Japanese social media. Japanese children and young people, whose identities seem to be increasingly in a state of flux, reflexively create and recreate themselves in everyday life by oscillating between different cultural value systems using their SNSs.

In contemporary mobile-saturated society, they are faced with opportunities and risks in the context of everyday life. Children and young people tend to trust the mobile Internet community as a closed, private time-space, and their trust sometimes make them vulnerable to privacy issues and the harmful effects of cyber-bullying. As mobile phones connect with each other twenty-four hours a day, giving rise to the term "fulltime intimate community," because of connectivity factors there is no time-space in which to escape from cyber-bullying.

In the process of globalization and digitalization, we face two opposing forces: de-traditionalization and reflexive traditionalization. Mobile phones and SNSs may give people opportunities to connect with each other beyond age, gender, class, location, and social status, which challenge the hierarchical, patriarchal, and seniority structure in Japan. However, they also reinforce traditional Japanese social and cultural norms within a large mobile Internet community. Mixi has become a social and cultural sphere where people are afraid to express themselves freely, an idea at odds with Habermas's idea of the "public sphere" (1989). They increasingly participate in the world of mobile Internet for connectivity, entertainment, information, and ontological security rather than to express publicly their own social, critical, and political opinions.

Thus, although Japanese youth have become regarded as having some of the highest levels of digital literacy in the world, it does not necessarily mean that they critically and politically participate in the online community to create a new form of democracy supporting the idea of global citizenship or everyday cosmopolitanism:

> The moral existential effort required to do anything with the experiences available via media technologies has to come from other sources—ultimately from within the situated lifeworld of the self. Without this, no amount of technological sophistication can make us online cosmopolitans.
>
> (Tomlinson, 1999, p. 204)

Before we exoticize young people and irresponsibly entrust them with our future, I believe there are many ways in which we have to support them in terms of the opportunities and risks that they face when engaging with the mobile Internet. There is a need for both a new type of digital literacy for mobile media, as well as global literacy for moral and cosmopolitan issues, beyond the dichotomies between online and offline and the local and the global. This will enable young people to minimize the risks of harm and maximize the opportunities to create a new cosmopolitan identity and culture in today's mobile-saturated global society.

References

Acquisti, A., & Gross R. (2006). Imagined communities: Awareness, information sharing, and privacy on the Facebook. In P. Golle & G. Danezis (Eds.), *Proceedings of 6th Workshop on Privacy Enhancing Technologies* (pp. 36–58). Cambridge, UK: Robinson College.

BBC News (2008). Japan police probe stab "warning." Retrieved September 10, 2010, from http://news.bbc.co.uk/1/hi/world/asia-pacific/7443233.stm

Bennett, S., Maton, K., & Kervin, L. (2008). The "Digital Natives" debate: A critical review of the evidence. *British Journal of Educational Technology*, *39*(5), 775–786.

Buckingham, D. (1998). Review essay: Children of the electronic age? Digital media and the new generational rhetoric. *European Journal of Communication*, *13*(4), 557–565.

Buckingham, D. (2006). Is there a digital generation? In D. Buckingham & R. Willett (Eds.), *Digital generations*. Mahwah, NJ: Lawrence Erlbaum Associates.

Bull, M. (2000) *Sounding out the city: Personal stereos and the management of everyday life*. Oxford: Berg.

Cohen, S. (1972). *Folk devils and moral panics*. London: MacGibbon & Kee.

de Certeau, M. (1984). *The practice of everyday life*. Berkeley: California University Press.

Facer, K., & Furlong, R. (2001). Beyond the myth of the "Cyberkid": Young people at the margins of the information revolution. *Journal of Youth Studies*, *4*(4), 451–469.

Flichy, P. (1995). *Dynamics of modern communication: The shaping and impact of new communication technologies*. London: Sage.

Giddens, A. (1990). *The consequences of modernity*. Cambridge, UK: Polity Press.

Giddens, A. (1991). *Modernity and self-identity: Self and society in the late modern age*. Cambridge, UK: Polity Press.

Habermas, J. (1989). *The structural transformation of the public sphere* (T. Burger, Trans.). Cambridge, UK: Polity Press.

Harada, Y. (2010). *Chikagorono wakamonoha naze damenanoka* [*Why are recent young people bad?*]. Tokyo: Koubunshasinsho.

Hashimoto, Y., Oku, R., Nagao, Y., & Shono, T. (2010). *Neo digital natives no tanjo* [*A birth of neo digital natives*]. Tokyo: Diamondosha.

Helsper, E. J., & Eynon, R. (2010). Digital natives: Where is the evidence? *British Educational Research Journal*, *36*(3), 503–520.

Ito, M., Okabe, D., & Matsuda, M. (Eds.). (2005). *Personal, portable, pedestrian: Mobile phones in Japanese life*. Cambridge, MA: The MIT Press.

Ito, Y. (2002). Climate of opinion, kuuki, and democracy. In W. Gudykunst (Ed.), *Communication yearbook 26* (pp. 266–296). Mahwah, NJ: Lawrence Erlbaum.

Kimura, T. (2010). *Digital natives no Jidai to jouhounettowakushakai tositeno nihonshakai* [*The age of digital natives and Japanese society as information network society*]. Division of University Corporate Relations—The Bridge between industry and the University of Tokyo. Retrieved September 10, 2010, from www.ducr.u-tokyo.ac.jp/vision-wg/pdf/07 kimura_vision-wg.pdf

Littlejohn, S. W., & Foss, K. (Eds.). (2009). *Encyclopedia of communication theory*. Newbury Park, CA: Sage.

Livingstone, S. (2008). Internet literacy: Young people's negotiation of new online opportunities. In T. McPherson (Ed.), *Unexpected outcomes and innovative uses of digital media by youth*. Cambridge, MA: The MIT Press.

Livingstone, S. (2009). *Children and the internet: Great expectations, challenging realities*. Cambridge: Polity Press.

Livingstone, S., & Haddon, L. (Eds.) (2009). *Kids online: Opportunities and risks for children*. Bristol: Polity Press.

Morley, D., & Robins, K. (1995). *Spaces of identity: Global media, electronic landscapes and cultural boundaries*. London: Routledge.

Naikakuhu [Cabinet Office]. (2009). *Seishonen no internet riyoukankyoujittai kousa* [*Survey of youth and internet use environment*]. Retrieved September 10, 2010, from http://www8.cao.go.jp/youth/youth-harm/chousa/h21/net-jittai/pdf-index.html

Nakajima, I., Himeno, K., & Yoshii, H. (1999). Ido-denwa riyono fukyu to sono shakaiteki-imi [Diffusion of cellular phones and PHS and its social meanings]. *Joho Tsuushin Gakkai-shi*, *16*(3), 79–92.

Nakane, C. (1967). *TateShakai no ningenkankei tanitsu shakai no riron* [*Interpersonal relationships in a vertically structured society*]. Tokyo: Koudansha Gendaishinsho.

NHK. (2008). *Digital natives: Portrait of the young people who will shape the next age*. Tokyo: NHK Shuppan.

Palfrey, J., & Gasser, U. (2008). *Born digital: Understanding the first generation of digital natives*. New York: Basic Books.

Prensky, M. (2001a). Digital natives, digital immigrants. *On the Horizon*, *9*(5), 1–6.

Prensky, M. (2001b). Digital natives, digital immigrants, Part II: Do they really think differently? *On the Horizon*, *9*(6), 1–6.

Scannell, P. (1988). Radio times: The temporal arrangements of broadcasting in the modern world. In P. Drummond & R. Paterson (Eds.), *Television and its audience: International perspectives*. London: British Film Institute.

Sekiguchi, T. (2001). Log on to the dark side. Retrieved September 10, 2010, from www.time.com/time/magazine/article/0,9171,131020,00.html

Selwyn, N. (2003). Doing IT for the kids: Re-examining children, computers and the "information society." *Media, Culture & Society*, *25*, 351–378.

Selwyn, N. (2009). The digital native—myth and reality. *Aslib Proceedings*, *61*(4), 364–379.

Shimoda, H. (2004). *Keitai literashi* [*Mobile literacy*]. Tokyo: NTT Shuppan.

Takahashi, T. (2003). *Media, audience activity and everyday life—The case of Japanese engagement with media and ICT*. Doctoral dissertation. The London School of Economics and Political Science, University of London.

Takahashi, T. (2008). Japanese young people, media and everyday life: Towards the internationalizing media studies. In K. Drotner & S. Livingstone (Eds.), *International handbook of children, media and culture*. London: Sage.

Takahashi, T. (2009). *Audience studies: A Japanese perspective*. London and New York: Routledge.

Takahashi, T. (2010). MySpace or Mixi? Japanese engagement with SNS (Social Networking Sites) in the global age. *New Media and Society*, *12*(3), 453–475.

Tapscott, D. (2009) *Grown up digital: How the net generation is changing your world*. New York: McGraw-Hill.

Tomlinson, J. (1999). *Globalization and culture*. Cambridge, UK: Polity Press.

Van Rompaey, V., & Roe, K. (2001). The home as a multimedia environment: Families' conception of space and the introduction of information and communication technologies in the home. *Communications*, *26*(4), 351–369.

Watson, J., & A. Hill (Eds.). (2000). *Dictionary of media & communication studies*. London: Arnold.

Yamamoto, S. (1977). *Kuuki'no kenkyu* [*A study of "Kuuki"*]. Tokyo: Bungeishunjuu.

6

ANALYZING STUDENTS' MULTIMODAL TEXTS

The Product and the Process

Mike Levy and Rowan Michael

Introduction

The debate about young people's use of emerging technologies suggests that the way literacy is viewed has undergone a fundamental shift to incorporate aspects of digital literacy (Pegrum, 2009). However, we need to be careful with terms such as "Digital Natives" that lead to an understanding of a whole generation as a homogeneous group. It is recognized increasingly that while a majority of students may possess a core set of technology-based skills, a very diverse range of skills and skill levels exist across the student population (Kennedy et al., 2008; Margaryan & Littlejohn, 2008). In other words, there is more variance across individuals than is suggested by broad generalizations such as the "Digital Native" or the "Net Generation." As Bylin says, "no two digital natives are created equal" and "each of them has varying degrees of access to digital technologies, literacy skills, and participation within their peer culture" (2009, p. 1). Other authors, such as VanSlyke, conclude that "while most of the younger students were proficient in using the Web, they could not adequately perform advanced searches or evaluate the validity of the resources they found" (2003, "A Counter Argument," ¶1). Bennett, Maton, and Kervin (2008) also found that new technology use by young people in the UK was far more complex than the digital native portrayal.

If a coherent group does exist, as terms like "Digital Natives" suggest, do members acquire their skills all at once, or do they develop over time? With English or mathematics we may have a sense of the students' abilities in a particular year level at school, whereas with ICT skills it seems we are more uncertain, both about when particular skills are acquired initially, and then how they develop and evolve over time. If there are differences between individual students, we need to be able to evaluate or measure them at a particular point in time as a basis for understanding how they evolve and develop. A number of research studies have been working in this direction. For example, researchers in Australia with the *National Assessment Program—ICT Literacy Years 6 and 10 Report, 2005* (Ministerial Council on Education, Employment, Training and Youth Affairs, 2007) developed a comprehensive ICT literacy scale against which the technological performances of students could be assessed. Considerable differences were found between the two cohorts (also in terms of gender, socioeconomic levels, and state boundaries). They found that 49 percent of Year 6[1] and 61 percent of the Year 10 student participants *were* able to reach a proficient, basic standard for their year level in searching and selecting information sources from the Internet for specific purposes and communicating that information for particular audiences with software applications. But 51 percent of Year 6 and 39 percent of Year 10 students did not. Also of concern was the finding that there was "much less frequent use of applications that involve creating, analyzing or transforming information" (p. 91). Where young people have been encouraged to transform their understanding of particular topics by designing a multimodal text,[2] positive and enhanced outcomes have been reported (Kimber, Pillay & Richards, 2007; Lehrer, Erickson & Connell, 1994; The New London Group, 1996). Such studies support the notion that digital transformations and designing can enhance the learning process. This recognition of the importance of developing young people's creative and critical productions with technology signals the need for closer attention by researchers and educators to the actual products that young people create in their learning activities. As Adlington and Hansford contend:

> Students often appear to be highly proficient with digital technologies, seemingly able to juggle multiple tasks at the one time . . . however, there are aspects of multimodal designs that need more careful scrutiny and explicit teaching is needed of the more subtle design elements. This is an area that teachers and researchers need to explore.
>
> (2008, p. 8)

Clearly, more empirical research is needed to understand more precisely what skills, knowledge, and literacies are available to young people, both collectively and individually.

Context of the Project

In this chapter, research conducted with students in Australian high schools will be used to examine some of the products and processes associated with the construction of a multimodal text. In the two case studies described in this chapter, we look closely at what students actually do when they are working at the computer. We work inductively—that is, try to locate patterns of activity and productivity from looking at a collection of instances. The first case study (Jenny) compares two multimodal products, the first produced in Year 8, the second by the same student two years later in Year 10. The second case study (Anna and Suzanne) focuses on process as two students work collaboratively to produce a website.

To help facilitate a deeper understanding of products and processes in multimodal text construction, the notion of task is central. It is important in terms of the product because the task goals provide the frame of reference for evaluation of the end result. It is important in terms of the process because we can relate the phases or steps prescribed in the task with those actually followed by the students during completion. In that way, we can also establish whether students are on-task or off-task at different stages of construction. In the present study the discussion of tasks in second-language learning specifically is used to inform our understanding of tasks more generally, while focusing on task-based learning and multimodal text construction with native speakers in a high school context. Broadly accepted, although poorly articulated, concepts such as multitasking—often ascribed as a "natural" ability of digital natives—can also be investigated more systematically (see Gardner & Levy, 2010). Finally, we can consider differences between broadly and narrowly defined tasks.

In order to clarify the notion of task further, it is most instructive to consider a disciplinary area where task goals and task types have been firmly embedded in both discussions of pedagogy and research for many years. Specifically, in the area of second-language learning, recent work concerning cognitive and socio-cultural approaches is most helpful in refining and focusing the task concept further because it illustrates important differences between task types and the learning objectives associated with them (Charbonneau-Gowdy, 2009; Compernolle & Williams, 2009). In this study, the discussion of tasks in second-language learning specifically is used to inform our understanding of tasks more generally, as in this study focusing on task-based learning and multimodal text construction with native speakers in a high-school context.

There has been much written on the nature of tasks in second-language learning (Candlin & Murphy, 1986; Ellis 2003; Levy & Stockwell, 2006; Skehan, 1998). The "task" has been a central construct both in research and practice in the classroom (see Ellis, 2003). There is not sufficient space here to provide an in-depth analysis, but it is important to note that the ways in which language learning tasks are defined has changed significantly over the last twenty years. Generally speaking one can readily detect a broadening out of the concept, at least as it is understood in language learning, from solely developing the students' communicative ability in a specific area of language to enriching the students' personal experience more broadly by enhancing awareness, motivation, creativity, and interpersonal skills (see Ribé & Vidal, 1993). This broader conceptualization of task and the many definitions and subtle interpretations has brought with it some complications; and to help resolve these difficulties, Skehan's (1998) notion of balance of pedagogical goals is most helpful.

According to Skehan (1998), for long-term language learning success, we need to ensure a balanced focus between the pedagogical goals of fluency, accuracy, and complexity in the long-term learning of the grammatical system. By complexity, Skehan means the learner's willingness to use more challenging and difficult language. Importantly, different tasks focus the learners' attention in specific ways: in Skehan's words, "task characteristics predispose learners to channel their attention in predictable ways." Therefore, he continues, "tasks may be chosen and implemented so that particular pedagogic outcomes are achieved" (p. 112). Importantly, an appropriate balance is required between tasks that focus upon fluency and accuracy, and meaning and form; in that regard, it becomes clear that students require reflective activities to develop language awareness, as well as productive activities, in order to become effective and autonomous learners. To achieve the desired balance, Skehan suggests cycles of task-based activity to accommodate different task goals (see also Willis, 1996).

These insights into the nature of the language learning task have important implications regardless of the fact Skehan was writing before the advent of Web 2.0 and network-based computer-assisted language learning (CALL) technology. By delineating more precisely our understanding of the language learning task, we are better able to distinguish general activity at the computer with language learning tasks, and on-task activity as opposed to off-task work. Skehan's analysis also provides a basis upon which actually to determine what the focus might be as students work at the computer in open-ended activities without a time limit and without a preset task to complete, as, for example, when they are active at the computer in the home environment. Further research utilizing Skehan's approach to task-based learning in examining the impact of new technologies on task-based learning, literacies, and the use of authentic materials would be beneficial.

The question of working to a plan, as in responding to a specified task goal, is different to unstructured, open-ended activity at the computer. If we do not know what the task is, we will not be able to determine whether learners are on or off task. A study by Darhower (2002) is noteworthy in this respect because it actually catalogues off-task discussion as well as on-task work. In the context of computer-mediated communication (CMC) and "chat" used to facilitate interaction among a class of students learning Spanish, Darhower describes a sample chat room task with six specific steps around the topic of movies. Darhower explains how in a number of chat room discussions, the learners decided to abandon the assigned task in favor of a topic of their choice. About one quarter of the chat episodes included a significant amount of off-task discussion, ranging from 15 percent to 48 percent of the entire chat episode. Three patterns of result were evident in relation to this paper: first, while some learners never strayed from the assigned topic particular individuals did so in all or nearly all of the chat sessions (Darhower, 2002, p. 262); second, while students often stayed on-task when the instructor was in the room, they went off-task immediately when the instructor left. Clearly, some students are better at staying on task than others. Third, learners often negotiated whether or not to go off-task, and then the topic to discuss. Sometimes conflicts occurred when learners negotiated whether to stay off-task or to return to the assigned task. This study employs a socio-cultural theoretical framework and emphasizes the development of learners' sociolinguistic competence through engaging in the chat sessions. Generally speaking, off-task work was not portrayed in a negative light on the basis that it contributed to social cohesiveness, a view consistent with the theoretical framework. Within another theoretical framework, emphasizing research on interaction and negotiation of meaning, and a more narrowly conceived language learning task, for example (e.g., Fernández-Garcia & Martínez-Arbelaiz, 2002), these off-task digressions are not discussed or reported (see Levy & Stockwell, 2006, for discussion). In such studies, off-task work is not even considered, perhaps with the assumption that the students are always on task. In fact, learner interaction with tasks can change the nature of the envisaged tasks, both in terms of outcome and process.

Rationale of the Project

The case study described here aims to elucidate further the nature of students' multimodal creations through the use of empirical study and observation. The study is drawn from a larger, longitudinal Australian Research Council funded study conducted by Griffith University from 2003 to 2008. This study, *Using and creating knowledge in the high school years: Performance, production, process and value-adding in electronic curricular literacy*, examined the processes undertaken by secondary students in online learning environments and the multimodal products that they generated. The goal in terms of product was to track the development of the participants' multimodal literacies over a two-year period by comparing two multimodal products created at the beginning and end of the period (see Levy & Kimber, 2009). The goal in terms of process was to gain a deeper understanding of how multimodal texts were created, especially when the students were working in pairs at the computer (see Gardner & Levy, 2010). In all, fourteen secondary schools participated in this study and we were able to track 115 students studying the subject Study of Society and the Environment (SOSE) from Years 8 and 10 (2004) to Years 10 and 12 (2006). The complete dataset consists of survey data, product data, process data, and screen capture data.

This chapter examines two portions of the overall dataset, which may be regarded as two independent case studies that focus upon product and process:

the first includes a comparative examination of two products (two websites) created by the same student in Year 8 and Year 10; and the second describes qualities and characteristics of the process as two students work together to create a website describing the impact of plastic bags on the environment with their conclusion. Process data were collected from on-screen activity by using video screen-capture software as students collaborated on the online task. This enabled us to capture screen activity and audio of the voices of the two students working at the computer simultaneously.

Of the students who were followed from Year 8 to Year 10, we initially reviewed all students' products from the years in question to identify general characteristics and trends among the multimodal features. From that analysis, we selected ten students who best represented the cohorts and the multimodal products of these students provided the core product data in this study. For the study on process, the student pair selected for in-depth analysis was determined through an incremental, cyclical process of elimination. We initially chose to focus on a small group represented by one school. Then, from this group, we selected the students who fulfilled the following three criteria: they had worked collaboratively in pairs, they had fully completed the task, and the video screen data recordings were intact and complete.

Teaching and Learning Aims and Objectives of the Project

Online tasks were developed in collaboration with a teacher advisory group. For the comparison of products in the first case study, both the 2004 and 2006 tasks were devised as cross-curricular, inquiry-based activities. The 2004 task required students to evaluate possible solutions in response to the environmental threats posed by plastic bags; the 2006 task followed a similar pattern, but with global warming as the topic. Each task was carefully structured and divided into three phases of development: *researching*, *designing*, and *reflecting*. Part of the research process required the student to complete two templates: first, a *concept map* to organize information acquired from web sources; and second, a *decision-making matrix* to facilitate transformation of the ideas in their concept map into a preferred solution, as required for their multimodal text. Following these preparatory stages, the students could create a multimodal text using a word processor, a presentation tool, or a web publishing program. In the two examples described here, the multimodal products were created using PowerPoint. The investigation of the students' processes of construction utilized the same tasks and topics. For the second case study, the two students created a website on the pros and cons of plastic bags followed by an evaluation using FrontPage. Three hours were requested for the completion of the tasks, either in one session or successive lessons.

The Evaluation and Assessment Criteria

In order to compare and contrast the products of Years 8 and 10, it was necessary to isolate particular characteristic features of the product that represented capacity in operational terms. Clearly it was not possible to make the comparison in every way at every level. We had to be selective. To achieve this goal we determined a 3 × 3, two-dimensional approach that evaluated the title slide/page, the headings, and knowledge representation of each multimodal text in terms of design, content, and cohesion. This approach to evaluation is now explained in a little more detail.

Through consultation with a teacher advisory group and an iterative process of careful identification and selection of elements, the research group reduced the features required when determining quality in multimodal texts to three key elements. Ultimately, we limited our field of view to *design*, *content*, and *cohesion* for our analysis. This approach allowed us to identify individual differences and develop understandings of the nature of digital, multimodal text production at and across different year levels. We were interested in design at both the macro and micro levels in each product, and the students developing ability to manage and work within this environment. For content, critical factors lay first in the students' capacity to locate and select pertinent sources; then learners were expected to demonstrate how successfully they could work with this knowledge to create new knowledge while continuing to engage their audience. The third criterion was cohesion, which referred to the way in which the various elements of the text were drawn together to achieve unity.

Still, to consider these three criteria across every part of the multimodal product was demanding and extremely time consuming. We wanted to develop an approach that was practical. Therefore, we devised a strategy that focused on three elements that we believed were sufficient to provide the necessary coverage for our purposes, that is, to allow analysis within and across a number of texts, and to allow description and comparative discussion of the most salient elements of multimodal text productions. We concluded that close examination of the following components of the product would serve that end:

- the first slide/page in the set (*title slide/page*);
- the choice and shape or wording in the headings of individual slides/pages throughout the set (*headings*); and
- the quality of knowledge revealed in each slide/page and the complete set (*knowledge representation*).

A series of questions was developed in each of the three categories above, to define the distinctive attributes and to provide a basis for comparison of multimodal products at different new levels (for detailed discussion, see Levy & Kimber, 2009).

Findings for Product and Process: Comparison, Discussion, and Implications

Product

The focus on design, content, and cohesion applied to the title slides, headings, and knowledge representation provides the basis for a comparison between the Year 8 and Year 10 products of a single student who we will call Jenny.

The title slides of the two presentations illustrate differences on many levels. The title slide at Year 8 contains striking, dissonant colors, and involves a dynamic build—that is, single elements of the slide are added piece by piece progressively by the viewer with a mouse click: in this way, the viewer governs when the next element is added to the slide. In our dataset we could not find evidence of a dynamic build in Year 10. The use of the dynamic build feature rather than the immediate presentation of a complete slide gives the creator the opportunity to introduce ideas to the reader incrementally and thereby induce various reactions stage by stage within the context of a single slide. In addition, Jenny's title slide at Year 10 is more controlled and restrained compared with Year 8. Perhaps in Year 10, Jenny has become more aware of the expectations involved in creating a PowerPoint presentation within a school environment, especially in the visual aspects. There appears to be less spontaneity and more of a sense of what is to be expected in this kind of multimedia text. The garish, mismatched colors in the earlier title slide contrast markedly with the colors chosen in the latter one, being understated and symbolic. In fact, a key difference is the directness of the text and image in conveying the author's position on the topic. In Year 8, Jenny's position on the topic was made very clear on the title slide; at Year 10, her position is neutral initially, and the viewer/reader has to wait for later slides in order to be able to recognize the author's position on the topic.

As far as slide headings are concerned, in Jenny's Year 8 product, there is evidence of experimentation with the options PowerPoint provides. As with the dynamic build of the title slide, the student is inventive and playful. Thus, in the Year 8 product, we find headings characterized by five different fonts and five different colors for each heading: the student is clearly experimenting with the shadow settings. In stark contrast, the headings across the slides at Year 10 are much more constrained. The evidence of experimentation is missing, although at the same time there is much more of a sense of appropriateness in choosing a font size, style, and color. From Year 8 to Year 10, this particular student moved from using a wide variation of strong colors to black and white, and towards a simplicity in style with the removal of additional font attributes such as shadows in the later product. Whereas the WordArt was varied in the earlier product, it was consistent in the latter one. There is a sense here perhaps of advancement on the one hand and of loss on the other. While the Year 10 product shows a strong sense of unity and cohesion appropriately within a set of conventions and expectations, there is perhaps a loss of energy and creativity compared with the Year 8 product. Maybe only later do students learn that this degree of variation is "inappropriate."

In Jenny's Year 8 and Year 10 products, one can detect similarities and differences across the years. Perhaps the most immediate apparent difference is the color scheme. At Year 8, when viewed in color, the choice of colors to the mature eye is rather shrill with many strong colors varying from slide to slide. In both cases there is a fairly logical progression of ideas from one slide to the next and generally there is one image to a slide. The images are powerful and ideologically value-laden in both presentations. However, one can detect more subtlety in the ideological positioning at Year 10: at Year 8 it is more direct, passionate, and emphatic, especially in the title and content slides. At the lower level, the reader or viewer of the presentation is left in no doubt about the author's position on the topic from the very first slide. In the Year 10 product the author's position is more restrained and circumspect, as shown by the headings formulated as questions at the top of each slide, although the final slide—where the full-screen image in a sense answers the question posed in the heading—still leaves the viewer in no doubt about the author's position.

The question heading juxtaposed with an image "answer" in opposition is a recurring technique used by the student. It was used in slide 3 and 5 in the Year 8 product and again in slide 4 in the Year 10 presentation. It is difficult to ascertain how common this practice is for students' multimodal products across each year, but it is interesting to see this technique reoccurring for Jenny.

As far as content is concerned, the similarities between the two products are instructive. In the Year 8 product, when we reviewed the content of the concept map and decision-making matrix, we found that when content needed to be transferred from one source to another Jenny completed these documents reasonably well. She completed all but one node of the concept map in her own words, and was able to give a strategy together with an explanation in the decision-making matrix. We concluded that the content, although limited in terms of breadth and depth, showed some evidence of sequencing and organization.

Two years later, in the Year 10 product—and where no structural templates were provided to aid content development—Jenny still appears to be able to transfer text from one location to another, but is unable to go to the next step—that is, to evaluate it and formulate her own opinion and to communicate it. At Year 10, Jenny is still having difficulty formulating her own views and drawing conclusions from the material she has read on the resource website. The later slides contain a mix of statements, some taken directly from the source website (slide 3), and some perhaps representing her own opinion, but not finally resolved or clearly formulated (slide 4). In everyday terms, Jenny is not on top of the material she has read and she has not processed it sufficiently so as to reach the point where she has formed an opinion that she can then communicate clearly. This will now be more difficult for her given that she does not have access to supporting documents such as the concept map and the decision-making matrix to help her process existing material and drive the development of her own opinions. In terms of form, there is also little consistency in the structure of bullet point items.

It cannot be proven from the data in this study whether the differences between the Year 8 and Year 10 products, even for a single student, are more to do with a higher degree of knowledge and experience with the tools, or a higher degree of enculturation in regards to the conventions and expectations of a PowerPoint presentation created within a high school context. It may well be a combination of both of these dimensions.

Looking more broadly across the dataset, it is not possible to draw conclusions about what we might term, "Year 8-ness" or "Year 10-ness." There is very considerable variation across individuals within the groups in each year level, especially in terms of the technical resources that are accessed, as well as differences between the groups at the two year levels. There are also some broad areas of commonality across students in both year levels, particularly concerning visual choices where students have clearly visited the same sites for their images; further, it is surprising how often the first image displayed—or at least, an image on the first page of images displayed after a web search—is selected for inclusion in the student's website.

Process

This section on process introduces the results of the second case study where Anna and Suzanne are working collaboratively using FrontPage to design a website responding to a task that required them to present the pros and cons of plastic bags and their conclusion. Working together with a computer is very unlike two people collaborating with pen and paper. There are at least three important differences. First, while typed words may appear immediately on screen, there is often a considerable wait time between the keying in of an instruction and a response from the computer, for example when loading or saving a file, or searching on the Web, especially with slow school intranets. Second, the length of the wait time is unpredictable and may be several minutes. There is also another kind of unpredictability. The result the computer provides to an instruction is often unexpected, as in the selection and ordering of items located in a web search. What follows are some of the process phenomena observed while the students were working together.

First, students took turns in operating the keyboard and the mouse. Quite often one student would be typing on the keyboard while the other was using the mouse. Interactional coordination was frequently observed across modalities, specifically between the two participants through talk and through the keyboard/mouse to the computer screen. Coordination between keyboard/mouse and talk was displayed in a variety of ways, from the simple to the complex, for example, from the coordination of speaking aloud the words while typing the same words to coordination between the end of typing a sentence by one participant with some talk by the other participant (see also Gardner & Levy, 2010).

Second, while much of the talk responded directly or indirectly to task requirements, there was also evidence of off-task discussion. This included anecdotes, reminiscences, jokes, or stories about friends. With this particular pair of students, off-task discussion tended to occur when a routine task was underway (e.g., saving a file in the required area on the intranet), or when the students were simply waiting for a response from the computer, as in a web search. Sometimes as soon as the computer returned a result, the off-task discussion was quickly drawn to a close, sometimes it continued a little longer. Various computer problems (e.g., the school intranet blocker) also at times led to off-task discussion.

Third, there was evidence of various kinds of multitasking within the local computing environment, although the particulars of the multitasking need further investigation. Examples included typing at the keyboard while listening to instructions from a partner, selecting items from pull-down menus while waiting on a return from a search, telling a story while typing in the words for a Google search, forward planning of what to do next when currently engaged in a routine task, etc. It was also interesting to see how cognitive demands often appeared to regulate the completion of more than one task simultaneously; for example, there was evidence to suggest that incoming talk appeared to be sensitive to how close to completion the current task was. In other words, students sometimes paused before talking to their partner, recognizing the demands of the work to hand, until the current sub-task was sufficiently complete.

In reflecting upon the process dimension of multimodal task construction, it is clear we have much to learn. There appears to be considerable adjustment in pair work as individual students create a working, collaborative relationship. During wait times, for example, participants will often continue to talk, sometimes about the task at hand, sometimes about an unrelated matter. These activities are usually brought to a close by the computer signaling the completion of a response to a command, as in the results of an image search. This will generally bring the learners back to the task at hand on the computer, and the computer response acts as a cueing device for the users to resume their onscreen work (see Uhlirová, 1994).

Pedagogical Implications

Observing and reflecting upon the products and processes of multimodal text creation quickly lead to pedagogical implications. Although an in-class time limit of three hours was imposed by teachers in these in-class studies, many individuals and pairs of students did not complete the task. Although it is difficult to generalize, many students did not have what might be termed a completion mindset. For example, one pair of students spent approximately 25 minutes discussing the pros and cons of a very large number of web backgrounds. Clearly, the students thought this a priority—understandably if they had not been instructed otherwise—but it left them little or no time to engage with any other aspects of the task. Working in a multimodal environment exposes students to an enormous number of options and choices. If time were relatively unlimited, as perhaps in the home environment, the amount of time spent on what might be considered relatively unimportant activities would not be problematic. However, on some occasions, especially in a more formal learning environment or in the workplace, it is beneficial to develop in students' time management skills and a sense of priorities in relation to the task at hand. Students may not develop these skills in informal learning environments. Also, it would appear that increased scaffolding of the task through the provision of start-up materials (e.g., a set of web backgrounds) rather than requiring students to start from scratch would ensure students engage with more complex decision-making and text production. In other words, specific tasks and task structure will lead to specific types of learning.

It is also clear from studies such as this one that the technology needs to work effectively and efficiently and in a timely manner. If students have to wait long periods before the results are returned, or if they have to navigate multiple levels within the school intranet to simply load or save, the temptation to move off-task is increased. As evidenced in the study above, these off-task discussions did not seem to support learning through developing social cohesiveness but rather served as "time fillers." Technological infrastructure, therefore, does play a part in supporting learning either "on task" and "off task," and poor infrastructure leads to a loss of time that students are engaged in learning.

Finally, applying Skehan's concept of cycles of task-based activity beyond language learning may also increase quality in both process and product. A balance must be achieved between students' use and development of skills and a reflective process to allow development of metacognitive awareness of their task and skill performance. Such reflection should include a range of skills that are required for task completion and include ICT skills; cognitive skills such as analysis, synthesis, summation, and logical organization of ideas; and focus and time management skills.

Conclusion

Characterizing young learners as a homogeneous group through the use of terms such as "Digital Natives" is problematic for a number of reasons, but the main one is that through a broad generalization such terms gloss over the need to identify and recognize difference. What we have learned from these case studies and the project as a whole is an acute awareness of the complexity of multimodal text production, and the multitude of differences that occur at many levels from one student to the next. Multimodal text production requires students to have sufficient time to complete the tasks, and we found repeatedly in this study that students did not finish in the allotted time. This may in part be due to out-of-school experiences—in the home, for example, where there may be no time limit. Further research into the way students engage with technology in the home environment is necessary, especially in terms of how it differs from technology engagement in the school environment. We also found that the scaffolding procedures for Jenny at Year 8, through the concept mapping decision-making matrix, were very helpful in guiding her towards a more complete, task-relevant outcome. In other words, specific task design will lead to specific learning outcomes.

The study also raised the critical importance of students needing to develop their reflective and evaluative processes in relation to the task, an example of which was Jenny's difficulty in synthesizing, analyzing, and making evaluative decisions about content without scaffolding in Year 10. Lessons can be learned from the literature on task-based language learning, and inclusion of task-based cycles that include reflective components may lead to increased quality of process and product. Such reflective tasks could be designed to be private, such as a reflective journal; public, for example blogs or bulletin boards; or public, shared, and interactive, such as wikis. In a similar way to the critical, evaluative, editorial skills that need to be developed by students when a draft essay is examined, a parallel suite of skills need to be developed for self-assessing web-based tasks such as the ones described here. The number of options available and the range of processes and sequences through which goals may be accomplished greatly complicate research endeavors in the field. Therefore, initially, studies should be descriptive and detailed, with a focus on what students actually do and the choices they make in relation to task goals. In this way, task goals may be further tightened and targeted to provide a clearer scaffold for student work until they gain the confidence and competence to work independently. This approach very much relates back to Skehan's framework for analysis discussed earlier, particularly: in relating task objectives to particular pedagogic outcomes; in achieving an appropriate balance between meaning and form; and in using the notion of cycles of task-based activity to accommodate different task goals, priorities, and points of focus at different times through the process of task completion.

From our analysis, it is also evident that regardless of their technical fluency, students still require traditional skills for successful task completion. Students' lexico-grammatical skills, such as spelling, sentence construction, and choice of lexis, all influenced their ability to complete the task and contributed to the quality of the final product. Students' ability at cognitive tasks, such as analysis, synthesis, organization of ideas, and summation, were all necessary as part of the research process and consequent content production. Time management skills and maintaining a task focus were also important. The essential nature of traditional skill development for students further indicates that today's students are not so different from previous generations: they still need to learn the same basic skills.

The case study above has demonstrated that students in school today are not a homogeneous grouping. They exhibit significant variation in technological skills and abilities, as well as traditional skills. Broad generalizations such as "Digital Natives" dilute the urgent need to gather specific information and data on performance (both process and product), and obscures the educational needs of the current generation, needs that are, as they have always been, specific to each individual student. In order for educational reform to meet the needs of today's students, continued empirical research must be undertaken into how students are learning ICT skills, what skills they need to be learning, and the outcomes of teaching and learning for ICT at different levels in schools. Further research into the specific types of learning produced by different tasks is also required.

Acknowledgments

The research reported in this paper was funded in part by the Australian Research Council 2003–2008. Chief investigators were Professor Mike Levy (The University of Queensland), Professor Claire Wyatt-Smith (Griffith University), and Dr Geraldine Castleton (Griffith University). The authors also wish to acknowledge the contribution of Dr Kay Kimber (Brisbane Girls Grammar School).

Notes

1 In the Australian education system the school year begins in February and finishes at the end of November. Students begin Year 1 the year they turn five and therefore students studying in Year 6 are 10–11 years old, Year 8 are 12–13 years old, Year 10 are 14–15 years old, and Year 12 are 16–17.

2 The term "multimodal text" refers to the way many "texts" are no longer simply constructed with the written word but are now constructed in often complex, multifaceted ways using graphics, animations, and audiovisual material. These texts contain multiple modes and therefore require meaning to be made and constructed in different ways (See Jewitt & Kress, 2003; Levy & Kimber, 2009).

References

Adlington, R., & Hansford, D. (2008, July). Digital spaces and young people's online authoring: Challenges for teachers. Paper presented at *2008 National Conference for Teachers of English and Literacy*, Adelaide, Australia. Retrieved August 5, 2010, from www.englishliteracyconference.com.au/files/documents/AdlingtonHansford-Digital%20spaces.pdf

Bennett, S., Maton, K., & Kervin, L. (2008). The "Digital Natives" debate: A critical review of the evidence. *British Journal of Educational Technology, 39*(5), 775–786.

Bylin, K. (2009). Minds for the future: Why digital immersion matters. [Weblog entry, October 19]. Retrieved August 5, 2010, from www.hypebot.com/hypebot/2009/10/minds-for-the-future-why-digital-immersion-matters.html

Candlin, C. N., & Murphy, D. F. (1986). *Language learning tasks*. In *Lancaster Practical Papers in English Language Education*. Volume 7. London: Prentice-Hall International.

Charbonneau-Gowdy, P. (2009). Awakening to the power of video-based web-conferencing technology to promote change. In R. Oxford & J. Oxford (Eds.). *Second languages teaching and learning in the net generation* (pp. 199–216). Manoa, HI: National Foreign Language Resource Centre University of Hawai'i at Manoa.

Compernolle, R. A., & Williams, L. (2009). (Re)situating the role(s) of new technologies in world-language teaching and learning. In R. Oxford & J. Oxford (Eds.) *Second languages teaching and learning in the net generation* (pp. 9–22). Manoa, HI: National Foreign Language Resource Centre University of Hawai'i at Manoa.

Darhower, M. (2002). Interactional features of synchronous computer mediated communication in the intermediate L2 class: A sociocultural case study. *The CALICO Journal, 19*(2), 249–277.

Ellis, R. (2003). *Task-based language learning and teaching*. Oxford: Oxford University Press.

Fernández-Garcia, M., & Martínez-Arbelaiz, A. (2002). Negotiation of meaning in non-native speaker non-native speaker synchronous discussions. *CALICO Journal, 19*(2), 279–294.

Gardner, R., & Levy, M. (2010). The coordination of talk and action in the collaborative construction of a multimodal text. *The Journal of Pragmatics, 42*, 2189–2203.

Jewitt, C., & Kress, G. (2003) (Eds.) *Multimodal literacy*. New York: Peter Lang.

Kennedy, G. E., Judd, T. S., Churchward, A., Gray, K., & Krause, K-L. (2008). First-year students' experiences with technology: Are they really digital natives? *Australasian Journal of Educational Technology, 24*(1), 108–122.

Kimber, K., Pillay, H., & Richards, C. (2007). Technoliteracy and learning: An analysis of the quality of knowledge in electronic representations of understanding, *Computers and Education, 48*(1), 59–79.

Lehrer, R., Erickson, J., & Connell, T. (1994). Learning by designing hypermedia documents. *Computers in the Schools, 10*, 227–254.

Levy, M., & Kimber, K. (2009). Developing an approach for comparing students' multimodal text creations. *Australasian Journal of Educational Technology, 25*(4), 489–508.

Levy, M., & Stockwell, G. (2006). *CALL dimensions: Options and issues in computer assisted language learning*. Mahwah, NJ: Lawrence Erlbaum Associates.

Margaryan, A., & Littlejohn, A. (2008). *Are digital natives a myth or reality: Student's use of technologies for learning*. Retrieved August 10, 2010, from www.academy.gcal.ac.uk/anoush/documents/DigitalNativesMythOrReality-MargaryanAndLittlejohn-draft-111208.pdf

Ministerial Council on Education, Employment, Training and Youth Affairs (MCEETYA). (2007). *National Assessment Program—ICT literacy Years 6 and 10 Report, 2005*. (Report No. NATASS230106). ACER. Retrieved August 10, 2010, from www.curriculum.edu.au/verve/_resources/NAP_ICTL_2005_Years_6_and_10_Report.pdf

The New London Group. (1996). A pedagogy of multiliteracies: Designing social futures. *Harvard Educational Review, 66*, 60–92.

Pegrum, M. (2009). *From blogs to bombs: The future of digital technologies in education*. Crawley: UWA Publishing.

Ribé, R., & Vidal, N. (1993). *Project work: Step by step*. Oxford: Heinemann.

Skehan, P. (1998). *A cognitive approach to language learning*. Oxford: Oxford University Press.

Tapscott, D. (1998). *Growing up digital: The rise of the net generation*. New York: McGraw-Hill.

Toffler, A. (1970). *Future shock*. New York: Random House.

Uhlirová, L. (1994). On the role of the PC as a relevant object in face-to-face communication. *Journal of Pragmatics, 22*, 511–527.

VanSlyke, T. (2003, May/June). Digital natives, digital immigrants: Some thoughts from the generation gap. *The Technology Source*. Retrieved August 10, 2010, from http://depd.wisc.edu/html/TSarticles/Digital%20Natives.htm

Willis, J. (1996). *A framework for task-based learning*. London: Longman.

7

CITIZENS NAVIGATING IN LITERATE WORLDS

The Case of Digital Literacy

Ola Erstad

Introduction

Increasingly, in the public debate on youth and popular culture, media have become the defining factor dividing generations. This cultural phenomenon started in the 1950s with music and film being targeted towards the age group between childhood and adulthood (Tropiano, 2006). These developments created new cultural expressions of musical genres and films with youthful themes. Other examples of the role of media in defining the cultural positions of youth versus adults are debates about media violence (Comerford, 1992) or music genres such as punk (Hebdige, 1979).

Children born after 1990 are the first generation growing up with digital media embedded in and increasingly dominating the media culture. For this new generation, digital media does not represent something "new." At the same time, a public discourse has been created around young people and new media, conceiving of them as hyper-competent and the creators of twenty-first-century skills (Tapscott, 1998, 2009; Nixon, 1999, 2005). However, there is a lot of uncertainty surrounding these conceptions of so-called "Digital Natives" and "Digital Immigrants" (Prensky, 2001), creating a need to nuance what young people can and cannot do with digital media and the implications such conceptions might have.

Not all young people are digitally competent, nor are they all interested in every aspect of the new media (Livingstone, 2009). They are also, to a large degree, unreflective of the broader implications of such media on our culture, as are most adults. Much research today celebrates the creative and communicative practices in which young people are involved. However, these practices do not include all, or even most, young people. Still, digital media are all around us, and something we relate to in different contexts. In this sense, education and learning are of key importance in a digital culture. Digital literacy or "digital competence," which is the term used in Nordic countries, bridges what young people know or do not know in using digital media, and how education could create the contexts that develop such skills, knowledge, and attitudes further (Erstad, 2010a, 2010b).

The aim of this chapter is to look closer at the term "digital literacy" as a way of understanding how young people relate to the digital culture they live in, and the role of education in developing their knowledge and skills further. To be a citizen today implies dealing with digital media in almost all aspects of life. The conceptual understanding of digital literacy is important in our explorations of citizenship in the twenty-first century and the competencies needed to take part in our present and future societies (Binkley, Erstad, Herman, Raizen & Ripley, 2009). The different literate worlds that young people move between, online and offline, relating to different ways of getting access to and interpreting information ("reading") and producing content in different modalities ("writing"), informs us about how we need to reorient what we mean by "being literate" in our culture.

I will look at this from a Nordic, primarily a Norwegian, perspective, since my research has mostly dealt with media use in this cultural setting, both inside and outside of schools. The first part of the chapter will present a discussion of different aspects of the so-called "digital generation" and emerging literate practices among young people. The second part focuses on digital literacy as a way of understanding how children and young people use different digital media and how this might be implemented in educational settings as an important social arena for knowledge-building in a digital society. However, we will turn first to the Nordic context.

The Nordic Context

The Nordic countries (Denmark, Sweden, Norway, Finland, and Iceland) are interesting partly because of the penetration of technologies in all aspects of society coupled with a high degree of access among young people. At the same time there is a public and political awareness about the importance of digital literacy related to education and not such a strong emphasis on testing as in many other countries. So this could very well be the land of the digital natives.

Access to computers, the Internet, and mobile phones with Internet capabilities among young people between the ages of sixteen and twenty-two is more than 90 percent, and in some areas up to 100 percent. So access is not an issue for most youths in these countries. During the last decade, the time spent on digital media among Nordic youth has been steadily growing in the age range from eight to twenty-four years (Nordicom, 2009). For example, 73 percent of all eight to eighteen year olds use the Internet daily (Norwegian Media Authority, 2008). In Norway, the annual study on children and youth media use done by Synovate shows that, on average, the time spent on media during a regular weekday has increased from four hours and forty-five minutes in 1991 to six hours and thirty-two minutes in 1999 to seven hours and fifty-eight minutes in 2009 (Erstad, 2010b). For the age group of sixteen-to-twenty-four year olds, 2009 marks the first year that the average time spent with media exceeded nine hours per day (nine hours and five minutes). Mobile phones were included in this study from 2006. Of course, this does not mean that more than nine hours are spent continuously every day, since most young people are multitasking—that is, spending time with different media at the same time, for example, watching TV, listening to music, being on Facebook, and sending texts.

Social networking sites have existed in the Nordic countries for some time. Some examples are "LunarStorm" in Sweden, "mPetreklanen" in Norway, and "Skum.dk" in Denmark. The development of these sites started around 1999–2000, and they have since then gained increasing popularity among young people, where Facebook in recent years has taken over as the main social media site (Erstad, Gilje & de Lange, 2007).

The technology push within the education systems in the Nordic countries has been central from the beginning of the 1990s onwards (Erstad & Quale, 2009). The main focus has been on the technology itself, and on getting access to computers and the Internet into schools. It is only in recent years that critiques, reflection, and issues around production and creativity have started to emerge in terms of the ways digital media are used in schools (Erstad & Gilje, 2008). An important aspect is, of course, that the education systems in the Nordic countries are different from education systems in other parts of the world. There has generally been a much stronger tradition of project-based learning, a strong emphasis on equal possibilities, and a high access to media within schools. Also, the broader social structure and the welfare society model, which are similar in all Nordic countries, have created a different framework for how people engage themselves in their own societies (Castells & Himanen, 2004).

Another aspect is the emphasis on *Bildung*, a concept from the German tradition, which can be used to understand the interrelationship between technological development and education (Drotner, 1991; Thavenius, 1995; Lovlie, 2003). No similar concept exists in the English language, but it is indicative of being or becoming "literate." The argument is that the growth of media culture as a resource for identity formation and learning breaks off from the elitist conception of *Bildung*. The ways in which young people use media culture today create new ways of conceptualizing what it means to become "literate" or competent in contemporary Western cultures.

A Digital Generation?

Over time, the study of the age group between childhood and adulthood has been seen as a struggle over cultural positions and between different scientific fields, especially psychology and sociology (Lesko, 1996). In particular, the influence of cultural studies has been predominant in its orientation towards meaning making, cultural settings, sign making, and performance among different subcultures of youth (Hebdige, 1979). In this part of the chapter I will use different perspectives on youth and digital media to provide some critical reflections of the general term "digital generation" (Buckingham & Willett, 2006).

Conceptions of Digital Youth

Conceptions of digital youth are entwined with generalizations about generational change popularized by the idea of digital natives and immigrants (Prensky, 2006). Further, these conceptions are supported by other popular notions of generational change, such as Generation X and Y, or "Generation Me" (Twenge, 2006).

The implications of such generational divides can be seen in Tapscott's book *Growing up Digital: The rise of the "Net Generation"* (1998), and a recent follow-up book called *Grown up Digital* (2009), as well as a similar book by Palfrey and Gasser called *Born Digital* (2008). These books are based on empirical data consisting of interviews with a large number of young people from around the world, even though the data themselves are not presented in any detail and are therefore difficult to evaluate from a methodological perspective. Such books have a tendency to over-generalize the extent to which children and young people are competent media users in a broad set of areas. From other research we know that there are huge differences both within and between different cultures and countries in how young people relate to and use digital media (Coiro, Knobel, Lankshear & Leu, 2008). One voice critical of such public conceptions of digital youth is Buckingham (2003), who argues for a more nuanced understanding of how young people relate to different media, creating a middle ground between media pessimists and optimists based on different sets of empirical data.

Another influence on the public perception of digital youth is the popular media discourse about new kinds of computer-related positional advantage in relation to educational and life-chance trajectories for children, especially targeted towards parents (Buckingham, Scanlon & Sefton-Green, 2001; Nixon, 1999, 2005). In addition, newspapers and magazines have added to the social construction of technology-savvy kids by presenting stories of how young people succeed as entrepreneurs in technology businesses or drop out of institutionalized education to be hired by media industries seeking their specialized technological competencies (Nixon, 2005).

Studying Digital Youth

Today, there is a lot of empirical data on digital youth. One line of research is directed towards quantitative studies of use patterns and frequencies. For example, in a recent study of media use among American youth, the Kaiser Foundation used the term "Generation M2" to describe the increasing time spent with such media by American youth, tracing developments from 1999 to 2009 (Rideout,

Foehr & Roberts, 2010). Another example is the study "UK Children Go Online" (Livingstone & Bober, 2005) and, further, the "EU Children Online" study. These studies document in a nuanced way the use of the Internet by a broad set of youth, showing that many young people are not very elaborate or reflective users.

However, in order to grasp the more qualitative aspects of media use, we need to specify certain focus areas of media use, such as the work by Gee (2003) on gaming cultures, Lankshear and Knobel (2006) on fan fiction cultures, or Buckingham and Willett (2009) on media production. In this way we get a better understanding of how specific groups of young people are engaged in using digital media for different purposes and the implications these ways of using media have for their broader social and cultural lives. Similar examples of the different ways children and young people are using different media and their implications are evident in recent research (Coiro, Knobel, Lankshear & Leu, 2008; Drotner & Livingstone, 2008).

Furthermore, the age-specific use of digital media is fluid. On certain social networking sites, age groups in their twenties and thirties are even higher consumers than youth. However, there are certain aspects of the contextual embedding that such media have for youth rather than for adults that do seem different (Buckingham & Willett, 2006).

The Emerging Practices of Digital Youth

Important in defining digital youth is examining the emerging practices using digital media and how these change over time. In this way we get a better understanding of the development of social patterns of media use, how they are distributed among the population as a whole, and the social, cultural, and educational implications they might have.

Using an ethnographic approach, Ito and colleagues have studied "digital youth" in the US (Ito et al., 2010). In what they describe as media ecologies, they manage to document the broader social and cultural contours, as well as the overall diversity, in youth engagement with digital media. The concept of ecology is used strategically to highlight that:

> The everyday practices of youth, existing structural conditions, infrastructures of place, and technologies are all dynamically interrelated; the meanings, uses, functions, flows, and interconnections in young people's daily lives located in particular settings are also situated within young people's wider media ecologies . . . Similarly we see adults' and kids' cultural worlds as dynamically co-constituted, as are different locations that youth navigate such as school, after-school, home, and online places.
>
> (Ito et al., 2010, p. 31)

By drawing on different case studies from specific communities, this research manages "to map the contours of the varied social, technical, and cultural contexts that structure youth media engagement" (p. 31). In their findings, they draw out certain genres of participation into what they describe as "friendship driven" and "interest driven." Further, they have identified different levels of commitment and intensity in new media practices, in what they describe as "hanging out," "messing around," and "geeking out." These genres of participation are then interpreted as "intertwined with young people's practices, learning, and identity formation within these varied and dynamic media ecologies" (p. 31). This research is important in the way it broadens our understanding of media use and participation in social media among young people.

One interesting term used by Watkins (2009) in analyzing media use, especially during the last two decades, is "digital migration." In his rich sets of data, Watkins shows both how young people gradually migrate from traditional mass media towards digital media, and also how they migrate between different online sites such as MySpace, YouTube, and Facebook, and also how mobile technologies are creating new patterns of use anytime, anywhere.

Another example is the ways in which digital media might influence the civic engagement of youth (Cassell, Huffaker, Tversky & Ferriman, 2006; Selwyn, 2002). In recent years, this has become an interesting area of research that documents how some groups of young people either become engaged in sites made for such purposes or create their own spaces to express their own opinions or make collective statements (Loader, 2007; Rheingold, 2008). Some research shows that the Internet can serve as an information resource and community-building tool for civic engagement and political participation among young people (Rainie & Horrigan, 2005). So perhaps the influence of the Internet on children and adolescents can play a positive role in their development, a role that other institutions in society are no longer filling?

This is an example of how skills in using digital media and navigating the Internet are the foundation for the development of broader cultural competencies of importance to our evolving democratic processes. Still, such digital practices represent a challenge of participation and navigation in the Internet culture, of who really participates, and of how competent young people as democratic participants are in navigating between different online spaces of importance for them.

Another important development is the new possibilities for user-generated content production represented by Web 2.0 and the new editing software that make the personal voice more apparent. Information and communication technologies can be used for producing and consuming narratives in a whole new way by people around the world, as seen on Internet sites such as MySpace and YouTube. Content can be downloaded from the Internet, remixed (Lessig, 2008), and put together in new ways, and then uploaded onto the Internet for others to use further in a potentially endless production process. This way of working with content fundamentally changes the traditional way of creating content as experienced through the printed book. This "production mode" and the new competencies of remixing (Erstad, 2008) have also raised issues about students' active role in knowledge practices.

In the popular press, these practices are often celebrated as the literacies of the young generation. Although these cultural practices have become more common, and are new in the sense that digital media change both how and what people produce, not all young people are involved in such practices; far from it. Potentially, most young people can take part in these production practices, but for different reasons they choose not to. These practices have primarily been studied as part of young people's everyday lives. However, such practices have increasingly found their way into more formal settings of school-based learning, for example, with digital storytelling in different subject domains. In this sense, issues of digital competency become important in taking up such cultural practices and framing them as learning practices of importance to the development of the skills and competencies needed in the twenty-first century.

A Generation of Digital Youth

Such a discussion about what we mean by a digital generation is important, not only to move beyond simple statements about "natives" and "immigrants," but also in terms of identifying what impact such technologies have on specific social practices in which people are involved.

There is great variation in how digitally competent and technologically interested young people are. Livingstone's (2009) studies of the bedroom cultures of young people using digital media in the UK are examples of research that raise critical questions about what we mean by "digital youth" and the role of media in young people's everyday lives. Such studies show that not all young people are as technology savvy as the public image might imply.

Similar issues have been raised concerning the concept of a "digital generation" (Buckingham & Willett, 2006). Such research shows that our broad descriptions of a digital generation should be applied carefully. We need to specify variations and digital divides among young people at different age levels, and in different cultural contexts, and also to specify different aspects of digital media, from gaming to social media, texting, and so forth. So, more correctly than as relating to a specifically digital generation, these developments can best be described as a transitional phase where digital media are still in transition and where young people today are experiencing a dual culture, between the old and the new, what Herring (2008) calls "a transitional generation."

To Be(come) Literate in the Digital Age

To be literate is an indication of how people adjust to social and cultural developments and to what extent they have the competencies needed to take part in every aspect of social life in a digital culture. My interest is mainly in the role of education in creating the learning environments needed for providing all children and young people with the competencies needed to become literate in a digital culture and enhance their everyday knowledge, experiences, and skills.

Most conceptions of digital literacy build on the research tradition defining literacy as embedded in specific social practices (Barton, 1994; Heath, 1983; Scribner & Cole, 1981; Street, 1984). A definition of literacy by Lankshear and Knobel (2006) encompasses these social practices that change over time. They define literacy as: "Socially recognized ways of generating, communicating and negotiating meaningful content through the medium of encoded texts within contexts of participation in Discourses (or, as members of Discourses)" (p. 65). This definition is not bound by certain technologies. It proposes to study literacies in practice (what people do with technologies and digital texts) and not as something pre-described. The important message is that digital literacy among young people today is of direct relevance to discussions about learning in schools, and it seriously confronts earlier conceptions of literacy and learning.

In addition, it is important to stress that digital literacy is related to *situational embedding*, that is, the use of technology within life situations. To understand such processes we have to look at different contexts where literacy is practiced and given meaning. This is especially important when relating it to how children and young people use digital technologies across contexts.

This implies that we have constantly to ask the more general question of what it means to "read" and "write" in a culture, and thereby how we learn (Pahl & Rowsell, 2005). In the *Handbook of Literacy and Technology*, with the subtitle *Transformations in a Post-Typographic World*, Reinking et al. (1998) present several perspectives on how the development of digital technologies changes conceptions of text, of readers and writers, and ultimately of literacy itself. This implies that digital literacy relates to changes in traditional cultural techniques such as reading and writing, yet meanwhile opening up new dimensions to what it means to be a competent reader and writer in our culture.

The key questions then become: What are the key literacies and competencies for the twenty-first century, and how can we develop an education system that is adjusted to face these challenges of competence development for the future? Also, what do young people really know about media, and what implications does this have for learning in educational settings? Technology serves as both a driver and a lever for these transformations.

Towards Frameworks and Assessments

During the last decade, several initiatives have been taken to develop typologies and frameworks for digital literacies. Some of the frameworks of digital literacy conceive of digital literacy in a narrow sense as skills that can be broken down into certain operations. However, other definitions and frameworks conceive of digital literacy more broadly.

TABLE 7.1 Different aspects and categories of digital literacy

Basic skills	Be able to open software, sort out and save information on the computer, and other simple skills in using the computer and software.
Download	Be able to download different information types from the Internet.
Search	Be aware of and know how to get access to information.
Navigate	Be able to orient oneself in digital networks and learning strategies in using the Internet.
Classify	Be able to organize information according to a certain classification scheme or genre.
Integrate	Be able to compare and put together different types of information related to multimodal texts.
Evaluate	Be able to check and evaluate the information one seeks to get from searching the Internet. Be able to judge the quality, relevance, objectivity, and usefulness of the information one has found. Be able to evaluate sources critically.
Communicate	Be able to communicate information and express oneself through different mediational means.
Cooperate	Be able to take part in net-based interactions of learning, and take advantage of digital technology to cooperate and take part in networks.
Create	Be able to produce and create different forms of information as multimodal texts, make web pages, and so forth. Be able to develop something new by using specific tools and software. Be able to remix different existing texts into something new.

Source: Translated from Erstad, 2010b

From my own research on the educational use of digital technologies, I have suggested a few categories to specify some aspects of digital literacy in school practices (Erstad, 2010b). This is thought of as different aspects of how we understand young people's use of digital technologies in learning activities at school, and as a tool for assessing what they can and cannot do with digital media.

Table 7.1 is one step in the direction of breaking down what we mean by digital literacy in terms of school practices. The categories consist of general competencies that are not connected to specific subjects in school or specific technologies. They can be taught and are not only related to what is learned in school settings, but also to situations outside the school.

Other frameworks have used "digital competence" as an overall term. One example is the European Commission Education and Training 2010 working group on "key competences". This program identifies *digital competence* as one of the eight domains of key competences, defining it as:

> The confident and critical use of Information Society Technologies for work, leisure and communication. These competences are related to logical and critical thinking to high-level information management skills, and to well developed communication skills. At the most basic level, ICT skills comprise the use of multi-media technology to retrieve, assess, store, produce, present and exchange information, and to communicate and participate in networks via the Internet.
>
> (European Commission, 2006, p. 14)

Digital competence in this framework encompasses knowledge, skills, and attitudes related to such technologies.

The critical point is to bring the policy agenda and the more normative research arguing for the necessity of digital literacy more in touch with studying knowledge practices, and how digital media create conditions for change and transition within such practices (Erstad, in press). However, the key challenge is to go deeper into the implications of increased use of new technologies in educational practices.

Some countries, such as Australia, the US, Norway, and Hong Kong, have developed specific tests to measure students' digital literacy. The first attempt was made by the International Society for Technology in Education (ISTE) in the US (see www.iste.org/standards.aspx), where students, teachers, and administrators can click on different online assignments and get a profile of their digital literacy skills.

In Norway, testing of digital competence was introduced in the ITU Monitor 2009 study (Hatlevik et al., 2009). The results show a strong relationship between students' digital literacy, their general school performance, and the educational background of the parents. The strength of this study is how it examines digital competence as interconnected with issues of access, school leadership, teacher competence, and school development.

A more elaborate test, in the sense that it uses more simulation tools and is not so related to specific school subjects, has been developed in Australia. This test is also more based on performance assessment in solving problems than just on skills in operating the technology. In their report from the first phase Ainley, Fraillon, and Freeman (2007) present the results from a study conducted in 2005 involving approximately 7,400 students from grades 6 and 10 in 520 schools across Australia. By having two year-groups, it also traces progressions in what the authors call ICT literacy.

The items distributed across the ICT literacy scale were used to develop a progress map that could be interpreted in terms of the skills and understanding demonstrated by students in their responses to the items. In this case, six proficiency levels were defined and descriptions were developed to characterize typical student performance at each level. The levels and the percentage on each level are used to summarize the performance of students overall, and to compare performances across subgroups of students.

For example, at Level 1 the students are expected to perform basic tasks using computers and software, to implement the most commonly used file management and software commands when instructed, and to recognize the most commonly used ICT terminology and functions. The scale then increases in complexityand performance level. At Level 4 the students are assessed on their abilities to generate well-targeted searches for electronic information sources and select relevant information from within sources to meet a specific purpose. In addition they are expected to create information products with simple linear structures and use software commands to edit and reformat information products in ways that demonstrate some consideration of audience and communicative purpose, and also to recognize situations in which ICT misuse may occur and explain how specific protocols can prevent this. At the highest level, Level 6, the focus is even more on the productive capabilities of students in integrating information through technical proficiency, careful planning, and review, and representing data as integrated, complete information products. Students at this level should also be able to design information products consistent with the conventions of specific communication modes and audiences and use available software features to enhance the communicative effect of their work (Ainley, Fraillon & Freeman, 2007). To what extent these items and levels are general competences that might work in other countries and cultures is difficult to know since we do not have many other scales to compare with. Still, this outline gives some indications of how we might create better indicators of digital literacy and student progression.

The data from the above-mentioned study (Ainley, Fraillon & Freeman, 2007) show that only 8 percent of Year 6 students performed at Level 4 or above compared to 61 percent of Year 10 students. In contrast, 51 percent of Year 6 students performed at Level 2 or below compared to 7 percent of Year 10 students. ICT literacy was strongly associated with socioeconomic background. Approximately two-thirds (68 percent) of Year 6 students whose parents were "senior managers and professionals" attained the proficient standard, compared to approximately one-third (32 percent) of students whose parents were in "unskilled manual, office and sales" occupations. Three-quarters (75 percent) of Year 10 students whose parents were "senior managers and professionals" attained the proficient standard, compared to just less than half (49 percent) of students whose parents were in "unskilled manual, office and sales" occupations.

There was no statistically significant difference between the sexes in the percentage attaining the proficient standard at either Year 6 or Year 10. There was no difference in ICT literacy associated with language background. The authors conclude that:

> One should not assume that students are uniformly becoming adept because they use ICT so widely in their daily lives. The results of the assessment survey suggest that students use ICT in a relatively limited way and this is

> reflected in the overall level of ICT literacy. Communication with peers and using the Internet to look up information are frequent applications but there is much less frequent use of applications that involve creating, analyzing or transforming information. There are substantial differences between Year 6 and Year 10 suggesting that considerable growth in ICT proficiency takes place over these four years. Within each Year level there are differences associated with socioeconomic background, indigenous status and remote geographic locations (compared to metropolitan locations).
> (Ainley et al., 2007, p. xiv)

This assessment approach to digital literacy is still in an initial phase, and several initiatives are now being taken in different countries. The important message from the Australian study is that this should not be seen only as a summative score of certain skills, but, to a larger extent, as formative assessment where students, both individually and collaboratively, perform to solve certain tasks of problem solving.

Digital Literacies in Educational Practices

In my own research I have tried to specify the more qualitative and practical consequences of digital literacy in school settings (Erstad, 2006). In this way one gets a more focused and detailed understanding of the use of digital media for educational purposes. Five dimensions can be elaborated, which highlight different aspects of how we understand digital literacies as part of school-based learning.

Dimension 1: Basic Skills

This has traditionally been expressed as certification of skills for teachers and students. It is a profile of how good you are at performing certain tasks in operating the computer, the Internet, or software. The problem with this approach is that the technology changes all the time, and it is difficult to develop standardizations that will last over time. And, as expressed by young people, handling the technology is something you explore and learn when needed (Erstad, 2007). Still, not all students have the same skills in operating the technology, and teachers should track the levels of their students as a starting point for how technology is used in learning activities.

Dimension 2: Media as Object of Analysis

One aspect of digital literacy in schools is the importance media and technology have as a knowledge domain in themselves. During the last forty years, media culture has become more and more evident at all levels of society. In this sense it has become a knowledge domain that is important for students to know about in itself. This has traditionally been part of media education in school, but since the impact of digital media, it has become an important part of many subjects in school. Issues such as media history, media genres, and media and power would then be important parts of school curricula.

Dimension 3: Knowledge Building in Subject Domains

This relates to how new technologies change fundamental issues within established school subjects. We have seen this before when the calculator was introduced in mathematics, and the disputes this created about how mathematics as a subject changed because of it. The same can be said about different digital media and software packages that are introduced in different subjects. How does it change the knowledge structures within the subject itself? What are considered core knowledge elements? How do students build knowledge and approach these knowledge structures? It is thereby seen that knowledge is interconnected with the cultural tools we have available, and that this changes over time.

Dimension 4: Learning Strategies

This dimension goes across different subject areas and is more about the ways students approach information and knowledge. This has been important before in the way students might have problems in developing good strategies for how they learn, and their self-regulated learning. Related to digital literacy this dimension has become even more important. Developments of information sources on the Internet put more challenges on the competences of students to orient themselves in searching for information, evaluating such sources, and the way they use information to build knowledge—also how students need to develop good strategies in how they can use information to learn more, in what is referred to as learning how to learn.

Dimension 5: Digital Bildung/Cultural Competence

This last dimension points towards broader issues around learning in our contemporary Western culture. Issues of what is called "digital *Bildung*," or cultural competence, are more concerned with the overall challenges of being part of a digital culture. It is about functioning optimally in a media culture and a knowledge society, and being able to be informed to make decisions of importance for oneself as a citizen and for society as a whole, for example, when elections become digitalized and political debates take place online. It is also about how learning is connected to identity and our communicative competence in using the different cultural tools available to us. This approach to learning and literacy is more holistic and integrated in terms of educating the digital generation.

Across Contexts of Learning and Literacy

In several studies (Coiro, Knobel, Lankshear & Leu 2008; Drotner & Livingstone, 2008) interviewing and observing young people about their relationship to and use of different digital media, it is evident that digital media in general are an embedded part of their everyday activities. They talk about it as something taken for granted, even though it seems many do not define such media as important, as in the impression given in the literature on digital generations mentioned above.

As part of a study that began in January 2009, four focus group interviews were conducted with twenty-eight young people (fifteen-to-sixteen year olds), divided by living in the East and West of Oslo, and by gender-specific groups (fourteen boys and fourteen girls). The theme for the interviews was about growing up in the East and West of Oslo, and the role of different media in their lives. Oslo is divided by a river that runs through the middle of the city. In general this division also indicates some distinct ethnic, religious, and socioeconomic differences between the West and East of Oslo, though there are differences within communities on each side. In the East the average socioeconomic level of families is much lower than in the West. The major immigrant groups that have come to Norway in the last thirty years live in the East of Oslo, with hardly any living in the West. The crime rates are higher in the East, but there are no major differences in the average school performances between the two areas.

The morning rituals in the two neighborhoods have similarities, but also differences. All of the students check whether they have received MSN or Facebook postings since the evening before. A few use the Internet to check news channels online, to see if something has happened during the night, which, they mention, might also be relevant for discussions at school the same day. For some of the students in the East, it is common to pray before going to school.

All of them, both east and west, also talk about school as an important social space. School is where they make and meet friends. During recess they hang out with friends, but also during school hours, when they are often bored, they have ways of staying in touch with friends. Available digital media such as the computer and mobile phones give them more possibilities for this. One girl from the West says about the social aspects of school that, "I was away from school on Friday because I was sick, and I had missed soooo much. They had talked about so many insanely strange things. I notice I like much more to be at school than at home."

After-school activities consist mainly of homework and organized activities such as football and dancing. Most of the students also spend much of their time hanging out with friends, in the East mostly in outdoor spaces, while in the West in private houses. The computer is present most of the time, except when they are training. As one girl from the West explains, "I can sit at the computer all day, during the night when I cannot sleep, or after school if I do not have anything else to do." The students turn on the computer as soon as they get home, and it serves as a multifunctional medium that they use to play and download music, to communicate with friends (mostly through Facebook and MSN), to see films with friends, check on YouTube, to search for information, and to use as a resource when doing homework. They usually log on to the learning management system at school to check what they have for homework, which has been put in a special file by the teacher. In addition, they also watch TV, especially news and special series. They also listen to music on their mobile phones or iPods throughout the day. Most of the boys play games several time a week, and they prefer online games where they can also play against friends using audio. The girls in the East play a bit, mostly physically active games such as those using the Nintendo Wii (boxing, golf, tennis, bowling), Xbox (dancing and Singstar), or PlayStation 3 (Guitar Hero). Girls in the West do not play games anymore.

As part of a wider conception of literacy and learning, these young people talk about different sites on the Internet as resources in their daily lives. This can be seen in the following examples:

> On YouTube you can learn all sorts of things. You can push "how to" and search whatever you want. I learned a song on guitar, another on piano, and also ideas for my knitting.
>
> (girl, West)

> *Girl 1:* One period I wrote a lot, created novellas and things like that.
> *Girl 2:* I did the same. I really like to write. In one period I was miserable; it was really great writing a lot.
> *Girl 1:* I have such a weird fantasy, so I have to get it out.
> *Girl 2:* Me, too. I write and write without stopping. It can be anything.
>
> (girls, West)

> In Football Manager I learn how to create a team, and how to take advantage of the team's finances so that it does not get into a deficit.
>
> (boy, East)

The question is, then, how this relates to school practices of using such technologies. According to the young people themselves, digital media are used very differently in schools, and for many of them there should also be a difference. Many seem critical of the extended use of such technologies in schools. There might be several reasons for this: that they have had bad experiences, that they are oriented towards getting good grades and see that occurring only through traditional ways of learning, or that they define a clear difference between learning-oriented activities with digital media in schools and more entertainment-oriented activities with such media outside of schools.

These young people use a wide variety of digital media that are part of their activities from the time they get up in the morning until they go to bed. Still, from an educational point of view, and relating to digital literacy, it is rarely expressed in a critical analytical way as something they reflect on. Digital media is something they "do stuff with." And that is why formal education becomes important.

Final Remarks—On Becoming a Digital Citizen

The argument in this article has been to develop a more cohesive approach in our conceptualizations of a new digital generation. It is rather, still, a generation that uses many different media, both analog and digital, in their everyday lives. At the same time it is clear that young people growing up today are experiencing important aspects of the implications of digital media in our culture. New conceptions of literacy, and what is now termed as digital literacy, exemplify many of the challenges of educating the digital generation.

During the last five years there has been an increasing international orientation towards defining twenty-first-century skills (Trilling & Fadel, 2009). This is partly about redefining known competences, such as problem solving and critical thinking, but also about new competences such as digital literacy, and the importance of knowledge creation and innovation. In addition to such key areas of competences, the orientation is towards the challenges that we face today concerning citizenship in a digital culture (Binkley et al., 2009).

However, there is one question that is of key importance for the educational prospects for a digital generation, and that is: to what extent will we see new divisions in our societies, locally, nationally, and globally, around who will become included and excluded? (Warschauer, 2003). The digital divide has mainly been discussed as an issue related to access, gender differences, and so forth. More important today is to see this as an issue of competence and literacy, or more generally as *Bildung* for a digital age. This would imply knowing how to navigate in the information jungle on the Internet, to create, to communicate, and so forth. This is where issues of digital literacy and empowerment come in.

In her book *Literacy for Sustainable Development in the Age of Information* (1999), Rassool argues that research perspectives on technology and literacy need to reconceptualize power structures within the information society, with an emphasis on "communicative competence" in relation to democratic citizenship. Digital technologies create new possibilities for how people relate to each other, how knowledge is defined in negotiation between actors, and how it changes our conception of learning environments in which actors make meaning. Empowerment is related to the active use of different tools, which must be based upon the prerequisite that actors have the competence and critical perspective to use them for learning. Literacy, seen in this way, implies processes of inclusion and exclusion. Some have the skills and know-how to use these processes for personal development, while others do not. Schooling is meant to counteract such cultural processes of exclusion.

What will the life of citizens be like in societies that are more and more dependent on digital media in every part of social life? How should we in our research efforts try to grasp what aspects of skills, competences, and literacies are important for being a citizen with the necessary knowledge base to take part in our society? This of course also raises some basic questions about the role of schools in our societies. Schools would then still be important social institutions as a learning space for all young people growing up, but just one of several learning spaces that children and youth relate to in their daily lives. In the next few years it will be critical to debate and research these issues and to move towards a better understanding of what citizenship in terms of twenty-first-century digital competences implies.

References

Ainley, J., Fraillon, J., & Freeman, C. (2007). *National Assessment Program: ICT literacy Years 6 & 10 Report 2005*. Retrieved May 24, 2010, from www.mceetya.edu.au/mceecdya/nap_ict_literacy,12183.html

Barton, D. (1994). *Literacy: An introduction to the ecology of written language*. Oxford: Blackwell.

Binkley, M., Erstad, O., Herman, J., Raizen, S., & Ripley, M. (2009). *Draft White Paper 1. Defining 21st Century Skills*. Retrieved May 24, 2010, from www.atc21s.org

Buckingham, D. (2003). *Media education: Literacy, learning and contemporary culture*. London: Polity Press.

Buckingham, D., & Willett, R. (Eds.). (2006). *Digital generations: Children, young people and new media*. Mahwah, NJ: Lawrence Erlbaum.

Buckingham, D., & Willett, R. (2009). *Video cultures: Media technology and everyday creativity*. Hampshire, UK: Palgrave Macmillan.

Buckingham, D., Scanlon, M., & Sefton-Green, J. (2001). Selling the digital dream: Marketing educational technology to teachers and parents. In A. Loveless & V. Ellis (Eds.), *Subject to change: Literacy and digital technology* (pp. 20–40). London: Routledge.

Cassell, J., Huffaker, D., Tversky, D., & Ferriman, K. (2006). The language of online leadership: Gender and youth engagement on the Internet. *Developmental Psychology*, *42*(3), 436–449.

Castells, M., & Himanen, P. (2004). *The information society and the welfare state: The Finnish model*. Oxford: Oxford University Press.

Coiro, J., Knobel, M., Lankshear, C., & Leu, D.J. (2008). *Handbook of research on new literacies*. New York: Lawrence Erlbaum.

Comerford, M. (1992). Den stora faktaslakten. En kritisk analys av Studio S:s videomassaker. [The big slaughter of facts. A critical analysis of Studio S's video massacre.] *Filmhäftet*, *77/78*, 71–81.

Drotner, K. (1991). *At skabe sig-selv* [*To create yourself*]. Copenhagen: Gyldendal.

Drotner, K., & Livingstone, S. (Eds.). (2008). *The international handbook of children, media and culture*. Los Angeles: Sage.

Erstad, O. (2006). A new direction? Digital literacy, student participation and curriculum reform in Norway. *Journal of Education and Information Technologies*, *11*(3–4), 415–429.

Erstad, O. (2007). Designing learning futures. *The virtual: Designing digital experience*. Proceedings from Virtual 06 Conference, Södertörn University, Sweden.

Erstad, O. (2008). Trajectories of remixing—digital literacies, media production and schooling. In C. Lankshear & M. Knobel (Eds.), *Digital literacies: Concepts, policies and practices* (pp. 177–202). New York: Peter Lang.

Erstad, O. (2010a). Conceptions of technology literacy and fluency. In P. Peterson, E. Baker & B. McGaw (Eds.), *International Encyclopedia of Education, Vol. 8* (pp. 34–41). Oxford: Elsevier.

Erstad, O. (2010b). *Digital kompetanse i skolen, 2. utgave* [Digital competence in the School, 2nd ed.]. Oslo: Universitetsforlaget.

Erstad, O. (in press). Digital literacies and schooling—Knowledge practices in transition. In S. Lampros (Ed.), *Pursuing digital literacy in the 21st Century*. New York: Peter Lang.

Erstad, O., & Gilje, Ø. (2008). Regaining impact—Media education and media literacy in a Norwegian context. *Nordicom Review, 29*(2), 219–230.

Erstad, O., & Quale, A. (2009). National policies and practices on ICT in education: Norway. In T. Plomp, R. Anderson, N. Law & A. Quale (Eds.), *Cross-national information and communication technology policy and practices in education* (pp. 341–352). Greenwich, CT: Information Age Publishing.

Erstad, O., Gilje, Ø., & de Lange, T. (2007). Re-mixing multimodal resources: multiliteracies and digital production in Norwegian media education. *Journal of Learning, Media and Technology, 32*(2), 183–199.

European Commission (2006). *Key competences for lifelong learning: A European reference framework*. Directorate-General for Education and Culture. Retrieved May 24, 2010, from http://europa.eu/legislation_summaries/education_training_youth/lifelong_learning/c11090_en.htm

Gee, J. P. (2003). *What video games have to teach us about learning and literacy*. New York: Palgrave Macmillan.

Hatlevik, O., Ottestad, G., Skaug, J., Kløvstad, V., & Berge, O. (2009). *ITU Monitor 2009*. ITU. Retrieved December 10, 2010, from www.itu.no/filestore/Rapporter_-_PDF/ITUMonitor2009_English.pdf

Heath, S. B. (1983). *Ways with words: Language, life, and work in communities and classrooms*. New York: Cambridge University Press.

Hebdige, D. (1979). *Subculture: The meaning of style*. London: Methuen.

Herring, S. C. (2008). Questioning the generational divide: Technological exoticism and adult constructions of online youth identity. In D. Buckingham (Ed.), *Youth, identity and digital media*. Cambridge, MA: The MIT Press.

Ito, M., Baumer, S. Bittanti, M., boyd, d., Cody, R., Herr-Stephenson, B., Horst, H. A. et al. (2010). *Hanging out, messing around, and geeking out*. Cambridge, MA: The MIT Press.

Lankshear, C., & Knobel, M. (2006). *New literacies: Everyday practices and classroom learning*. New York: Peter Lang.

Lesko, N. (1996). The past, present and future conceptions of adolescence. *Educational Theory, 4*, 453–472.

Lessig, L. (2008). *Remix: Making art and commerce thrive in the hybrid economy*. New York: Penguin Press.

Livingstone, S., & Bober, M. (2006). *UK children go online*. Final report of key project findings. Retrieved February 2, 2011, from www.lse.ac.uk/collections/children-go-online

Livingstone, S. (2009). *Children and the Internet*. Cambridge, UK: Polity Press.

Loader, B. D. (2007). Introduction: Young citizens in the digital age: Disaffected or displaced? In B. Loader (Ed.), *Political engagement, young people and the Internet* (pp. 1–18). London: Routledge.

Lovlie, L. (2003). Teknokulturell danning [Technocultural *Bildung*]. In R. Slagstad, O. Korsgaard & L. Lovlie (Eds.), *Dannelsens forvandlinger* [*The changes of Bildung*]. Oslo: Pax Forlag.

Nixon, H. (1999). Creating a clever, computer-literate nation: A cultural study of the media, young people and new technologies of information and communication in Australia 1994–1998. Unpublished Ph.D. thesis. The University of Queensland.

Nixon, H. (2005). Cultural pedagogies about ICTs and education in a globalised cultural economy. In M. Apple, J. Kenway & M. Singh (Eds.), *Globalizing education: Policies, pedagogies and politics* (pp. 45–60). New York: Peter Lang.

Nordicom. (2009). *Young people in the European digital media landscape. A statistical overview with an Introduction by Sonia Livingstone and Leslie Haddon*. Gothenburg: Nordicom, University of Gothenburg.

Norwegian Media Authority. (2008). *Safe Use—A survey of 8 to 18 year olds' use of digital media 2008*. Fredrikstad, Norway: Norwegian Media Authority. Retrieved May 24, 2010, from www.medietilsynet.no/no/Trygg-bruk/Ressurser

Pahl, K., & Rowsell, J. (2005). *Literacy and education: Understanding the new literacy studies in the classroom*. Thousand Oaks, CA: Sage.

Palfrey, J., & Gasser, U. (2008). *Born digital: Understanding the first generation of digital natives*. New York: Basic Books.

Prensky, M. (2001). Digital natives, digital immigrants. *On the Horizon*, *9*(5), 1–6.

Prensky, M. (2006). *Don't bother me Mom—I'm learning! (How computer and video games are preparing your kids for twenty-first century success—and how you can help!)*. New York: Paragon House.

Rainie, L., & Horrigan, J. (2005). *A decade of adoption: How the Internet has woven itself into American life*. Washington, DC: Pew Internet and Family Life.

Rassool, N. (1999). *Literacy for sustainable development in the age of information*. Clevedon: Multilingual Matters.

Reinking, D., McKenna, M. C., Labbo, L. D., & R. D. Kieffer (Eds.). (1998). *Handbook of literacy and technology: Transformations in a post-typographic world*. Mahwah, NJ: Lawrence Erlbaum.

Rheingold, H. (2008). Using participatory media and public voice to encourage civic engagement. In W. L. Bennet (Ed.), *Civic life online: Learning how digital media can engage youth* (pp. 97–118). Cambridge, MA: The MIT Press.

Rideout, V. J., Foehr, U. G., & Roberts, D. F. (2010). *Generation M2: Media in the lives of 8- to 18-year-olds. A Kaiser Family Foundation Study*. Menlo Park: Kaiser Family Foundation. Retrieved May 24, 2010, from www.kff.org/entmedia/8010.cfm

Scribner, S., & Cole, M. (1981). *The psychology of literacy*. Cambridge, MA: Harvard University Press.

Selwyn, N. (2002). *Literature review in citizenship, technology and learning*. Bristol, UK: Nesta Futurelab.

Street, B. (1984). *Literacy in theory and practice*. Cambridge, UK: Cambridge University Press.

Tapscott, D. (1998). *Growing up digital: The rise of the net generation*. New York: McGraw-Hill.

Tapscott, D. (2009). *Grown up digital: How the net generation is changing your world*. New York: McGraw-Hill.

Thavenius, J. (1995). *Den motsägelsefulla bildningen* [*The contradictory Bildung*]. Stockholm: Brutus Östlings Bokförlag Symposium.

Trilling, B., & Fadel, C. (2009). *21st century skills. Learning for life in our times*. San Francisco: Jossey-Bass.

Tropiano, S. (2006). *Rebels & chicks: A history of the Hollywood teen movie*. New York: Back Stage Books.

Twenge, J. M. (2006). *Generation me*. New York: Free Press.

Warschauer, M. (2003). *Technology and social inclusion: Rethinking the digital divide*. Cambridge, MA: The MIT Press.

Watkins, S. Craig (2009). *The young & the digital: What the migration to social-network sites, games, and anytime, anywhere media means for our future*. Boston: Beacon Press.

8

BEYOND GOOGLE AND THE "SATISFICING" SEARCHING OF DIGITAL NATIVES

Gregor E. Kennedy and Terry S. Judd

Introduction

Over lunch early last year a doctoral student from our research group was reporting back from her work in the field. Her Ph.D. project was considering the use of technology in high school genetics education and she had recently been out in schools conducting observations and interviews with students and their teachers. She told a story of how a teacher in the classroom forgot a key piece of administrative information and how one student—quick as a flash and without being asked—stepped in and used Google to locate and provide the information the teacher required. Later on students were asked to complete a genetics worksheet on mitosis that contained a number of relatively complex short-answer questions. Our doctoral student observed the class as it worked in pairs with a number of online resources that were provided, and was bemused—and somewhat shocked—to see some students typing entire worksheet questions into Answers.com and being disappointed that more coherent results were not returned.

This anecdote in part exemplifies the conundrum we will explore in this chapter. How students, who are so clearly familiar and apparently adept with Internet tools, are at times so poor at using the Internet academically. We will consider how the Internet and the many digital tools available on the Web have affected the way students seek and gather information in the context of higher education. Our chapter, like this book, is set against the framing of students as "Digital Natives"—young people who due to their digital upbringing are said to be adept and pervasive users of a wide range of technologies. This characterization of young people has been with us for about a decade, and while some of its original proponents have softened their position somewhat (Prensky, 2001a, 2001b, 2009) others continue to advocate strongly for it (Tapscott, 2009).

We begin by reviewing the evidence about higher education students' use of technology, particularly their use of Internet-based tools. We then provide a brief description of how the use of information and communication technologies has evolved in higher education settings, and argue that information-seeking behavior, a key component of information literacy, has been fundamentally affected by the information technology revolution. This leads into a review of empirical research on university students' information-seeking behavior with an emphasis on their use of web-based tools. On the basis of this review, we align students' "satisficing" information-seeking behavior and attitudes with a well established educational construct: a surface approach to learning. In the final section we consider the implications of our review for higher education and examine how our characterization of students accords with Prensky's (2009) notion of digital wisdom.

The overarching aim of our thesis is to move beyond commonly held views of students as digital natives. By questioning this stereotype and by reviewing evidence about students' use of technology for scholarly information seeking we aim to arrive at a more sophisticated understanding of students who are engaged in tertiary education, which may be useful in informing policy and practice.

Empirical Research on Digital Natives

While the "Digital Native" construct rapidly took hold in the popular psyche, the empirical research needed to validate it lagged well behind. The majority of this research, including our own, has focused on the degree to which young people use technology—what technologies and technology-based tools young people are using and the extent to which they are using them.

Over the last five years or so, a comprehensive series of medium-to-large-scale studies of students' and young peoples' technology adoption and use have been conducted by a range of organizations and institutional researchers. These include the EDUCAUSE Centre for Applied Research (ECAR) and Pew Internet series of studies from North America; the Joint Information Systems Committee (JISC), British Educational Committee and Technology Agency (BECTA), and the Oxford Internet Institute series of studies and the work of Jones and others from the UK (Jones & Healing, in press; Jones & Ramanau, 2009; Jones, Ramanau, Cross & Healing, 2010; Selwyn, 2008); Australian studies by Kennedy and others (Kennedy et al., 2009; Kennedy et al., 2008a; Kennedy et al., 2007; Kennedy, Judd, Dalgarno & Waycott, in press; Kennedy et al., 2008b; Waycott et al., 2010; Gray, Chang & Kennedy, 2010; Oliver & Goerke, 2007); and South African studies by Czerniewicz and Brown (Czerniewicz & Brown, 2006, 2007, in press). While few if any of these studies are directly comparable, they do appear to describe a student population that is far from uniform in its response to technology. Yes, there are those that are avid adopters and appropriators of digital devices and the technologies they support, but a far greater proportion of students appear to be only selectively attached to or engaged with many new and some everyday technologies in both their social and learning lives.

Certainly, if we focus on ownership or access to core devices (computers and mobile phones) and familiarity with and use of core technologies (e.g., email, web search) the overall impression does suggest a generation of inveterate owners and users. The 2009 ECAR study of undergraduate students and information technology (Smith, Salaway, Caruso & Katz, 2009) reports that 98.8 percent of the more than 10,000 students surveyed owned a computer (88.3 percent owned laptops), 90 percent sent text messages and used social networking sites, on average on a daily basis, and the median time spent online each week was 21.3 hours. In a recent UK-based study (Jones, Ramanau, Cross & Healing, 2010), the authors report unrestricted computer access by students at 99.6 percent, mobile ownership at 97.8 percent and daily mean use of email and text messaging. Digital equity emerges as an issue in the recent South African study by Czerniewicz and Brown (in press), with 22 percent of students having no off-campus access to a computer. However, mobile phone ownership was extremely high at 98.5 percent and did not appear to be linked to students' socioeconomic status. Being able to access online information is also a core activity for a strong majority of students. In a recent US-based Pew Internet study, 55 percent of all Internet users aged between 18 and 29 used a search engine on a typical day (Fallows, 2008). Search engine use is likely to be even higher among tertiary students, with eight in ten students from the 2009 ECAR study stating that they "like to learn through running Internet searches" and the same proportion rating their ability to "effectively and efficiently search for information" as either very skilled or expert (Smith et al., 2009).

Most current students seem comfortable with the idea that they are avid users and adopters of new technologies. According to the 2009 ECAR study, 87 percent of students rate themselves as either early (ahead of their peers) or mainstream (on a par with their peers) adopters of new technologies. This comfort seems warranted in the case of social networking, which, led by a wave of student adopters, has made a rapid transition from emerging to mainstream technology that is now embraced by many in the wider community (see usage data presented by McCarthy, 2008). Its use within the student community has reached such high levels that it at least matches and probably exceeds that of email (Judd, in press). The uptake of other key technologies, including blogs, wikis, and file sharing (including photo sharing), which have been around since before the advent of social networking sites, has been considerably slower and patchier (Kennedy et al., 2007, in press; Jones et al., 2010). Students' use of these technologies may continue to rise, particularly in educational contexts, given that many have been integrated into the learning management systems that have been embraced by most tertiary institutions. However, this depends largely on educators' ability to utilize these technologies in educationally meaningful and engaging ways.

Technology adoption and use also varies according to student demographics, with age, gender, discipline, and socioeconomic differences reported across a number of studies. Significant age differences are often apparent even within a relatively narrow band of ages. And while these generally follow a pattern of increasing technology use with decreasing age (e.g., use of social networking sites—Smith et al., 2009) this is not always the case (see Kennedy et al., in press). Male students tend to be heavier users of technology than females (Kennedy et al., in press; Smith et al., 2009) and are much more likely to consider themselves as early adopters of new technologies (55 percent versus 25 percent—Smith et al., 2009). Some of the clearest gender differences exist in relation to gaming, with young males substantially more likely than females to play games regularly (Lenhart, 2008; Smith et al., 2009). Discipline-based differences have been reported in some studies (greatest in engineering, lowest in education—Smith et al., 2009; highest in medicine, lowest in creative arts—Selwyn, 2008) but not others (Kennedy et al., in press). Other notable demographic differences have been found for on-campus versus distance education students (Jones et al., 2010), students at metropolitan as compared to rural and regional campuses (Kennedy et al., in press) and international versus local students (Gray et al., 2010; Kennedy et al., in press).

The emerging (and evolving) picture, then, is one of high levels of technology access, ownership, and use for core devices and core technologies among tertiary students—which largely reflects (albeit at somewhat higher levels) existing trends in the broader population. Beyond that, the adoption and use of newer technologies is lower and patchier, and is nuanced by social and demographic factors. Given this picture, and the fact that young peoples' use of technology is not as ubiquitous as some commentators have made out, the findings from this research have led many to question the idea of the universal digital native student.

Information Technology and Information Literacy at University

Despite, and in a way because of these findings, most commentators and researchers would support the notion that the rise of the Internet has brought about major changes in many aspects of culture and society. It has fundamentally changed the ways in which activities and exchanges are carried out across sectors as diverse and important as commerce and banking, entertainment, the arts, and education. The way many of us pay bills, buy music, read and receive news, book holidays, and catch up with friends has been altered. While numbers of our old routines have remained, in many instances these routines have been added to, augmented, and, in some cases, supplanted by applications of the Internet.

Within the higher education sector, the arrival of the Internet saw the introduction of email and simple web pages in teaching and learning settings. Over time, as bandwidth and computing power increased, it became possible to develop and deliver learning activities based around multimedia resources that made use of images, animation, and video and required higher levels of user interaction.

In the late 1990s learning management systems (LMSs)—software applications that bundled together communications technologies, content and assessment delivery, and course management tools—were widely adopted as enterprise "learning" technology systems. Students were able to log into their institutional LMS to access course notes and readings, participate in discussions, check timetables, or contact their lecturer. In more recent times we have witnessed the rise of social or Web 2.0 technologies such as social networking, blogs, and wikis.

The Internet has also clearly affected the way in which higher education students locate and access information and resources to support their learning. Much has been written about information literacy and students' information-seeking behavior, the key elements of which are represented by various conceptual and behavioral models (see, for example, the Seven Pillar model—SCONUL, 1999; Big Six Model—Eisenberg, 2008; see also Lorenzo and Dziuban, 2006). These models typically propose that individuals follow an information seeking process that starts with them recognizing the need to find a particular piece of information, and ends with them locating and applying it in a meaningful way. In line with this, Eisenberg (2008) defines information literacy as "the set of skills and knowledge that allows us to find, evaluate, and use the information we need, as well as to filter out the information we don't need" (p. 39). His "big six" model has the stages of (i) task definition, (ii) information seeking strategies, (iii) location and access, (iv) use of information, (v) synthesis, and (vi) evaluation. Information literacy skills, including their component skills of independent research, problem solving, critical thinking, and inquiry, are widely regarded as key competencies expected of graduates by most universities. In this chapter we are primarily interested a subset of students' information literacy skills: the digital (and non-digital) strategies university students use to locate and access information and resources for their studies.

Students' Information Seeking Behavior with the Internet

Not so long ago—perhaps even within the last ten years—students were largely reliant on hard copies of materials for their studies (reading packs, textbooks, journals, monographs). While they could search for some resources electronically via scholarly reference databases (e.g., Psych-Info, ERIC, MedLine), the rapid expansion of the Internet and online publishing has dramatically improved students' capacity to find and access resources from both academic and non-academic sources. All that is required is a computer, Internet access, and for access to sanctioned scholarly content, the necessary authentication.

But how do students approach the task of finding study-related information using the Internet? How do they negotiate online scholarly databases and authoritative sources of information, and integrate these with tools and sources such as Google and Wikipedia? A review of the literature over the last five years suggests that while students are often strategic and efficient information seekers within the digital landscape, they can also express frustration and impatience in their own searching abilities and skills.

We have been assessing students' use of information sources for a number of years in our own research. Through a series of longitudinal studies, we established that students' on-campus use of generalist online tools, particularly Google and Wikipedia, increased markedly between 2005 and 2009 (Judd & Kennedy, in press a). However, students' use of specialist online tools over the same period, including the university library and Google Scholar, was consistently low. In the case of Google Scholar, it was used in less than 2 percent of the 25,000 individual computer sessions we analyzed.

In another study, we analyzed the Internet searches of 842 first-, second- and third-year biomedical students (Judd & Kennedy, in press b). We were particularly interested in how these students used five key Internet sites—Google, Wikipedia, eMedicine, National Institute of Health (NIH), and the university's library[1]—to gather biomedical information related to their problem-based learning curriculum. We found that students were heavily reliant on Google and Wikipedia. When combined these were the only sites used in 80 percent of first-year students' computer sessions that involved some sort of biomedical inquiry. This figure dropped across year levels, with third-year students solely relying on Google and Wikipedia at about half the rate of first-year students. Other more authoritative sites—NIH, eMedicine, the library—showed significantly less use overall, but their use did increase across year levels with third-year students using them in 17–36 percent of their inquiry sessions. Despite their heavy reliance on Google and Wikipedia, students routinely rated them as the least reliable of the five sites.

In a second set of analyses, we just considered students' use of Google for biomedical enquiries and conducted a content analysis of pages that were visited after each Google search. We developed a three-tiered classification of the reliability of the resources students were accessing and reviewing. For example, high reliability resources included peer-reviewed journal articles, online textbooks, and referenced resources from reputable sources such as universities, public research institutions, and professional organizations. In contrast, low reliability informational sources included resources from commercial sites (advertising medical products and services), sites without an explicit health or biomedical focus, and any resources from sites of unknown provenance. We found that first-year students were more inclined to rely on low reliability sources than third-year students and vice-versa for high reliability sources.

We concluded from this research that when it came to using the Internet for biomedical enquiries, the behavior of students in our sample was best characterized by expediency. Students knowingly preferenced less reliable tools and sources in their search for study related information in order to access and gather information quickly and easily. They preferenced simple and easy search and informational tools that were guaranteed to return results, over tools that were less familiar and perceived to be more effortful even though their use would likely lead to more relevant and reliable results. While this pattern of information seeking seemed to diminish as students progressed in their university careers, it nonetheless persisted as a significant component of their information seeking strategies through the undergraduate years.

Other researchers have established similar patterns of results, albeit with some variation. Griffiths and Brophy (2005) present a comprehensive review and empirical analysis in their paper on students' searching behavior. In the Evaluation of the Distributed National Electronic Resource (EDNER) project students were set fifteen tasks "designed to be typical of information seeking in an academic environment" (Griffiths & Brophy, 2005, p. 545). They found that search engines dominated the sites students accessed first when looking for academic information. Sixty-four percent of students visited a search engine first, the majority of which (45 percent) were Google searches. Significantly fewer students accessed the university's online catalogue, with only 10 percent of students visiting this first. Among the reasons students liked to use a search engine, and Google in particular, was because it was straightforward and easy to use, it seemed to have whatever a student wanted, and it meant that students did not have to access a range of databases. In addition to their findings about students' high reliance on search engines and low use of academic resources, Griffiths and Brophy pointed to the difficulties that students have in locating information and resources and the fact that they "may trade quality of results for effort and time spent searching" (2005, p. 550).

In their review of the information behavior of the "Google generation," Rowlands and colleagues (2008) found that 89 percent of college students use a search engine to begin their scholarly information seeking and only 2 percent use the library website. In their review, they also more generally characterize, based on detailed log file analysis, what they saw as new scholarly information-seeking behavior. One aspect of this characterization is the tendency towards horizontal information seeking; that is "skimming activity, where people view just one or two pages from an academic site and then bounce out, perhaps never to return" (p. 294). When referring to young people's information-seeking behavior particularly, they point to the difficulties students have conducting effective searches and determining the relevance, accuracy, and authority of sources, despite their technological abilities.

In a departure from these findings, Head (2007) conducted an exploratory study of humanities and social science majors' use of Internet and library resources for research. Head's results suggest that students used course materials and library searches as their first port of call when conducting academic inquiries. Internet-based tools such as Google and Wikipedia were the third type of resource used by these students. It is perhaps not surprising that in the first instance, students sought out and relied upon information contained in the course readings provided by their lecturers. This material—effectively recommended for their academic work—is likely to be highly relevant and reliable and does not need to be found or evaluated by students. For this reason, Head's (2007) results are not directly comparable to our own studies and those, for example, of Griffiths and Brophy (2005) where course "texts" were not included in an analysis of students' information-seeking behavior. Moreover, these findings should be tempered to some extent given the sample was students who were in "the upper division" and were "more seasoned with the research process than lower division students" (Head, 2007, p. 2). Despite all this, a clear message from this paper is that regardless of type of student and the strategies and tools used, students had difficulty conducting "college-level research" and were challenged by the tasks of accessing appropriate resource material, narrowing down their search topics to make them more manageable, and were overwhelmed by the scope and range of resources available to them.

More recent research from Head in *Project Information Literacy* has shown that undergraduate students typically use a small set of information sources that are familiar to them, close at hand, convenient, and quick (Head & Eisenberg, 2009). Again rather than Google, the first ports of call for students when conducting research for their studies were the course readings provided by the lecturer. Again, it is not surprising that students surveyed and interviewed in this investigation start their research on a set piece of academic work with the resources that have been provided to them. When moving beyond these sanctioned resources, Head and Eisenberg (2009) found that "Google was the go-to resource for almost all of the students in the sample. Nearly all of the students in the sample reported always using Google for both course-related research and everyday life research" (p. 15). Their information seeking strategies are "based on efficiency and utility" (p. 21) and suggest a "less is more approach to dealing with the proliferation of information resources available . . . in the digital age" (p. 15). While many students did report using scholarly research databases, the authors noted that "As a whole the findings suggest that students in our sample favoured sources for their brevity, consensus, and currency over other qualities and less so for their scholarly authority" (p. 21).

The critical question here is not whether university students are using tools like Google and Wikipedia in their studies; it is clear that the vast majority are, which is unsurprising given their truly remarkable reach, scope, and utility. The central issue is determining how students are using these tools and whether they are going beyond them as part of their everyday scholarly information seeking. There is evidence, particularly based on the work of Head and Eisenberg (2009, 2010), that students are simply using resources such as Wikipedia to "scope" the academic "problem" they are researching. However, there is also ample evidence to suggest that many students are relying extensively—and sometimes solely—on tools such as Google and Wikipedia for their scholarly information seeking and are doing so in a fairly unsophisticated manner. Moreover, evidence from our own research shows that often students are *not* going beyond Google, and when they do they often select popular web-based resources of questionable academic value.

Satisficing Search Strategies as Approaches to Learning

When combined with broader studies of young people's use of technology, our review of students' scholarly information-seeking behavior shows that despite near-ubiquitous use of the Internet for information seeking and communication, students are challenged by *scholarly* information seeking at university. When drawn together, the empirical research shows that undergraduate students often engage in relatively superficial scholarly information-seeking behavior and over-value expediency in their searches. Their attitudes and values appear to be more closely aligned with expediency and familiarity than with precision and effort. The question for us now is, what are the implications of these behaviors in an academic context; what does it mean for students' scholarly work and their academic development? In short, does it really matter that they exhibit strategic and expedient approaches to scholarly information seeking on the Internet?

Head and Eisenberg (2009) touched on these questions when they compared students' approaches to conducting course-related research with the "gold-standard" epitomized by what is advocated by the library. While not stated explicitly, differences between the two approaches implied deficiencies in the student approach. As an alternative response to the question of whether we should be concerned about students' scholarly information seeking on the Internet, below we contend that students' behavior, attitudes, and values surrounding scholarly information seeking reflect a culture of "satisficing" decision-making that is in turn indicative of a surface approach to learning.

The social scientist Herbert Simon is attributed with coining the term "satisficing" in the area of decision-making to describe the decisions individuals take that are satisfactory but are not "maximal" or optimal (Simon, 1955, 1957). When presented with a range of options that could be pursued, a satisficing decision is one that is acceptable to an individual based on some personal criterion, but it is a decision or course of action that is known not to be the "best" one. A cost-benefit analysis is often associated with satisficing decisions; an individual makes a judgment balancing the effort required to gain the maximum or best outcome. Satisficing decisions are made when it is judged that the effort required for a particular outcome is high and a decision is taken to arrive at an acceptable outcome with reduced effort. Satisficing decision-making is not poor, exactly; rather, these decisions are strategic and known to be less than what is best in the given circumstances.

We feel this term—satisficing—accurately captures and describes students' online information-seeking behavior in academic contexts. Students often adopt, and appear to be comfortable with, a "near enough is good enough" approach that is expedient and somewhat superficial, and in doing so eschew the precision, depth, and persistence that we usually associate with finding and appraising the best scholarly information and resources. Moreover, there are clear parallels between students' satisficing information-seeking behavior and established educational research on students' approaches to learning.

In the seminal work by Marton and Säljö (1976a, 1976b), students were observed to adopt one of two approaches to a learning task. Students who adopted a "deep" approach to the learning task were inclined to focus on trying to comprehend the meaning behind learning material, whereas students who adopted a "surface" approach to the learning task tended to focus on simply reproducing what was contained within the learning material with little concern for understanding the overall meaning. These constructs—deep and surface approaches learning—have been highly resilient in educational research. Marton and Säljö's original work laid the foundation for many similar and popular conceptions of students' approaches to learning, including Biggs' (1987) deep and surface approaches and Entwistle, Hanley, and Hounsell's (1979) meaning and reproducing orientations.

The way in which surface approaches to learning, or "surface learners," have been described varies in the literature in part because the construct encompasses both the achievement goals and motivation of students, and the cognitive or learning strategy they adopt. Regardless, a surface approach to learning is associated with an uncritical or superficial approach to learning material and information, a desire to reproduce material, cognitive strategies such as rehearsal and repetition, and academic behavior such as lack of persistence, minimal effort, selection of tasks based on difficulty, and the avoidance of challenging and effortful tasks (see Ames, 1992; Ames & Archer, 1988; Elliot, 1999; Kaplan & Midgley, 1997; Meece, Blumenfeld & Hoyle, 1988; Pintrich, 2000; Pintrich & Schrauben, 1992). The tone—and in some cases the exact note—of these descriptions is consistent with the types of Internet-based searching behaviors that students have been shown to adopt. Indeed, one of the most prominent researchers on approaches to learning, John Biggs, describes the overall learning strategy that arises from a surface approach as one "that is 'satisficing,' but not satisfying, task demands by investing minimal time and effort consistent with appearing to meet requirements" (Biggs, 1993, p. 6).

While some researchers have suggested that there may be advantages to both a deep and surface approach to learning, depending on the context (Hidi & Harackiewicz, 2000), traditionally a deep approach to learning has been encouraged by educators. For example, a surface approach may be useful when attempting to memorize vocabulary. Or a student may strategically adopt a surface approach during their course for pragmatic reasons associated with time constraints or pressures that come from outside the university. But the reason why deep approaches are encouraged by educators is that they have been associated with positive or "adaptive" student learning outcomes (Biggs, 1979, 1993; Marton & Säljö, 1976a, 1976b; Prosser & Trigwell, 1999). While surface approaches are typically associated with superficial retention and recall of largely fact-based information, deep approaches are associated with greater—or deeper—conceptual understanding of the material that is presented.

Key thinkers in the academic community have highlighted the somewhat vexed relationship between the development of students' scholastic abilities and their satisficing searching with powerful information seeking tools. For example, Courant raises the legitimate concern that:

> Ubiquitous access to information poses a risk that the special character of scholarly work and understanding can often be skipped altogether, because it is now easy to obtain answers to questions that are "good enough", via any number of tools that are immediately, freely, and conveniently available on the web.
>
> (2008, p. 202)

Similarly, Head and Eisenberg suggest that faculty, administrators, and librarians on the front line face "some of the most challenging times any of us have ever seen" (2009, p. 34). For them a "perfect storm" is brewing whose origin is based on factors that are broader than students' information-seeking behavior, but does include the concern that:

> . . . many students' information-seeking competencies end up being highly contextual, a set of predictable skills developed for passing courses, not for lifelong literacy and professional goals beyond college. As a result, we see the very important pedagogical goals of deep learning and critical thinking are at risk of being greatly impeded within the academy.
>
> (p. 34)

The Wisdom of Moving Beyond Google

In this chapter we are not suggesting that the rise of the Internet and tools and services such as Google and Wikipedia have created or caused a problem in undergraduate students' scholarly information-seeking behavior. Undergraduate students had difficulties finding and using appropriate information for their studies well before the invention of Google (see Maughan, 2001). However, we are suggesting that:

- there is little evidence to suggest that students' generally high use of traditional web technologies has resulted in more sophisticated scholarly information-seeking behavior when using the Internet;

- the behavior and attitudes of students when it comes to scholarly information seeking is indicative of "satisficing" search strategies that are associated with a surface approach to learning in higher education;
- undergraduate students' experiences with easy-to-use and useful tools such as Google and Wikipedia mean that they are more likely to rely on these tools when undertaking more rigorous academic inquiries.

Based on our review here we, like others, have speculated that students who have grown up with the Internet have developed a set of deeply held expectations about searching for information, based on their experience with tools such as Google and Wikipedia (Brabazon, 2007; Griffiths & Brophy, 2005). From a cognitive psychology perspective, students may come to university with a well-developed "script" for Internet-based searching that places a premium on speed and ease. When searching for information in an academic context this can lead to two problems. First, students may quickly become disappointed and frustrated with the functionality and ease of use of online academic tools and services. This in turn may result in heavy reliance on familiar tools that are known to produce results. Second, in an academic context where the relevance, reliability, and authority of information are highly valued, the quality of information sources and resources returned from students' easy and familiar "searching scripts" might be challenged. A tension exists, therefore, between the need to provide students with a simple interface to the array of academic resources now available online, and the need to ensure students are aware that their "search script" requires updating—that effort and skill are required to search for, find, and use high quality academic resources. It is not enough to simply provide students with an academic Google—we already have this in the form of the excellent but under-utilized Google Scholar—the aim should be to have students appreciate the educational value of being able to undertake and capitalize on sophisticated online information seeking.

A critical issue here is that students have an array of tools and services at their fingertips that give them easy *access* to information, but these same tools that students preference are not optimized to support scholarly information seeking. The "pagerank" algorithm that underpins Google's search results associates relevance with "visibility" (the more pages that link to a given page the higher its ranking). And while this system is highly effective, a high pagerank does not guarantee a page's relevance or its reliability, which are critical qualities for scholarly information. Thus, the pagerank system cannot be used as a proxy for individual judgments about the relevance and reliability of particular information sources. Similarly, while Wikipedia entries can provide a useful overview of a topic, they are of unknown provenance and lack the authority of peer-reviewed sources, characteristics that are openly acknowledged by the Wikipedia organization (Reliability of Wikipedia, 2010; Wikipedia: Good articles, 2010). In this context, students need to be clear about the value and utility of different types of reference tools and resources they use for academic purposes. As Nicholson notes:

> Google . . . delivers fantastic volume but the measure of relevance is still pretty crude . . . Wikipedia provides a great first cut at coherently organised material plus a good set of relevant links. But if reliability is a critical objective, then sources like Britannica, or research journals, or original documents become progressively more important.
>
> (2006, p. 14)

The implication of Nicholson's comment is that some tools and resources—particularly when combined with a satisficing approach to study—are likely to be inappropriate for many of the educational tasks that students are asked to complete during their undergraduate studies, in which reliable and authoritative sources are required.

A broader implication is that within higher education—and no doubt at other levels of education as well—there needs to be a greater emphasis on how to search for, locate, evaluate, and apply the mass of information available online. The proliferation of "smart" and "user-friendly" tools and services that negotiate the expanding "infosphere" places *more* not less pressure on educators to assist students in honing their information literacy skills. The information age has made sophisticated information seeking skills *more* needed by students not less. Prudent information seeking will be mandatory in the twenty-first century, not an optional extra or something relegated to a "smart" tool or an "expert" system. The "smarts" and the expertise need to be developed within the individual as well as within the technology.

What we are looking for in our students is perhaps what one of the original proponents of the digital native student has called "Digital Wisdom" (Prensky, 2009). Prensky sees digital wisdom as arising both from the use of digital technology and in its use. It is reflected in soundness of judgment, knowing what is important, and an ability to solve problems and consider a number of issues when coming to a decision or judgment. These are clearly key attributes of a sophisticated information seeker. Prensky defines digital wisdom as "the ability to find practical, creative, contextually appropriate, and emotionally satisfying solutions to complicated human problems" (2009, p. 3). Those with digital wisdom:

> . . . look for the cases where technology enhances thinking and understanding . . . and make careful judgments about what digital enhancements are appropriate and when . . . They investigate and evaluate the positive as well as the negatives of new [digital] tools and figure out how to strike the balance that turns tools into wisdom enhancers.
>
> (2009, p. 8)

Based on our review above, do today's students show digital wisdom when seeking out scholarly information? The answer is largely "no." While students can find creative and emotionally satisfying solutions to information-seeking problems, often their solutions are not contextually appropriate. They often seem to eschew technologies that could truly assist with their thinking or understanding, and make use judgments based on perceptions of effort and expediency; in general, they find it difficult to strike a balance between powerful new search tools and other more effortful ways of finding and locating scholarly information.

It is perhaps not surprising that many of today's undergraduate students are not "digitally wise" when it comes to scholarly information seeking. Prensky notes that his concept of digital wisdom must be "learned and taught" (2009, p. 7). It is only through this process that students will come to understand that the arrival of new technologies and tools is typically accompanied by a tradeoff (Carr, 2008). When it comes to Google and scholarly information seeking this tradeoff needs to be made explicit to students. Students need to be fully aware that when they rely too much on Google for their studies something is gained—a remarkable ability to locate information that can be useful; but something is also lost—hard-won but essential skills in finding, evaluating, and using high quality online information.

Conclusion

While the popularity and ubiquity of the Internet and the information contained on the Web has not created a new problem—undergraduate students have always been admonished to develop more sophisticated research skills—in this chapter we have argued that a generation of students that has grown up with Google may over-value expediency when locating and selecting appropriate scholarly information. This is consistent with previous commentary, for example, by Tara Brabazon, who in *The University of Google* argues that Google is "facilitating laziness, poor scholarship and compliant thinking" among students (2007, p. 15) and that "Google is a one-size-fits-all response to information sharing and assumes that the user has the literacy to not only utilize the search engine but the interpretative skill to handle the results" (p. 20).

The empirical research reviewed in this chapter suggests that while students are strategic in their information seeking for study, their behavior is marked by satisficing strategies. We have shown how these strategies correspond with a surface approach to learning that has traditionally been regarded as having limited educational value. We have argued that, somewhat counter-intuitively, this places more not less onus on faculty to support "Digital Native" students in the development of their information literacy skills, particularly in the area of Internet-based information seeking.

As we suggested at the outset of this chapter, our aim was to move the debate about students' use of technology in education beyond stereotypical views of students as "Digital Natives." The evidence we have provided above suggests that only a small proportion of students fit the "Digital Native" mold, and despite most students being avid Internet users, the majority are not sophisticated *scholarly* users of the Internet. It is perhaps time, therefore, to dispense with manifestly inadequate labels and categories, and begin focusing on how we, as educators, can help students move beyond Google so they can harness the Internet for greater academic advantage.

Note

1 The last three sites being recommended by faculty.

References

Ames, C. (1992). Classrooms: Goals, structures, and students' motivation. *Journal of Educational Psychology, 84*(3), 261–271.

Ames, C., & Archer, J. (1988). Achievement goals in the classroom: Students' learning strategies and motivation processes. *Journal of Educational Psychology, 80*(3), 260–267.

Biggs, J. (1979). Individual differences in study processes and the quality of learning outcomes. *Higher Education, 8*, 381–394.

Biggs, J. (1987). *Student approaches to learning and studying*. Melbourne: Australian Council for Educational Research.

Biggs, J. (1993). What do inventories of students' learning processes really measure? A theoretical review and clarification. *British Journal of Educational Psychology, 63*(1), 3–19.

Brabazon, T. (2007). *The university of Google: Education in a (post) information age*. Aldershot: Ashgate.

Carr, N. (2008). Is Google making us stupid? What the Internet is doing to our brains. *Atlantic Magazine*, July/August. Retrieved July 10, 2010, from www.theatlantic.com/magazine/archive/2008/07/is-google-making-us-stupid/6868

Courant, P. (2008). Scholarship: The wave of the future in the digital age. In R. Katz (Ed.), *The tower and the cloud higher education in the age of cloud computing* (pp. 202–211). Boulder, CO: EDUCAUSE.

Czerniewicz, L., & Brown, C. (2006). *The virtual mobius strip*. Centre for Educational Technology Research Report. Retrieved July 10, 2010, from www.cet.uct.ac.za/virtualmobiusreport

Czerniewicz, L., & Brown, C. (2007). *Disciplinary differences in the use of educational technology*. Paper presented at Proceedings of Second International E-learning Conference, New York.

Czerniewicz, L., & Brown, C. (in press). Debunking the "Digital Native": Beyond digital apartheid, towards digital democracy. *Journal of Computer Assisted Learning*, Special Issue.

Eisenberg, M. B. (2008). Information literacy: Essential skills for the information age. *Journal of Library & Information Technology, 28*(2), 39–47.

Elliot, A. J. (1999). Approach and avoidance motivation and achievement goals. *Educational Psychologist, 34*(3), 169–189.

Entwistle, N., Hanley, M., & Hounsell, D. (1979). Identifying distinctive approaches to studying. *Higher Education, 8*, 365–380.

Fallows, D. (2008). *Search engine use*. Pew Internet & American Life Project. Retrieved July 10, 2010, from www.pewinternet.org/Reports/2008/Search-Engine-Use.aspx

Gray, K., Chang, S., & Kennedy, G. (2010). Use of social web technologies by international and domestic undergraduate students: Implications for internationalising learning and teaching in Australian universities. *Technology, Pedagogy & Education, 19*(1), 31–46.

Griffiths, J. R., & Brophy, P. (2005). Student searching behavior and the web: Use of academic resources and Google. *Library Trends, 53*, 539–554.

Head, A. J. (2007). Beyond Google: How do students conduct academic research? *First Monday, 12*(8). Retrieved July 10, 2010, from http://firstmonday.org/htbin/cgiwrap/bin/ojs/index.php/fm/article/viewArticle/1998/1873

Head, A. J., & Eisenberg, M. B. (2009). *How college students seek information in the digital age*. Project Information Literacy progress report "Lessons Learnt." Retrieved July 10, 2010, from http://projectinfolit.org/pdfs/PIL_Fall2009_Year1Report_12_2009.pdf

Head, A. J., & Eisenberg, M. B. (2010). How today's college students use Wikipedia for course-related research. *First Monday, 15*(3). Retrieved July 10, 2010, from http://firstmonday.org/htbin/cgiwrap/bin/ojs/index.php/fm/article/viewArticle/2830/2476

Hidi, S., & Harackiewicz, J. M. (2000). Motivating the academically unmotivated: A critical issue for the 21st Century. *Review of Educational Research, 70*(2), 151–179.

Jones, C., & Healing, G. (in press). Net generation students: Agency and choice and the new technologies. *Journal of Computer Assisted Learning*, Special Issue.

Jones, C., & Ramanau, R. (2009). Collaboration and the net generation: The changing characteristics of first-year university students. *Proceedings of the 9th International Conference on Computer Supported Collaborative Learning* (pp. 237–241). Rhodes, Greece.

Jones, C., Ramanau, R., Cross, S., & Healing, G. (2010). Net generation or digital natives: Is there a distinct new generation entering university? *Computers and Education, 54*(3), 722–732.

Judd, T. S. (in press). Facebook versus email. *British Journal of Educational Technology*.

Judd, T. S., & Kennedy G. E. (in press a). A five-year study of internet use by undergraduate biomedical students. *Computers & Education*.

Judd, T. S., & Kennedy G. E. (in press b). Expediency-based practice? Medical students' reliance on Google and Wikipedia for biomedical inquiries. *British Journal of Educational Technology*.

Kaplan, A., & Midgley, C. (1997). The effect of achievement goals: Does level of perceived academic competence make a difference? *Contemporary Educational Psychology, 22*, 15–435.

Kennedy, G., Dalgarno, B., Bennett, S., Gray, K., Waycott, J., Judd, T., et al. (2009). *Educating the net generation: A handbook of findings for practice and policy*. Sydney: Australian Learning and Teaching Council.

Kennedy, G., Dalgarno, B., Bennett, S., Judd, T., Gray, K., & Chang, R. (2008a). Immigrants and natives: Investigating differences between staff and students' use of technology. *Hello! Where are you in the landscape of educational technology? Proceedings ascilite Melbourne 2008* (pp. 484–492). Retrieved December 10, 2010, from www.ascilite.org.au/conferences/melbourne08/procs/kennedy.pdf

Kennedy, G., Dalgarno, B., Gray, K., Judd, T., Waycott, J., Bennett, S., Mason, K., Bishop, A., Chang, R., & Churchward, A. (2007). The net generation are not big users of Web 2.0 technologies: Preliminary findings. In *ICT: Providing choices for learners and learning. Proceedings ascilite Singapore 2007*. Retrieved July 10, 2010, from www.ascilite.org.au/conferences/singapore07/procs/kennedy.pdf

Kennedy, G., Judd, T. Dalgarno, B., & Waycott, J. (in press). Beyond natives and immigrants: Exploring the characteristics of net generation students. *Journal of Computer Assisted Learning*.

Kennedy, G., Judd, T., Churchward, A., Gray, K., & Krause, K.-L. (2008b). First year students' experiences with technology: Are they really digital natives? *Australasian Journal of Educational Technology*, *24*(1), 108–122.

Lenhart A. (2008). *Teens, video games and civics*. Washington DC: Pew Internet & American Life Project. Retrieved July 10, 2010, from www.pewinternet.org/Reports/2008/Teens-Video-Games-and-Civics.aspx

Lorenzo, G., & Dziuban, C. (2006). *Ensuring the net generation is net savvy*. EDUCAUSE Learning Initiative Paper 2. Boulder, CO: EDUCAUSE. Retrieved July 10, 2010, from http://net.educause.edu/ir/library/pdf/ELI3006.pdf

Marton, F., & Säljö, R. (1976a). On the qualitative difference in learning I—Outcome and process. *British Journal of Educational Psychology*, *46*, 4–11.

Marton, F., & Säljö, R (1976b). On the qualitative difference in learning II—Outcome as a function of the learner's conception of the task. *British Journal of Educational Psychology*, *46*, 115–127.

Maughan, P. D. (2001). Assessing information literacy among undergraduates: A discussion of the literature and the University of California-Berkeley assessment experience. *College & Research Libraries*, *62*, 71–85.

McCarthy, C. (2008). ComScore: Facebook is beating MySpace worldwide. *The Social, C/Net News.Com*. Retrieved July 10, 2010, from http://news.cnet.com/8301-13577_3-9973826-36.html

Meece, J. L, Blumenfeld, P. C., & Hoyle, R. H. (1988). Students' goals orientations and cognitive engagement in classroom activities. *Journal of Educational Psychology*, *80*(4), 514–523.

Nicholson, P. J. (2006). *The role of intellectual authority*. Notes for remarks to the Association of Research Libraries 148th Membership Meeting Ottawa, Canada, May 18, 2006.

Oliver, B., & Goerke, V. (2007). Australian undergraduates' use and ownership of emerging technologies: Implications and opportunities for creating engaging learning experiences for the Net Generation. *Australasian Journal of Educational Technology*, *23*(2), 171–186.

Pintrich, P. R. (2000). An achievement goal theory perspective on issues in motivation terminology, theory, and research. *Contemporary Educational Psychology*, *25*, 92–104.

Pintrich, P. R., & Schrauben, B. (1992). Students' motivational beliefs and their cognitive engagement in classroom academic tasks. In D. H. Schunk & J. L. Meece (Eds.), *Student perceptions in the classroom* (pp. 149–183). Hillsdale: Lawrence Erlbaum.

Prensky, M. (2001a). Digital natives, digital immigrants. *On the Horizon*, *9*(5), 1–6. Retrieved July 10, 2010, from http://web.me.com/nancyoung/visual_literacy/site_map_and_resources_files/Digital_Natives_Digital_Immigrants.pdf

Prensky, M. (2001b). Digital natives, digital immigrants, Part II: Do they really think differently? *On the Horizon*, *9*(6), 1–6. Retrieved July 10, 2010, from http://web.me.com/nancyoung/visual_literacy/site_map_and_resources_files/Digital_Natives_Digital_Immigrants.pdf

Prensky, M. (2009). H. sapiens digital: From digital natives and digital immigrants to digital wisdom. *Innovate*, *5*(3). Retrieved July 10, 2010, from www.innovateonline.info/pdf/vol5_issue3/H._Sapiens_Digital-__From_Digital_Immigrants_and_Digital_Natives_to_Digital_Wisdom.pdf

Prosser, M., & Trigwell , K. (1999). *Understanding learning and teaching: The experience in higher education*. Buckingham: Open University Press.

Rowlands, I., Nicholas, D., Williams, P., Huntington, P., Fieldhouse, M., Gunter, B., Withey, R., Jamali, H., Dobrowolski, T., & Tenopir, C. (2008). The Google generation: The information behaviour of the researcher of the future. *Aslib Proceedings. New Information Perspectives*, *60*(4), 290–310.

SCONUL (1999). *Information skills in higher education*. Briefing paper prepared by The Society of College, National and University Libraries (SCONUL). Retrieved July 10, 2010, from www.sconul.ac.uk/groups/information_literacy/papers/Seven_pillars2.pdf

Selwyn, N. (2008). An investigation of differences in undergraduates' academic use of the internet. *Active Learning in Higher Education*, *9*(1), 11–22.

Simon, H. A. (1955). A behavioral model of rational choice. *Quarterly Journal of Economics*, *69*, 99–118.

Simon, H. A. (1957). *Models of man*. New York: Wiley.

Smith, S. D., Salaway, G., Caruso, J. B., & Katz, R. N. (2009). *The ECAR study of undergraduate students and information technology, 2009*. Boulder, CO: EDUCAUSE Center for Applied Research.

Tapscott, D. (2009). *Grown up digital: How the net generation is changing your world*. New York: McGraw-Hill.

Waycott, J., Bennett, J., Kennedy, G., Dalgarno, B., & Gray K. (2010). Digital divides? Student and staff perceptions of information and communication technologies. *Computers and Education*, *54*, 1202–1211.

Wikipedia. (2010) Wikipedia: Good articles. Retrieved July 10, 2010, from http://en.wikipedia.org/wiki/Wikipedia:Good_articles

Wikipedia. (2010). Reliability of Wikipedia. Retrieved July 10, 2010, from http://en.wikipedia.org/wiki/Reliability_of_Wikipedia

9

ACTUAL AND PERCEIVED ONLINE PARTICIPATION AMONG YOUNG PEOPLE IN SWEDEN

Sheila Zimic and Rolf Dalin

Introduction

Many studies have shown that there is a high adoption rate with regard to the Internet by young people (Findahl & Zimic, 2008; Lenhart & Madden, 2005; Livingstone & Haddon, 2009). In Sweden more than half of five year olds are using the Internet and there are almost no non-users among teenagers and young adults (Findahl & Zimic, 2008). This engagement with the online world has augmented the image of participating young people, even though questions have rarely been asked in relation to what they really participate in and if that kind of participation is what is expected from them as members of the information society (Livingstone, 2009). Another issue that is often ignored in relation to young people involves the social factors that mediate their engagement with digital technologies. Because of young people's high Internet usage and the established image of digital natives, the risk of a digital divide among young people has not, until recently, been generally discussed (Bennett, Maton & Kervin, 2008; Facer & Furlong, 2001; Livingstone & Helsper, 2007; Selwyn, 2009). Several researchers have found that online behavior differs among boys and girls of different age groups and with different social backgrounds (Hargittai & Hinnant, 2008; Lee, 2008; Livingstone, Bober & Helsper, 2005). Further, skills were found to be very important for young people in relation to online opportunities, principally in relation to participation (Livingstone & Helsper, 2007).

In a previous study (Zimic, forthcoming), digital skills, self-efficacy, and attitudes towards new technology were compared across levels of the perceived feeling of participation in the information society. The aim was to learn more about what participation means to young people. The study indicated that the skills and attitudes considered as being the most important for participation were actually not rated as the most important among the young people themselves. Instead of strategic skills, which are considered to be at the highest skill level, information literacy had the strongest relationship with the perceived feeling of participation (Zimic, forthcoming).

Following the tradition of previous work of questioning the images of digital natives (Bennett et al., 2008; Facer & Furlong, 2001; Livingstone & Helsper, 2007; Selwyn, 2009), this chapter aims to question the concept of digital participation in relation to young people's own feeling of participation in the information society. Thus, the relation between Internet activities and the perceived feeling of participation is analyzed in an attempt to answer the research question: *Which Internet activities merit the perceived feeling of participation in the information society among twelve-to-thirty-one year olds in Sweden?*

Finding out how Internet usage differs between young people who feel more or less engaged with the information society, can provide a better understanding of the reasons relating to varied levels of perceived participation. In this way, the rather stereotypical images of young people's online participation can be replaced with a more nuanced understanding.

What is Participation Online?

Participation is in many ways considered to be a democratic issue, meaning that it is a human right to be able to express opinions and become actively involved in society. In relation to children and young people this issue is stated in article 12 of the UN Convention on the Rights of the Child:

> State Parties shall assure to the child who is capable of forming his or her own views the right to express those views freely in all matters affecting the child, the views of the child being given due weight in accordance with the age and maturity of the child.
>
> (UNICEF, 1989)

Carpentier (2007) argues that the definition of participation oscillates between the minimalist and the maximalist variations of democracy and politics. Whereas the minimalist approach is limited to the elections of political representatives who organize their decision-making, the maximalist approach considers both representation and participation in the sphere of political decision-making, but also in other societal spheres such as the economy, culture, and media. Therefore, participation is practiced partially in the way it is perceived, but the practice also structures the definition of participation (Carpentier, 2007). In relation to participation on the Internet, the concept e-participation is often used. The concept was initially strongly associated with voting online, but actually refers to electronic solutions in all the democratic processes (Rose, Grönlund & Viborg, 2007). However, e-participation is still often associated with taking part in civic and political activities

(Livingstone et al., 2005; Montgomery, 2008; Turnšek, 2007), which are not always seen as typical forms of participation among young people (Loader, 2007). Extending the concept of participation by including activities such as communicating, peer-to-peer connection, seeking information, interactivity, webpage/ content creation, as well as visiting civic/political websites (Livingstone, Bober & Helsper, 2005) showed that young people are participating in various ways online.

In accordance with Carpentier (2007), Bennett et al. (2009) touch on the issue of the political-ideological task of defining participation in relation to being a good citizen. They suggest that there are two types of citizenship—*dutiful* citizenship and *actualizing* citizenship. These two forms of citizenships have distinct meanings for different age groups in many democracies. Older citizens tend to feel more obliged to participate in elections and government-centered activities whereas young citizens tend to favor more personally expressive or self-actualizing politics. These forms of expression occasionally occur in elections, but more often than not they emerge in direct action networks organized around specific issues such as global warming. The opportunity offered by Web 2.0 experiences favors the type of actualizing citizenship, while the other forms of dutiful citizenship are more traditional and include participation in elections and engagement in party politics (Bennett et al., 2009). It appears as if the opportunities associated with social networking sites and other types of Web 2.0 based technologies that support actualizing citizenship are regarded as the way young people are participating in civic and political activities. This would suggest that many young people are actualizing citizens rather than dutiful citizens, giving support to the image that young people are disengaged from traditional mainstream party politics (Bennett et al., 2009).

Yet another image labels young people as progressive, even rebellious, assuming that it is a "natural" part of being young, which according to Lindgren (2009) is a common misconception about younger generations. The expectations regarding youngsters' participation in the information society builds upon stereotypes both in relation to the image of youth and that of technology. The image of technology often reflects a deterministic view, meaning that the generational differences are seen to be produced by technology, rather than as being a result of social, historical, and cultural factors (Buckingham & Willett, 2006).

How is young people's participation online best approached? First of all, the Internet as media, in comparison to other media such as TV, is often considered to be more "active" and to encourage participation (Carpentier, 2007). Olsson (2006) studied the media use of politically active Swedish youth, and he found that they are critically aware and calculating in relation to traditional media use as well as digital media use. They were also aware of what is considered "low status" media consumption and "high status" media consumption. The question is whether there is a common awareness among young people in relation to participation online. This leads to another question, namely, what kind of Internet media consumption or Internet activities indicate a low or high degree of participation online?

This question will be addressed in the chapter by using the concept "participatory culture" (Jenkins, 2009) in order to explore the extent to which the Internet activities expected for participation merit the feeling of participation. As stated previously, by extending the concept of participation it was found that young people do take part in a range of online opportunities and gain new experiences in relation to participation. However, not all young people are engaged and they do not all engage in the same way (Livingstone et al., 2005). Rheingold (2008) suggests that the young bloggers, video producers, and social networking users certainly cannot be called passive media consumers. He points out the importance of making online opportunities interesting for young people because they engage in activities that they can relate to and find meaningful for their lives. In addition, he implies that adults should improve their listening in relation to young people. There is a requirement for an audience and the belief that one's opinions are being heard (Rheingold, 2008). The importance of believing that one's opinions will be heard is one of the points defining participatory culture (Jenkins, 2009). Participatory culture is here understood to have:

> 1. relatively low barriers to artistic expression and civic engagement
> 2. strong support for creating and sharing creations with others
> 3. some type of informal mentorship whereby what is known by the most experienced is passed along to novices
> 4. members who believe that their contributions matter
> 5. members who feel some degree of social connection with one another (at least, they care what other people think about what they have created).
>
> (Jenkins, 2009, pp. 5–6)

According to a study conducted by the Pew Internet & American Life Project (Lenhart & Madden, 2005) more than a half of all American teens—and 57 percent of teens who use the Internet—could be considered "media creators." However, Jenkins et al. (2009) state that the number of young Americans who are embracing the new participatory culture has been underestimated since the Pew study did not consider new forms of expression. In a more recent study by Pew (Smith, Lehman Schlozman, Verba, & Brady, 2009) it has been shown that those who take part in civic life online are similar to those who participate offline—well-educated and with high socioeconomic status. However, social media appears to be of considerable importance for civic engagement since many of those who are engaged use email, instant messaging, and blogs for civic and political purposes (Smith, Lehman Schlozman, Verba, & Brady, 2009). Montgomery has investigated the "youth civic web"—platforms built for young people in order to invite them to participate. She concludes that interactive media is helping to provide young people with some of the essential skills for civic and political engagement by allowing them to learn about the critical issues of the day; insert their own voices into the public discourse; and actively participate in a range of political issues (Montgomery, 2008).

Simultaneously, critical voices exist that define the Internet in terms of creative and participating media (Carpentier, 2007; Haggren et al., 2008). Haggren, Larsson, Nordwall, and Widing (2008) suggest that the old structures of audience versus media creators have not disappeared. Rather, the power structures are categorized into complex digital structures, making it more difficult to notice them. It is not the media *per se* but Internet users who decide whether they are going to participate (Haggren et al., 2008). Carpentier (2007) also implies that the participatory potential of media technologies remains dependent on the way they are used, which means that, in practice, Web 2.0 technologies can be used in top-down non-participatory ways (Carpentier, 2007).

By exploring the relation between Internet activities related to participatory culture and the perceived feeling of participation we can better understand what importance these activities have in terms of the participation of young people in the information society.

Mode of Procedure

This study is based on data collected from an annual national survey about the Internet usage of Swedish people, which is part of the international World Internet Project (www.worldinternetproject.net). The survey was conducted between February and May 2009. A random sample of 2,353 people from all around Sweden within the age range of twelve and above, answered a wide range of questions about their Internet usage. Initially the survey was conducted as a panel study and the inevitable "drop offs" were compensated for by random sampling by age. Two different surveys were conducted, one involving respondents of sixteen and above and one with young people from twelve (born in 1997) to sixteen years (born in 1993). The main reasons for conducting two different surveys were that people younger than sixteen required parental permission to participate but, additionally, in order to obtain a larger sample of the young people to be able to perform statistical analyses when the youngest groups are studied separately.

Table 9.1 shows the distribution within the sample of the age groups 12–31 years. The age groups 12–16 and 17–19 years are weighted by 0.5 in order to match the proportions of the Swedish population.

The questions regarding participatory culture were selected from the survey to determine whether they matched some of the five points regarding participatory culture mentioned previously (Jenkins, 2009). An overview of the questions can be found in Table 9.2.

TABLE 9.1 Sample sizes for 12–31 year olds

Age	*Frequency*	*Percent*
12–16	286	33
17–19	231	27
20–25	173	20
26–31	168	20
Total	**858**	**100**

TABLE 9.2 Questions related to the concept of "participatory culture"

Variable	*Question*	*Measure*
Writing a blog	*Do you write a blog?*	0 = No; 1 = Yes
Community member	*Are you a member of a community online?*	0 = No; 1 = Yes
Price comparisons	*How often, if ever, do you use the services for price comparisons in order to compare prices for a service or a product?*	0 = Never or Occasionally 1 = Monthly, Weekly, Daily
Uploading video clips	*How often, if ever, do you upload video clips online on web pages such as YouTube?*	0 = Never or Occasionally 1 = Monthly, Weekly, Daily
Uploading photos	*How often, if ever, do you upload photos? For instance on a blog, webpage, or community?*	0 = Never or Occasionally 1 = Monthly, Weekly, Daily
File sharing	*Do you ever use services for file sharing such as BitTorrent, Kazaa, DC++ or the Pirate bay?*	0 = Never or Occasionally 1 = Monthly, Weekly, Daily
Political information	*How often, if ever, do you use the Internet to search for political information?*	0 = Never or Occasionally 1 = Monthly, Weekly, Daily
Information about society	*How often, if ever, do you use the Internet to search information about the society?*	0 = Never or Occasionally 1 = Monthly, Weekly, Daily
Governmental information	*How often, if ever, do you use the Internet to search for official information from the government or municipalities?*	0 = Never or Occasionally 1 = Monthly, Weekly, Daily

It is possible for all of Jenkins' five items defining participatory culture in relation to blogs and communities to be supported. Blogs and communities are allowing people to express their creativity and they could be related to civic engagement. The purpose of communities and blogs is to share content with others, receive comments, and discuss specific issues with other people. This matches the description of participatory culture in points 1 (low barriers to artistic expression and civic engagement), 2 (creating and sharing), 4 (believe the contributions matter), and 5 (social connection). Point 3 regarding informal mentorship could also be supported; however, in this case it is not defined as being the primary reason for blogs and communities. The informal mentorship is more visible when using services for price comparisons or file sharing, where it is possible to read other people's comments regarding a product. File sharing and posting video clips and photos are mostly supported by the requirements of creating and sharing but also in believing that the creations matter to others. The information regarding politics, society, and governmental information are not primarily defined by the concept of participatory culture, but they are considered to be very important for participation at large. All of the questions were dichotomized in order to be able to compare the results but also to reduce the complexity in the regression model. The question regarding price comparisons was also used in a previous study to measure the strategic skills in using computers and the Internet. In this case it is used only as an Internet activity.

The dependent variable with regard to the perceived feeling of participation was analyzed by asking the question: *You have now answered a range of questions about different media and you have probably heard or read about surfing the Internet, using email, and information technology. Do you feel part of this new information society?* The answers were: *No, not at all*; *Yes, but only a little*; *Yes, to a large extent*; and *Yes, completely*. The question is not an attempt to measure actual participation in the information society but an indicator of people's subjective feeling, which we believe to be useful information in order to explore what participation really means. In the regression analyses the answers were dichotomized into *low* and *high* degree of perceived participation in the information society. A low degree of participation is categorized by *No, not at all* and *Yes, but only a little* and the high degree of participation is categorized by the answers *Yes, to a large extent* and *Yes, completely*.

Young Swedes' Online Participation

In order to obtain an overview of what young Internet users do online across a range of Internet activities, their use or non-use of these activities were analyzed for the age groups 12–16, 17–19, 20–25, and 26–31 years, respectively.

Some differences between age groups were found, as could be expected. The youngest group (12–16 years) was shown to be significantly different in comparison with the older age groups and for that reason the Internet activities are presented separately for 12–16 year olds and the 17–31 year olds. The young ones (12–16 year olds) use the Internet mostly for communication and entertainment-oriented opportunities, while the older age group (17–31 year olds) have a broader use of Internet applications. Communication related activities include: using email, instant messaging, and online communities. There is an almost equal usage of these among the 12–16 year olds and 17–31 year olds. The entertainment activities used to an equal extent by the two age groups involve watching videos (70 percent), listening to music (85 percent), and uploading video clips (10 percent). All the other Internet activities are used more by the older age group. The only activity the youngest group scores considerably higher on is playing games online (78 percent vs. 52 percent). Those between seventeen and thirty-one years do not primarily use the Internet for communication and entertainment but, additionally, to obtain information about different aspects, such as information about society, comparing prices, and looking at maps to discover information about road directions. These findings suggest that Internet activities related to participatory culture are unable to explain the variance in perceived feelings of participation among the two age groups. Approximately 26 percent of 17–31 year olds feel a low degree of participation, while this is felt by 45 percent of the 12–16 year olds (see Figure 9.1).

In the next step the dichotomies of perceived feeling of participation were analyzed within each of the two age groups. For 12–16 year olds there was no clear pattern for specific activities among those perceiving their participation as high. File sharing, making voice calls, and comparing prices were the three activities that were considerably higher among those perceiving a high degree of participation in the information society. However, the rates were very low and did not differ significantly between the dichotomies of perceived feeling of participation. On the contrary, for the older age group in this sample, a clearer pattern was

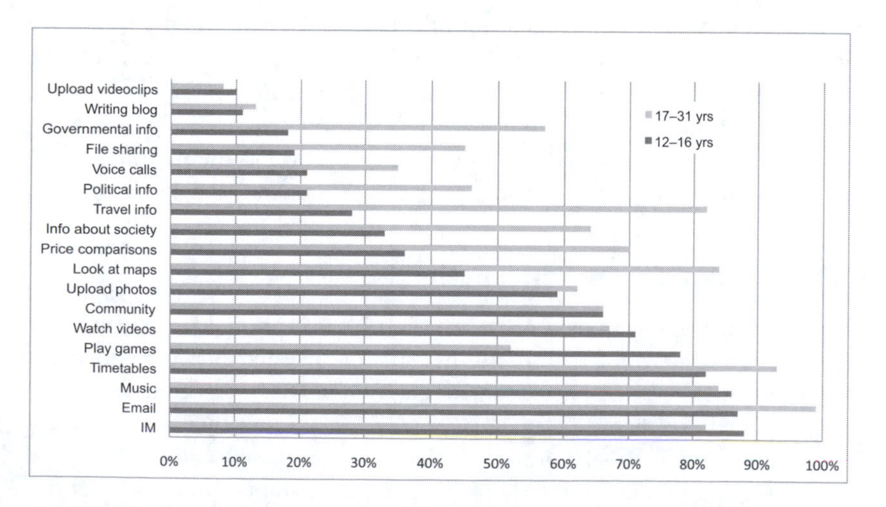

FIGURE 9.1 Internet activities by age group

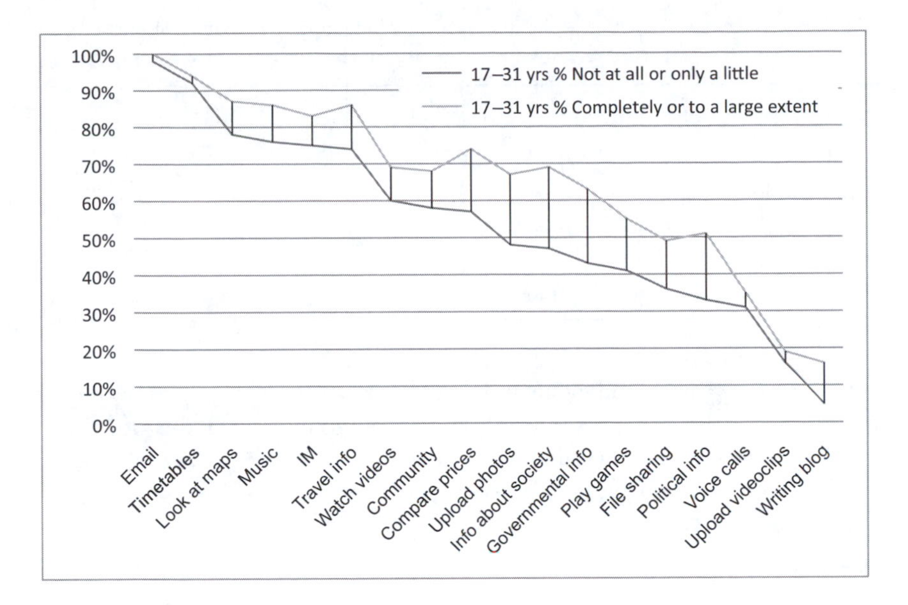

FIGURE 9.2 Internet activities among 17–31 year olds according to perceived feeling of participation

found. In Figure 9.2 it can be seen that those perceiving a high degree of participation consistently score higher on all the Internet activities included in this analysis. Some of the activities do indeed stand out, such as uploading photos; searching for information about society; obtaining information from the government and municipalities; file sharing; writing blogs; searching for political information; and comparing prices. These differ by 11 to 24 percentage points between those perceiving a low degree of participation and those perceiving a high degree of participation.

Some of the activities mentioned are defined by the concept of "participatory culture" used in this study in order to analyze the perceived feeling of participation. It is information concerning society, politics and governmental information, uploading videos and photography, and, finally, file-sharing. In the regression analysis, all of the activities defined as being related to participatory culture were included, together with the social factor gender. Table 9.3 presents the final model, which was felt to best explain the variance in the perceived feeling of participation. The Internet activities that merit the feeling of participation in the information society among 17–31 year olds are writing blogs and searching for information about society. Gender could not explain the variance in the perceived feeling of participation. This means that under the control of gender, the Internet activities shown in Table 9.3 could explain the variance in the perceived feeling of participation. However, this does not mean that the rates

TABLE 9.3 Regression analyses—Gender, writing a blog, and information about society on the perceived feeling of participation in the information society

	B	*S.E.*	*Wald*	*df*	*p-value*	*Exp(B)*
Gender	0.213	0.244	0.760	1	0.383	1.237
Writing a blog	1.203	0.496	5.890	1	0.015	3.329
Information about society	0.935	0.280	11.104	1	0.001	2.546
Constant	0.603	0.189	10.180	1	0.001	1.827

between young men and women engaging in writing blogs and searching information about society are equal. It means that young men and women who feel a high degree of participation tend to engage in these activities to a higher extent than those feeling a low degree of participation.

Discussion

The results suggest that the young people perceiving a low degree of participation in information society do not have as broad an Internet usage as those perceiving a high degree of participation. This was also the case with the youngest age group in the sample (12–16 year olds) who primarily use the Internet for communication and entertainment-oriented activities. In accordance with previous studies (Hargittai & Hinnant, 2008; Livingstone & Helsper, 2007) Internet usage diverges between younger and older adolescents.

Those perceiving their participation as low do not have low rates throughout all the Internet activities. They use email and they search for practical information such as time tables almost as much as those perceiving their participation as high. However, in relation to searching for information from the government, municipalities, or civic and political information and activities such as comparing prices and sharing files, the rates are much lower for those perceiving their participation as low in comparison to those perceiving their participation as high. In the regression analyses it was found that information about society and writing blogs could explain the variance in the perceived feeling of participation. This indicates that some of the activities labeled as "participatory culture" (Jenkins, 2009) do set users apart in relation to the perceived feeling of participation.

It is interesting that political, governmental, and society information appear to be important for young people in order to feel part of the information society, which is a traditional, or according to Carpentier (2007), a minimalistic approach to defining participation. In this study, the results indicate that both the political or society-oriented activities and Web 2.0 supported activities such as writing blogs appear to be important for young people in order to feel part of the information society. It is interesting that the youngest do not have a common definition regarding what participation is and they have a rather limited Internet use, thus it is important to be critical about what we expect from young people in relation to participation in the information society. It was surprising that gender is not significant for the feeling of participation. According to Livingstone, Bober, and Helsper (2005), girls and boys tend to engage in different types of Internet activities. However, in this study it was found that blogs and searching for information about society were important both for young women and men in order to feel a high degree of participation.

Limitations

The construction of variables regarding the activities related to participatory culture was restricted by the data at hand and therefore does not totally cover the concept of participatory culture. The question regarding price comparisons also measures a type of strategic skill when using the Internet, but in this chapter the question is used only to explore the specific Internet activity of comparing prices. A more problematic issue is the question regarding participation in the information society. It is a broad question, and does not specifically say what is meant by "being a part of the information society." However, the aim was not to measure the actual participation but to obtain an idea about how young people define participation in the information society. There is reason to believe that the youngest age group did not understand this question or rather they could not define participation on their own. There were no consistent patterns in Internet usage among those perceiving their participation as high as compared to those perceiving it as low.

Using the concept "information society" could also be problematic since it might mean that people automatically think of using information as being crucial in becoming a part of the information society. This is, however, almost unavoidable regardless of what concept is being used. The concept "digital society" might have had the effect of making people believe the more technically advanced Internet activities are the most important for participation. The information society is also a commonly used term to describe the society we live in today, and for that reason it is used in this study. As stated previously, the present study is an exploratory examination of what participation in the information society could mean to young people by examining which Internet activities merit the feeling of participation.

Implications and Concluding Remarks

This study follows the tradition of other research implying the importance of questioning the image of digital natives (Bennett et al., 2008; Facer & Furlong, 2001; Selwyn, 2009). In this study, it is done by exploring the concept of digital participation by analyzing the relationship between Internet activities (labeled "participatory culture") and the perceived feeling of participation in information society. The image of digital natives presumes that young people are competent in their use of ICT, and thus they are assumed to be participating in various ways in the digital world. However, in what way they are participating and what is really meant by digital participation are questions that still need further exploration (Livingstone, 2009).

This study has attempted to explore which Internet activities merit the feeling of participation among young Swedes. By linking the Internet activities to the perceived feeling of participation we can better understand which activities young people themselves think it is important to engage in, in order to feel part of the information society. Thus, it is felt that the risk of ascribing young people certain characteristics in relation to Internet use has been minimized.

The findings suggest that broad use of the Internet and the activities considered significant for participation at large, such as engaging in civic issues by finding information about society, are important for young people in order to feel part of the information society. Using the Internet does not automatically guarantee participation in the information society, hence assistance is required in order to engage them in relevant activities. There is some support for using the definition of Internet activities related to "participatory culture" (Jenkins, 2009) since the activity of writing blogs merits the feeling of participation.

The research question is answered in relation to the definition of participation within this study, namely participatory culture and civic engagement. Writing a blog and searching for information about society are two of the activities that merit young people's own feeling of participation. Since it is unclear how digital participation should be defined, young people's own feeling of participation provides important information regarding what participation might mean to young people. It is recommended that future research should turn its attention to exploring further what is really meant by digital participation, how young people are expected to participate, and also how young people themselves define digital participation. Finally, when approaching young people (younger than sixteen years), it has to be borne in mind that it is not always possible to ask direct questions relating to participation, as there is a risk they might not be able to relate to this sort of questioning.

References

Bennett, L. W., Wells, C., & Rank, A. (2009). Young citizens and civic learning: Two paradigms of citizenship in the digital age. *Citizenship Studies*, *13*(2), 105–120.

Bennett, S., Maton, K., & Kervin, L. (2008). The "Digital Natives" debate: A critical review of the evidence. *British Journal of Educational Technology*, *39*(5), 775–786.

Buckingham, D., & Willett, R. (2006). *Digital generations: Children, young people, and new media*. Mahwah, NJ: Lawrence Erlbaum Associates.

Carpentier, N. (2007). Theoretical frameworks for participatory media. In N. Carpentier, P. Pruulmann-Vengerfeldt, K. Nordenstreng, M. Hartmann, P. Vihalemm, B. Cammaerts, H. Nieminen (Eds.), *Media technologies and democracy in an enlarged Europe: The intellectual work of the 2007 European media and communication doctoral summer school* (pp. 105–122). Tartu: Tartu University Press.

Facer, K., & Furlong, R. (2001). Beyond the myth of the "cyberkid": Young people at the margins of the information revolution. *Journal of Youth Studies*, *4*(4), 451–469.

Findahl, O., & Zimic, S. (2008). *Unga Svenskar och Internet 2008: En rapport som baseras på en pilotstudie av barn och ungdomars Internetanvändning*. Hudiksvall: World Internet Institute.

Haggren, K., Larsson, E., Nordwall, L., & Widing, G. (2008). *Deltagarkultur*. Göteborg: Bokförlaget Korpen.

Hargittai, E., & Hinnant, A. (2008). Digital inequality: Differences in young adults' use of the internet. *Communication Research*, *35*(602), 602–621.

Jenkins, H. with Purushotma, R., Weigel, M., Clinton, K., & Robison, A. J. (2009). *Confronting the challenges of participatory culture: Media education for the 21st century*. Cambridge, MA: The MIT Press.

Lee, L. (2008). The impact of young people's internet use on class boundaries and life trajectories. *Sociology*, *42*(1), 137–153.

Lenhart, A., & Madden, M. (2005). *Teen content creators and consumers*. Washington DC: Pew Internet & American Life Project.

Lindgren, S. (2009). *Ungdomskulturer* (1. uppl. ed.). Malmö: Gleerup.

Livingstone, S. (2009). *Children and the Internet: Great expectations, challenging realities*. Cambridge, UK: Polity Press.

Livingstone, S., & Haddon, L. (2009). *EU kids online: Final report. LSE, London: EU Kids Online*. EC Safer Internet Plus Programme, Deliverable D6.5.

Livingstone, S., & Helsper, E. (2007). Gradations in digital inclusion: Children, young people and the digital divide. *New Media & Society*, *9*(4), 671–696.

Livingstone, S., Bober, M., & Helsper, E. (2005). Active participation or just more information? *Information, Communication & Society*, *8*(3), 287–314.

Loader, B. (2007). *Young citizens in the digital age: Political engagement, young people, and new media*. London & New York: Routledge.

Montgomery, K. C. (2008). Youth and digital democracy: Intersections of practice, policy, and the marketplace. In W. L. Bennett (Ed.), *Civic life online: Learning how digital media can engage youth* (pp. 25–50). Cambridge, MA: The MIT Press.

Olsson, T. (2006). Active and calculated media use among young citizens: Empirical examples from a Swedish study. In D. Buckingham & R. Willett (Eds.), *Digital generations: Children, young people, and new media* (pp. 115–130). Mahwah, NJ: Lawrence Erlbaum Associates.

Prensky, M. (2001). Digital natives, digital immigrants. *On the Horizon*, *9*(5), 1–6.

Rheingold, H. (2008). Using participatory media in public voice to encourage civic engagement. In W. L. Bennett (Ed.), *Civic life online: Learning how digital media can engage youth* (pp. 97–118). Cambridge, MA: The MIT Press.

Rose, J., Grönlund, Å., & Anderson, V. K. (2007). Introduction. In A. Avdic, K. Hedström, J. Rose, Å. Grönlund (Eds.), *Understanding eParticipation: Contemporary Ph.D. eParticipation research in Europe* (pp. 1–16). Örebro: Örebro University Library.

Selwyn, N. (2009). The digital native-myth and reality. *Aslib Proceedings*, *61*(4), 364–379.

Smith, A., Lehman Schlozman, K., Verba, S., & Brady, H. (2009). *The internet and civic engagement*. Washington DC: Pew Internet & American Life Project.

Turnšek, M. (2007). "The Digital Youth Revolt?": Young people and eParticipation. In A. Avdic, K. Hedström, J. Rose, Å. Grönlund (Eds.), *Understanding eParticipation: Contemporary Ph.D. eParticipation research in Europe* (pp. 201–214). Örebro: Örebro University Library.

UNICEF. (1989). *Convention on the Rights of the Child*, Document A/RES/44/25 C.F.R.

Zimic, S. (forthcoming 2011). Predicting the participation in information society. In E. Dunkels, G-M. Frånberg, C. Hällgren (Eds.), *Interactive media use and youth: Learning, knowledge exchange and behaviour*. Chapter 12. Hershey: IGI Global.

10

YOUNG CHILDREN, DIGITAL TECHNOLOGY, AND INTERACTION WITH TEXT

Rachael Levy

Introduction

There is no doubt that ICT and digital media have had a major impact on the ways in which young children today learn, play, work, and socialize. Indeed, there exists a substantial body of research that reveals the various ways in which such media has infiltrated the social and cultural practices of everyday life. In their study of young children's (aged from birth to six) use of popular culture, media, and new technologies, Marsh et al. (2005, p. 5) surveyed 1,852 parents and carers of children and concluded that "young children are immersed in practices relating to popular culture, media and new technologies from birth" and that young children are "growing up in a digital world and develop a wide range of skills, knowledge and understanding of this world from birth."

Further study has suggested that the "domestication of technology" (Holloway & Valentine, 2003, p. 100) means that ICT has become ingrained into family life and has a bearing on the ways in which physical spaces are created in the home as well reconfiguring the "time-spaces" of the family, in terms of activity. Moreover, it has been documented that young children are actually demonstrating an ability to handle screen texts even when they are not exposed to computers in their own home. Bearne et al. reported that "very young children show expertise in on-screen reading, even where homes have no computers" (2007, p. 11), because the ways in which such texts are handled is now embodied within a culturally valued discourse. More specifically, research has also indicated that young children are developing strategies within their home environments that allow them to access and read a variety of digital texts with fluency (Levy, 2009a). This suggests that many young children may be developing the knowledge and skills of "digital literacy" (Glister, 1997) before they even arrive in the school setting and are thus "native" users of digital technology.

Yet, if this is the case then serious issues must be addressed with regard to the implementation of early years pedagogy. In particular, many researchers have argued that schools need to recognize the "new textual landscape" (Carrington, 2005) of modern communication systems, and accommodate this within the early years curriculum. Yet such recommendations may be based on the assumption that skills of "digital literacy" are essentially homogenous in nature, and that young children experience interaction with technologies in similar ways. This chapter addresses this assumption and questions whether young children are inherently "native" users of digital technology, through reference to case study data collected from three young children at the time of entry into the formal education system in the UK. In doing so, this chapter also explores the relationship between children's interactions with digital technology and interaction with text in general. However, in order to do this, it is useful to first examine how the term "digital literacy" has been defined in the literature.

Digital Literacy and Text

Much has been written about the diversity of literacy practices that are constantly emerging into contemporary life (Cope & Kalantzis, 2000; Lankshear & Knobel, 2003). This means that definitions of the term "literacy" have been brought very much into question as researchers grapple to find ways in which to describe the rapidly changing discourses associated with text analysis and text production. As Marsh and Singleton (2009, p. 1) point out, "technology has always been part of literacy." In other words they are arguing that in order to read or write, one needs to have certain tools (paper, pencil, computer screen, etc.), yet the "nature of that technology inevitably influences the literacy experience" (Marsh & Singleton, 2008, p. 1). For this reason, literacy practices that have been somehow mediated by new technologies have been termed "digital literacies" (Carrington & Robinson, 2009).

Yet others have debated the extent to which definitions of the term "digital literacy" should include the encoding and decoding of alphabetic print. For example, Kress (2003) argues that literacy refers to "lettered representation" and that we need to find other ways in which to describe how screen and digital texts are read and utilized in terms of their broader symbolic representations. Merchant (2007, p. 121) agrees that the term "digital literacy" relates to more than a general confidence in handling screen texts, and should be oriented towards the "study of written or symbolic representation that is mediated by new technology." In other words, he appears to be arguing that the term "digital literacy" can help to redefine conceptualizations of literacy as an ability to understand the many sign and symbol systems in existence within texts today as well as the ways in which children make sense of them within their home environments. Marsh (2005) also acknowledges that while the term "points towards the ways in which lettered representation is being transformed and shaped by digitised technologies"

(p. 4), she also recognizes that "there are distinct aspects of text analysis and production using new media" (p. 5) that cannot be described in the same way as the more traditional literacy practices.

This issue is extended in the work of Albers, Frederick, and Cowan (2009), who point out that young children entering the school system today are not only regular users of a variety of digital and paper texts, but are developing the skills "to help them make sense of complex multimodal features" (Levy & Marsh, in press). This suggests there is something specific about the ways in which digital texts are used, and produced, that differs from traditional constructions of reading and writing, and in this sense constitutes a "digital literacy."

Yet it would be naive to suggest that the term "digital literacy" is therefore divorced from traditional constructions of reading and writing. In a recent review of research into technology and early childhood settings, Burnett (in press) argues that it is now apparent that "complex interactions . . . occur between children, technology, and their wide-ranging experiences of literacy." This issue is taken further still in the work of Prensky (2009) who speaks of the concept of "Digital Wisdom"; this being the capacity to capitalize on the rapidly changing landscape of technology, and use it *wisely*. Recognizing that the affordances, and indeed potential affordances, of the digital age are by no means confined to the technology itself, but are embedded within "the relationship between mind and machine" (Prensky, 2009, p. 4). Prensky argues that in order to succeed in the future, humans will need to "intelligently combine their innate capacities with their digital enhancements" (p. 3). From this position, it could be argued that "digital literacy" describes an ability to skillfully utilize one's knowledge of text construction and analysis (be it paper, digital, popular culture, and so on) in order to continuously develop one's ability to handle digital media.

Clearly there is still much debate surrounding the term "digital literacy." However for the purposes of this chapter it seems most useful to apply this broader definition of the term that recognizes the ways in which children apply their experiences of literacy in a variety of forms to their interactions with digital texts. Given Prensky's assertion that we should be concerning ourselves with the relationship children develop between cognition and digital media, this definition maintains a focus on how children form such relationships, rather than attempting to understand the minutia of skill in handling digital technology. Yet, if we are to promote "digital wisdom" in the way Prensky is suggesting then there are some issues that need to be addressed, especially in relation to the education of young children.

First, in order for children to function as competent and confident users of text in the twenty-first century, I would argue that we need to view the relationship between traditional and digital media as reciprocal. In other words, though I agree that we need to find ways in which to help children to build on their experiences with traditional media in order to inform their interactions with digital texts, it is equally important to understand how the use of digital texts informs young children's relationships with texts of all kinds. Much as we may embrace the affordances offered by changes in technology, we must also acknowledge that the school discourse is not only rooted in traditional constructions of literacy (Marsh, 2003), but that it is also responsible for shaping children's perceptions of aspects of literacy (Levy, 2009b).

As a consequence, this chapter has three related concerns. On the basis of case study data collected from young children (aged three and four years old) this chapter first explores young children's interactions with digital texts, and questions the assumption that there is uniformity to the ways in which young children handle such texts. Building on this, the chapter examines how interactions with digital texts can influence young children's relationships with texts in general, before turning to consider the implications of this for pedagogic practice.

Three Children: A Case Study

The findings discussed in this chapter draw from a larger longitudinal study that was designed to investigate young children's (aged three to six) perceptions of reading at the time of entry into the formal education system. Given that little previous research has attempted to understand young children's perceptions of reading, this collective case study was highly exploratory in nature and employed a variety of participatory techniques (described below) in order to access the voices of the twelve children in the study. It was decided to focus on children as they began school so that the influence of the home and school discourse could be investigated. In a general sense, this study aimed to understand how these young children came to develop definitions of reading, through their interactions with a variety of texts at home and at school, as well as understand the factors that influenced their perceptions of themselves as readers in the light of these definitions. More specifically, given that the role of phonics teaching has recently been the subject of considerable debate in the UK, especially as a result of the Rose Review (2006) (see Wyse & Styles, 2007)—which has recommended that the teaching of reading in early years should be based on synthetic phonic instruction—this study attempted to understand whether children's perceptions of print reading were influenced by the medium (including paper and screen texts) within which the print was situated.

While the overall study revealed much about the ways in which these children formed constructions of reading (Levy, 2008b), it was striking to note that these children were not only interacting differently with digital technology, but that such interactions appeared to influence the children's individual relationships with texts in general. In order to illustrate this point, this chapter now examines data gathered from three of the children in the study; Shaun (Nursery—aged four), Caitlyn (Nursery—aged four), and Joseph (Reception—aged five).

Data were collected in three phases over the course of the year. Most of the data were collected directly from the children, using a range of participatory techniques as described below. However, parents and children were also interviewed in their homes in order to gain an understanding of the ways in which technology was used by the children at home. Although the focus was firmly situated on the children, teachers were also interviewed so as to provide the study with a broader context. This meant that as the study progressed, profiles could be developed for each of the children on the basis of data collected from the children at home and at school, direct observation, and interviews with teachers and parents. A variety of activities were conducted over the course of the year in order to investigate the children's perceptions of reading in general. Given the extent of the study, it is not possible to describe each of these activities in detail; however, the next section provides a brief overview of the activities that were designed to explore specifically the children's interactions with digital texts.

Research Tools

Although home visits were conducted in order to observe the children's interactions with digital media in the home, and to allow parents the opportunity to speak about such interactions, most of the data were collected from the children themselves within the school setting. This involved the use of three main activities; the *Charlie Chick* interview, the *Small World Play* activity and the *Computer Assisted Interview*. Each of these activities were repeated throughout the three phases of the study and each included the use of a wide variety of sub-activities where artifacts such as pictures, photographs, and card games were used to facilitate a research conversation with the child.

The *Charlie Chick Interview* used a glove puppet (Charlie Chick) to mediate a conversation between researcher and child. Within the context of the conversation the children were asked to tell the puppet about the various activities they engaged with at home and at school, including their use of digital technology. Games were also introduced, via the puppet, to explore the children's beliefs about learning to perform various skills, such as reading books and reading words on the computer, alongside other activities such as painting a picture, riding a bike, and so on. This again provided an opportunity to encourage the children to talk about their perceptions of using digital media and discuss issues of perceived difficulty in comparison with using paper texts.

Small World Play artifacts were also used throughout the study to facilitate play-oriented research conversations by creating a "home scenario" as a basis for role play. As this scenario included a television, video, and computer, as well as general household furniture (such as table and chairs) and a family of dolls, the activity encouraged the children to talk about the ways in which they perceive technology to be used within the home environment.

Finally, the children were also presented with regular opportunities to use computers as part of the data collection. In the first phase of the study they were invited to show Charlie Chick how to use the computer and talk about their own interactions with computers at home and at school. Although the children were given opportunities to download games of their own choice, if they wished, the children were also encouraged to play some pre-specified games for reasons of comparison. Research into computer games for young children has identified that over the years consumer software has tended to blend educational philosophies with interactive gaming and entertainment genres, thus producing "edutainment" (Ito, 2009). In other words, many of the games designed for young children tend to offer educational value as well as entertainment. For this reason, the pre-specified games chosen for the children reflected this and included a nursery rhyme game that invited the children to participate in the creation of a story as well as a *Bob the Builder* game downloaded from a website, which encouraged the children to participate in a variety of activities involving manipulation and interaction.

The data were analyzed using a grounded theory approach (Glaser & Strauss, 1967; Harry, Sturges & Klinger, 2005) where cycles of analysis were allowed to inform subsequent phases of data collection. This helped to build the profiles for each child in the study, which illustrated how these children were developing skills in handling aspects of digital technology. The profiles further revealed the children's attitudes towards this media and the impact these interactions had on their wider relationships with text.

Young Children Interacting with Digital Technology

This next section explains how three children, Shaun, Joseph, and Caitlyn, were using aspects of digital technology at home and school, and the implications this had towards their individual interactions with texts in general. Findings from the study showed that although these three children were all demonstrating a variety of skills in handling various technologies, and an enthusiasm for using computers in particular, their individual interactions with digital media differed substantially from one another. This resonates with a study conducted by Plowman, McPake, and Stephen (in press) that surveyed 346 families in Scotland, and concluded that while children and parents are active users of digital technology, patterns of interaction differed from family to family and an increase in technological items in the home did not necessarily relate to the amount of use of technology by the children. However, the case study data in this chapter further suggests that it is also important to consider the ways in which children's interactions with digital technology at home has an influence on children's relationships with screen and paper texts in school.

Shaun

Shaun's teacher reported that he showed a particular interest in using the computer in the nursery, in comparison with other children in the class. She stated that Shaun will "spend ages on some games" and "can do loads on the computer." She then went on to explain that he had been confidently and competently playing a new computer game that very morning, reporting that "he knew how to play that game—finding the dice and stuff," even though no-one had taught him how to play the game. Yet, it appeared that Shaun actually had very little experience in using computers in his home. Shaun's parents reported that the family does have a computer, but it is used "only occasionally" (Shaun's mother), partly because it is kept in an upstairs bedroom and is difficult to access, and also because it "is not running a hundred percent" (Shaun's father).

As a result, Shaun's interaction with interactive games in the home was generally not mediated by the computer, but by the television. During the first home visit, Shaun's father explained that Shaun really enjoys using the interactive games on Sky television. Shaun was then observed using the remote control to access and play various games on the television. In addition to this, he was also reported to play games on his father's mobile phone and on small handheld games consoles.

It was clear that although Shaun was both highly confident and competent in using computer technology in school, he appeared to have received very little instruction in how to use this technology, from within either the home or school setting. It therefore appeared that although Shaun's exposure to the computer within his home environment was minimal, he had developed certain "funds of knowledge" (Moll, Amanti, Neff & Gonzalez, 1992) through his engagement with other forms of media that provided him with the digital skills, or "digital literacy," to access such texts outside of the school with fluency.

Joseph

Given that Bearne et al. (2007) also discovered that young children show skills in reading screen texts, even when they are not exposed to computers in their homes, this suggests that other children may also be able to transfer their digital skills from one context to another. However, this does not imply that there is uniformity in the acquisition of such skills, especially in terms of implication for the classroom context. As with Shaun, Joseph also had little access to computers outside of school, yet his teacher reported that Joseph "loves" the computer and "thinks it should be his turn all the time" to use it in school. Moreover, although Joseph does not use a computer in his home, he was also observed using the interactive games on television with independence. What is more, he also reported that he enjoyed playing "games on Daddy's phone," which he described in detail. He reported:

> The buttons you use for the games—that's left, right, and the up—and the middle one. You're only meant to use that one because you shoot the ball up, and the middle one shoots the ball and breaks all the bricks.

While Joseph and Shaun both demonstrated an ability to transfer their digital skills from home into school, the acquisition of these skills and the impact of this upon their wider interactions with texts differed substantially. While Shaun's interactions with digital texts appeared to support his abilities and confidences in handing paper texts, the same could not be said for Joseph. Joseph appeared more comfortable using print within the context of the computer, in comparison with paper-based media. For example, he consistently reported, during the first phase of the study, that he thought it was easier to read words on computers than in books. When asked why he thought this was the case he replied, "because books have lots of words and computers doesn't [*sic*]." Moreover, having reported in the *Small World Play* activity that a girl looking at a book would find it "hard," while the same girl would find it easy to look at the computer, Joseph explained that it was easier to read and write words on the computer because "you can hear them in your head."

Throughout the initial phases of the study, Joseph not only demonstrated a competence in using print within the context of the computer, but consistently reported that he thought it was easier to read print on the computer rather than in books. Yet even though Joseph remained very enthusiastic about using computers throughout all phases of the study, his confidence in reading print on the computer seemed to decrease over this period. For example, during a game within the *Charlie Chick Interview,* he reported that it was "easy" to learn to read words on the computer during the first phase of the study, but claimed that it was "hard" by the final phase. As Joseph consistently reported that it was "hard" to read words in books throughout all three phases, this suggests that Joseph came to regard print reading on the computer as being just as difficult as print reading in paper-based contexts. Joseph's profile strongly suggests that as time went by, he no longer believed that his own strategies to use print within the context of the computer were authentic. As a consequence, he appeared to lose confidence in his ability to handle print within the context of the computer, though he remained enthusiastic about computer use in general.

As these case histories show, Shaun and Joseph both appeared to acquire digital literacy skills within the context of their home media use, and both seemed able to transfer these skills across the boundaries of setting (from home into school) and from one media text to another (from the context of the interactive television, mobile phone, etc., in the home, to the context of the computer in school). However, the ways in which digital media use impacted upon the children's wider interactions with text implied a significant difference between the two boys. As Joseph was less confident in his abilities to decode print, using phonetic decoding strategies, he seemed to lose confidence in his abilities to handle print within the context of paper *and* screen media over the course of the year. In other words, Joseph had developed strategies to make sense of print and symbol systems with the context of digital media use; however, as these strategies were not recognized in school, the digital technology of the classroom did not seem to support Joseph's literacy development and interactions with texts in general. This differed substantially from Shaun's profile, whose interactions with digital technology seemed to support his school based literacy practices and helped to create a comfortable space in between the discourses of home and school.

Caitlyn

Caitlyn's profile provides further evidence to suggest that we cannot make assumptions about the ways in which children not only use digital media but also about the impact this has on their interactions with texts in the classroom. Caitlyn (Nursery—aged four) was reported to use the computer extensively in her home, from the first phase of the study. As Caitlyn's mother was a teacher, Caitlyn had access to a variety of computer games that were intended for use with children in the junior classes at school (aged seven to ten). During the first home visit, Caitlyn's mother expressed her surprise at Caitlyn's ability to use computer texts unaided in the home. For example, speaking of Caitlyn's use of one particular mathematics game, she stated, "I don't know how she does it actually, because it has got writing in it." She then went on to say that she believed Caitlyn has "worked out that some of the questions are adding and some of them are matching and some are 'more or less' questions," before reiterating, "I don't know how she does it all by herself, but she always gets it right."

However, even though Caitlyn was reported to have become "so proficient" in using the computer in her home, Caitlyn did not appear to transfer these skills into the classroom context. During classroom observations, Caitlyn did not seem to use the computer very much, despite the fact that it was generally available for the children to use. Moreover, when asked to comment on Caitlyn's interactions with the computer, Caitlyn's teacher also reported that she is "not overly" interested in using the computer in school.

Caitlyn's interactions with the computer therefore differed greatly from those observed in Shaun and Joseph's profiles. Whereas these boys seemed to develop digital literacy skills in the home, and then transfer these skills into the school setting, where they were then applied to the medium of the computer, Caitlyn appeared to confine her interactions with the computer to her home context. Although one can only speculate as to the reasons why this was the case, the project data does warn that one cannot assume that there is a uniformity to the ways in which young children apply their digital skills. Findings from the overall project revealed that Caitlyn was not alone in confining her digital skills to the home context, as this was identified as being the case for all three of the girls in the Nursery cohort (Levy, 2008a).

This suggests that it is possible that issues of gender may have an impact on the ways in which children interact with digital media at home and school. Certainly other studies have reported gender differences with regard to older children's use of screen texts. For example Holloway and Valentine's (2003) work in secondary schools revealed that even though there were clear differences within the groups of boys and girls studied, the girls still tended to be less interested in computers than the boys. Moreover, Facer et al. (2003) discovered that boys and girls tended to use the computer for different purposes. However, both of these studies stressed that it is often inappropriate to describe children's attitudes and behavior towards computer technology in terms of simple boy–girl distinctions, and that the formation of attitude towards such technology is situated within the complex discourse of socio-cultural theory.

This further suggests that more research is certainly required within the early years context to develop an understanding of how young children not only acquire digital skills, but apply them. Though we can only really guess as to the impact of factors such as gender, what is clear is that digital technology has played a unique role in the lives of the three children discussed in this chapter. Moreover, this data further suggests that the extent to which these children viewed digital texts as fitting, or not fitting, within the school discourse on "literacy," has had an impact on their individual interactions with texts in general. In order to clarify this issue, it is useful to draw upon aspects of "third space theory" (Bhabba, 1994) to facilitate an understanding of how digital technology can feature within the complex dynamics of home and school constructions of literacy.

Digital Technology and the "Third Space"

For some time now, the application of third space theory has been used within a variety of different disciplines to explore the space "in between" (Bhabba, 1994, p. 1) two or more discourses or conceptualizations. In particular, third space theory has been used to investigate issues of literary identity, which is influenced by the meeting of several different "funds of knowledge" (Moll et al., 1992). For this reason, researchers have found that third space theory is especially useful in helping to explore continuities and discontinuities between the discourses of home and school (Cook, 2005; Levy 2008b; Pahl & Kelly, 2005). Using Moje et al.'s (2004, p. 44) positioning of third space theory as a space of "cultural, social and epistemological change" through which different "funds of knowledge" or discourses are brought into "conversation" with each other (see Figure 10.1), this chapter now turns to examine the role of digital technology within this "conversation."

As described earlier, both Shaun and Joseph seemed to have developed a certain "digital literacy" that allowed them to transfer the digital skills they developed within the home, into the school setting. However, as they moved through the year of data collection, Joseph appeared to lose confidence in his ability to handle print within the context of the computer as well as within paper texts. This suggests that aspects of the school discourse caused disruption for Joseph, in terms of the ways in which he saw himself to be a reader of text in general. However, Shaun's interactions with computer technology did not seem to be influenced in this way,

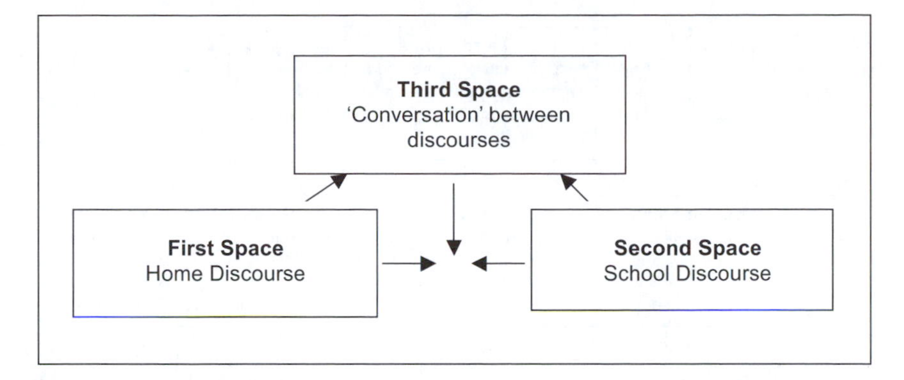

FIGURE 10.1 An application of Moje et al.'s (2004) construction of "third space theory"

and actually appeared to promote continuity between the discourses of home and school.

As stated, Shaun demonstrated a great confidence and proficiency in his ability to use unfamiliar computer texts in the Nursery. As Shaun moved up into the Reception year (ages four to five), he continued to use computer texts regularly in the classroom and appeared confident in applying a variety of strategies to make sense of these texts. Throughout all three phases of the study, Shaun demonstrated that he could transfer these skills from one medium or setting to another, thus suggesting that digital technology helped Shaun to navigate the boundaries of home and school. Given that Shaun also showed confidence and competence in his ability to read paper texts, it appears that there was much continuity between the discourses of home and school for Shaun (see Figure 10.2). His own constructions of literacy seemed to include both digital and paper based media and he appeared comfortable in handling a variety of texts both at home and at school.

However, the same could not be said for Caitlyn. As discussed, Caitlyn seemed to have developed a range of strategies in her home to help her to access and make meaning from computer texts. Yet Caitlyn appeared reluctant to bring these strategies into the school setting and was rarely to be seen using the computer in school. Moreover, the project data revealed that Caitlyn also owned a remarkable ability to create sophisticated narratives based on the pictures in books. Though unable to decode print, she was observed using the pictures in books to expressively narrate stories, both at home and in the nursery. Caitlyn's mother seemed to place great value on these skills, which she described as "incredible." Moreover, she reported that when Caitlyn is constructing a narrative based on the pictures in books, she uses "really advanced phrases" that are "absolutely amazing."

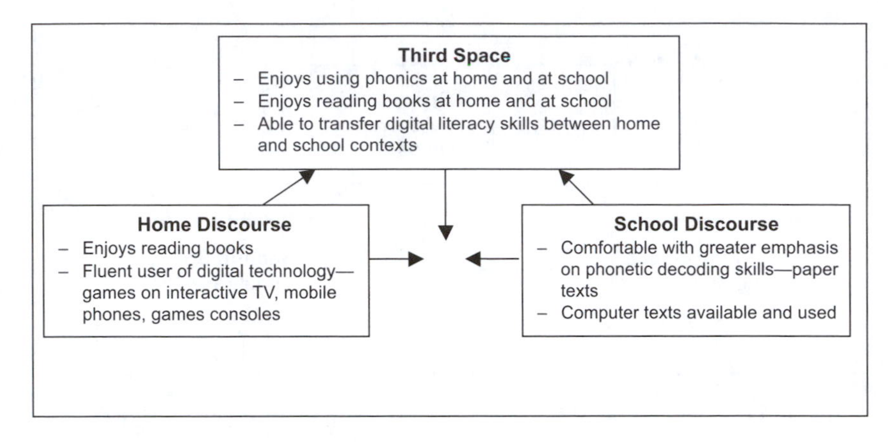

FIGURE 10.2 Shaun: Third space in between discourses of home and school

However, even from these early years, Caitlyn seemed very concerned that this was not *real* reading. For example, when asked how she knew what her stories were about, she replied, "I need to look at these bits [*pointing to the print*]. And see if they sound. And if they're the right letters." This suggests that Caitlyn was very aware of what the school system expected, in terms of reading being defined as the decoding of print in books. As a consequence, although it was reported that Caitlyn did occasionally continue to create these narratives with books when she moved into Reception, this reading also became increasingly confined to her home context.

This suggests that schooled constructions of literacy, and perhaps reading literacy in particular, caused considerable disruption for Caitlyn, as her own strategies to make sense of texts were perceived to be without value in the school system. It has been well documented that visual and iconic aspects of text have become central to the literacy texts encountered by children today (Kress, 1997, 2000). Yet, in reference to this work, Marsh reported in an interview with Kathy Hall (2003) that "schools have been rather slow to recognise the changing landscape of communication . . . [and still hang] on to the printed text as the primary form of communication." Caitlyn's profile indicates that such constructions meant she "shut down" on various aspects of her own meaning-making strategies, which included reading visual image on screen and in books. As she became increasingly aware of what she perceived to be the "correct" discourse of school, she showed considerable reluctance to employ any of these picture-reading skills, or digital skills, when handling texts in the classroom. Therefore, in contrast to Shaun's case, Caitlyn's digital skills did not appear to promote continuity between the discourses of home and school and were confined to the home context along with specific aspects of her book reading skills (see Figure 10.3).

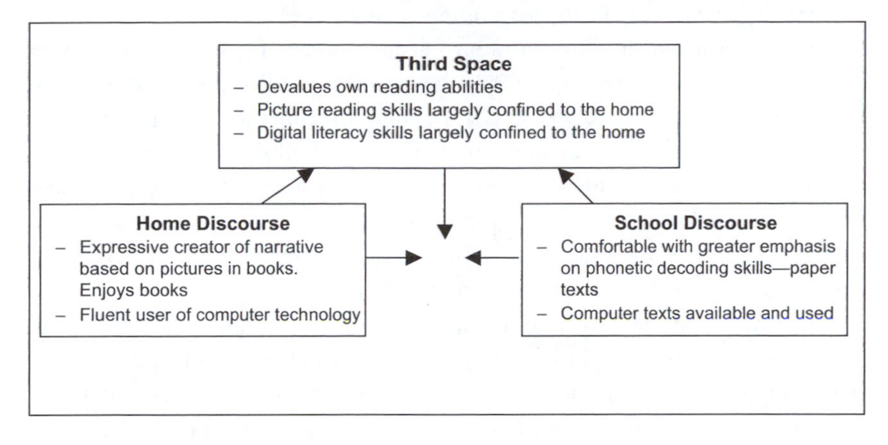

FIGURE 10.3 Caitlyn: Third space in between discourses of home and school

Conclusion

This chapter supports the claim that young children are immersed in "digital practices" from an early age (Marsh et al., 2005) and that they often develop skills in handling screen texts, even when they are not exposed directly to computers in their own homes (Bearne et al., 2007). It was clearly the case that all three children discussed in this chapter were using digital texts extensively from their earliest years, and that through this interaction they were developing skills in handling a variety of different texts. What is more, interactions with digital technology appeared to support these children in learning how to make sense of a variety of sound, symbol and visual systems, inherent within texts in general (Levy, 2009a). However, even among the small cohort discussed in this chapter, it was clear that the children had different responses to digital technology, especially in relation to its perceived place within the school discourse.

This has several implications for pedagogic practice. First, these findings suggest that it is not wise to assume that children are in any way "native" users of digital technology. While it is clear that many young children are indeed competent users of such texts, this study indicates that there can be substantial variance in the ways in which young children interact with technologies across the boundaries of home and school settings. For Shaun, digital technology seemed to contribute to his ability to find continuity between the discourses of home and school. He appeared to be comfortable and confident in his ability to handle a variety of paper and screen texts, and he was able to transfer the skills he had acquired in handling these texts across the boundaries of home and school. However, for Joseph and Caitlyn, perceptions of the schooled discourse on literacy seemed to prevent them from transferring their own skills and strategies in this way. As discussed, like Shaun, Joseph appeared to have developed digital skills in the home that initially allowed him to access computer texts with fluency in the classroom, despite the fact that he was not exposed to computers in his own home. However, the narrow discourse of school seemed to be responsible for Joseph losing confidence in his abilities to read print within the context of paper *and* screen texts in the classroom. Moreover, Caitlyn's story further suggested that not only did she confine her use of digital technology to her home, but she did not feel comfortable in using many of her own strategies to make sense of book and screen texts, within the school setting.

This strongly suggests that as definitions of literacy continue to grow and change, especially in the light of technological advancement (Carrington, 2005), there is an urgent need for schools to find ways to build on the skills and strategies young children develop in their homes in order to make sense of texts in general. Based upon Prensky's (2009) relational construction of "digital wisdom," I have argued in this chapter that "digital literacy" can be more usefully described in terms of the ways in which interactions with technology have an impact upon relationships with text, rather than the acquisition of digital skill alone. Findings from this case study data revealed that these three children not only demonstrated differences in the ways in which they transferred their digital skills from one setting into another, but that narrow constructions of literacy operating within the school discourse actively prevented two of these three children from capitalizing on their digital skills in order to form strong relationships with text. In fact, rather than encouraging "digital wisdom," the school discourse appeared to obstruct some children's interactions with screen and paper texts in the school setting, especially in relation to their confidence in handling print within these media.

While studies have observed children in print-centric early years classrooms demonstrating a desire to engage with the kinds of technology and new media that are part of their everyday experiences outside of school (Wohlwend, 2009), this study strongly indicates that schools need to find ways in which to not only include such technologies in the classroom, but actively build on the skills and strategies young children develop in their homes in order to make sense of digital texts, and thus develop aspects of "digital wisdom." Rather than replacing children's own "home" skills and strategies with a narrow paper-based discourse on literacy, schools should aim to build on the unique constructions and skills in handling texts that children display on entry into the school system. This may also mean that schools can play an active role in helping children to develop a range of encoding and decoding skills, situated within the visual and iconic media of digital texts, in order to help young children become confident and efficient users of many different texts in modern society.

References

Albers, P., Frederick, T., & Cowan, K. (2009). Features of gender: An analysis of the visual texts of third grade children. *Journal of Early Childhood Literacy, 9*(2), 234–260.

Bearne, E., Clark, C., Johnson, A., Manford, P., Motteram, M., & Wolstencroft, H. (2007). *Reading on screen*. Leicester: UKLA.

Bhabha, H. K. (1994). *The location of culture*. New York: Routledge.

Burnett, C. (in press). Technology and literacy in early childhood educational settings: A review of research. *Journal of Early Childhood Literacy*.

Carrington, V. (2005). New textual landscapes, information and early literacy. In Marsh, J. (Ed.), *Popular culture, New media and digital literacy in early childhood* (pp. 13–27). Oxford: RoutledgeFalmer.

Carrington, V., & Robinson, M. (2009). *Digital literacies: Social learning and classroom practices*. London: Sage.

Cook, M. (2005). A place of their own: Creating a classroom "third space" to support a continuum of text construction between home and school. *Literacy, 39*(2), 85–96.

Cope, B., & Kalantzis, M. (2000). *Multiliteracies: Literacy learning and the design of social futures*. London: Routledge.

Facer, K., Furlong, J., Furlong, R., & Sutherland, R. (2003). *Screenplay: Children and computing in the home*. London: Routledge.

Glaser, B. G., & Strauss, A. L. (1967). *The discovery of grounded theory: Strategies for qualitative research*. Chicago: Aldine.

Glister, P. (1997). *Digital literacy*. New York: John Wiley and Sons.

Hall, K. (2003). *Listening to Stephen read: Multiple perspectives on literacy*. Buckingham: Open University Press.

Harry, B., Sturges, K., & Klinger, J. K. (2005). Mapping the process: An exemplar of process and challenge in grounded theory analysis. *Educational Researcher, 34*, 3–13.

Holloway, S. L., & Valentine, G. (2003). *Cyberkids: Children in the information age*. London: RoutledgeFalmer.

Ito, M. (2009). *Engineering play: A cultural history of children's software*. Cambridge, MA: The MIT Press.

Kress, G. (1997). *Before writing—Rethinking the paths to literacy*. London: Routledge.

Kress, G. (2000). Multimodality. In B. Cope & M. Kalantzis (Eds.), *Multiliteracies: Literacy, learning and the design of social futures* (pp. 179–200). London: Routledge.

Kress, G. (2003). *Literacy in the new media age*. London: Routledge.

Lankshear, C., & Knobel, M. (2003). *New literacies: Changing knowledge and classroom learning*. Milton Keynes: Open University Press.

Levy, R. (2008a). Becoming a reader in a digital age: Children's self-perceptions as they start school. Unpublished Ph.D. Thesis. University of Cambridge.

Levy, R. (2008b). Third spaces are interesting places: Applying "third space theory" to nursery-aged children's constructions of themselves as readers. *Journal of Early Childhood Literacy, 8*(1), 43–66.

Levy, R. (2009a). "You have to understand words . . . but not read them": Young children becoming readers in a digital age. *Journal of Research in Reading, 32*(1), 75–91.

Levy, R. (2009b). Children's perceptions of reading and the use of reading scheme texts. *Cambridge Journal of Education, 39*(3), 361–377.

Levy, R., & Marsh, J. (in press, 2011). Literacy and ICT in the early years. In D. Lapp & D. Fisher (Eds.), *The handbook of research on teaching the English language arts* (3rd ed.). Mahwah, NJ: Lawrence Erlbaum Associates.

Marsh, J. (2003). One-way traffic? Connections between literacy practices at home and in the Nursery. *British Educational Research Journal, 29*(3), 369–382.

Marsh, J. (2005). Children of the digital age. In J. Marsh, J. (Ed.), *Popular culture, new media and digital literacy in early childhood* (pp. 1–10). London: RoutledgeFalmer.

Marsh J., & Singleton, C. (2009). Editorial: Literacy and technology: Questions of relationship. *Journal of Research in Reading, 32*(1), 1–5.

Marsh, J., Brookes, G., Hughes, J., Ritchie, L, Roberts, S., & Wright, K. (2005). *Digital beginnings: Young children's use of popular culture, media and new technologies*. Sheffield: Literacy Research Centre, University of Sheffield.

Merchant, G. (2007). Writing in the future in the digital age. *Literacy, 41*(3), 118–128.

Moje, E. B., Ciechanowski, K. M., Kramer, K., Ellis, L., Carrillo, R., & Collazo, T. (2004). Working toward third space in content area literacy: An examination of everyday funds of knowledge and discourse. *Reading Research Quarterly, 39*(1), 40–70.

Moll, L. C., Amanti, C., Neff, D., & Gonzalez, N. (1992). Funds of knowledge for teaching using a qualitative approach to connect homes and classrooms. *Theory into Practice, 31*(2), 132–141.

Pahl, K., & Kelly, S. (2005). Family literacy as a third space between home and school: Some case studies of practice. *Literacy, 39*(2), 91–96.

Plowman, L., McPake, J., & Stephen, C. (in press). The technologisation of childhood? Young children and technology in the home. *Children and Society*.

Prensky, M. (2009). *H. sapiens digital: From digital immigrants and digital natives to digital wisdom*. Retrieved May 10, 2010, from www.innovateonline.info/pdf/vol5_issue3/H._Sapiens_Digital-__From_Digital_Immigrants_and_Digital_Natives_to_Digital_Wisdom.pdf

Rose, J. (2006). *Independent review of the teaching of early reading*. Nottingham: DfES.

Wohlwend, K. (2009). Damsels in discourse: Girls consuming and producing identity texts through Disney Princess play. *Reading Research Quarterly, 44*(1), 57–84.

Wyse, D., & Styles, M. (2007). Synthetic phonics and the teaching of reading: The debate surrounding England's "Rose Report." *Literacy, 41*(1), 35–42.

PART III

Beyond Digital Natives

11

INTELLECTUAL FIELD OR FAITH-BASED RELIGION

Moving on from the Idea of "Digital Natives"

Sue Bennett and Karl Maton

Introduction

For the past decade the general notion of "Digital Natives" has attracted considerable attention in both academia and the popular media. While proponents of the idea use a variety of labels, such as "Net Generation," or "millenial learners," the claim they make is essentially the same: younger generations have grown up with digital technologies as part of their everyday worlds and so behave and think differently to older generations to whom these technologies have been introduced later in life (Howe & Strauss, 2000; Palfrey & Gasser, 2008; Prensky, 2001; Tapscott, 1998, 2009). This chapter critically examines the idea of "Digital Natives" by identifying findings from research that can shed light on questions about young people's aptitude for and interest in digital technologies. We analyze the key features of claims about digital natives and consider their possible implications for education and educational research. In short, we argue that most claims made about digital natives lack a rigorous and transparent empirical basis and do little to progress educational thinking or policy. It is time, we argue, to move this debate on, not simply to more nuanced versions of the idea, such as "Digital Wisdom" (Prensky 2009), but rather beyond the very notions and ways of thinking that underpin claims made about digital natives. Indeed, we suggest that moving on from the grounds of this debate is necessary to provide firmer foundations for educational technology research as a serious intellectual field and avoid becoming akin to a faith-based religion.

Research about Digital Natives

Among the host of claims made about young people in relation to technology, the most widespread stem from Prensky's (2001) article in which he describes young people as "Digital Natives" who are immersed in the world of digital technology and compares them to older "Digital Immigrants" who struggle to adapt to this brave new world. This simple typology has exhibited widespread appeal and been influential in the way arguments over the impact of digital technologies on young people have been shaped (e.g., Barnes, Marateo & Ferris, 2007; Brooks-Young, 2006; Gaston, 2006; Gros, 2003; Long, 2005; McHale; 2005; Skiba, 2005). (Here we are discussing the version of Prensky's claims that has influenced debates; we discuss his recent ostensible revisions of these ideas further below). Its appeal appears to lie in apparently commonsense confirmation by casual (and highly selective) observations of the behaviors of young people. However, Prensky's ideas have evoked intense criticism by scholars for their lack of rigor, exemplified by the absence of empirical evidence in the 2001 article. Nonetheless, his claims have stimulated a body of research that comprehensively dispels many of the sweeping generalizations made by Prensky and others and which has alerted educators and institutions to the diversity of technology practices among what may appear at first glance to be homogenous generational groups. Added to the existing tradition of research concerned with technology adoption inside and outside education (e.g., Buckingham, 2007; LaRose, Mastro & Eastin, 2001; Teo, 2009), this work is providing some valuable and often counter-intuitive insights into the potential role of technologies in education.

In discussing the findings of this body of research, it is important to note that we shall focus here on the results of empirical studies that are publicly reported in ways that allow scrutiny of the basis of their claims; that is, the authors provide details of the selection or recruitment of participants, data collected, instruments used, means of analyzing data, and how these relate to the conclusions made. For this reason, we do not include some popular non-fiction books on the topic (e.g., Palfrey & Gasser, 2008; Tapscott, 2009) because, though they may describe their claims as based on empirical research, they offer insufficient detail of that research to evaluate the veracity of those claims. Thus, where we describe claims as "unevidenced," we mean they either lack empirical support or at least transparent empirical evidence that can be evaluated by others.

A useful starting point for discussing the body of academic research are studies concerned with young people's access to various technologies. Access to technology in schools has long been of interest to educational technology researchers, as access is the obvious precursor to use (e.g., CEO Forum, 1999). Furthermore, because it is relatively easy to measure with self-report items, many recent surveys have collected this information from school and university students. Such surveys show high levels of access among much of the student population to what would now be considered baseline technologies of desktop/laptop computers, broadband Internet, and, in the case of older students, mobile phones (Kennedy et al., 2009; Margaryan & Littlejohn, 2008; Oliver & Goerke, 2007). More expensive, specialized devices have been shown to have lower levels of ownership (Bennett, Maton & Carrington, in press; Maton & Bennett, 2010; Salaway, Caruso, &

Nelson, 2008). These results support the notion that technology is highly accessible and therefore *potentially* well-integrated into young people's lives.

An important finding emerging from access studies of school-aged children—which are better at capturing a broad cross-section of the population than studies of university students because of the social profile of the latter—is that socio-economic status is a factor in technology access even in affluent societies (e.g., Aslanidou & Menexes, 2008; Eamon, 2004; Facer & Furlong, 2001; Jenkins, 2009; Livingstone & Helsper, 2007; OECD, 2010; Otto et al., 2005). Other studies of the ways access is managed in and outside school settings also highlight the various ways access can be provided or restricted according to the positive or negative values placed on digital technologies as a learning or recreational tool (Downes, 2002; Kerawalla & Crook, 2002; Thrupp, 2008; Youn, 2008). Taken together, these findings call into question the claim that *all* young people have equal access to digital technologies.

Access, however, is not usage. So, to explore technology practices beyond access, some researchers have begun to investigate the prevalence of different technology uses. The purpose is to develop a more sophisticated understanding of how different types of technology-supported practices feature in young people's lives. Several important themes emerge from these studies. First, some activities are more widespread and more frequent than others. For example, a greater proportion of survey respondents in studies (e.g., Kennedy et al., 2009; Maton & Bennett, 2010) indicated they use digital technologies for communicating and consuming information than for creative or gaming activities. Studies across age groups also suggest that different types of technology uses are prominent at different developmental stages (Helsper & Eynon, 2010; Kent & Facer, 2004; Livingstone & Helsper, 2007). On the basis of this type of data, Green and Hannon (2007) have characterized different ideal typical users ("digital pioneers," "creative producers," "everyday communicators," and "information gatherers"), and Kvavik (2005) has posited that students like to use technologies for convenience, communications, and control.

Overall, the findings suggest that rather than a homogenous population of always connected digital natives, young people's technology activities and interests are widely varying, beyond a core set of common activities involving communication and information retrieval. A significant body of research also suggests that factors such as socioeconomic status, gender, educational background as well as age influence the extent and type of technology supported activities (Brown & Czerniewicz, 2008; Hargittai & Hinnant, 2008; Helsper & Eynon, 2010; Jones et al., 2010; Kennedy, Wellman & Klemant, 2003; Korupp & Szydlik, 2005; Li & Kirkup, 2007; Selwyn, 2008). Qualitative studies are beginning to provide insights into the reasons for these variations, pointing to differences in opportunity, value, disposition, and perceived need across different contexts (e.g., Thrupp, 2008; Waycott et al., 2010).

Moving beyond technology use, research is also exploring the notion of ICT-related skills as an indicator of whether young people fit the image of tech-savvy digital natives. Again, research findings challenge this claim, suggesting that while some individuals may be skilled across a range of technologies, many are adept with only a limited set of common technology skills (Margaryan & Littlejohn, 2008; Salaway, Caruso, & Nelson, 2008). Furthermore, studies highlight disparities among young people in proficiency with digital technologies due to socioeconomic background, location, school computer use, and home computer use (e.g., Ainley et al., 2010). Research focusing on what seem to be highly developed skills, such as information seeking, go further to demonstrate the dangers of assuming that everyday skills are a sufficient basis for making claims about educational skills. For example, many young people may have the ability to find information using digital technology but lack the information literacy skills to make effective decisions about the information sources they find (Coombes, 2009; Singh, Mallan & Giardina, 2008). Considered together, these studies are a further reminder of the diversity of young people's technology skills and help move us away from the unhelpful stereotype of the "cyberkid" that casts young people as natural and always successful computer users (Selwyn, 2003).

In summary, it is clear that the claim that young people are digital natives has little or no basis in empirical evidence and that blanket statements about generational differences, however nuanced, provide little if any insight into current or future educational needs (cf. Bennett et al., 2008; Bennett & Maton, 2010). Instead, there exists a range of access, use, and skills, and it is this diversity that may pose far more significant challenges to educational institutions and systems than a proclaimed wave of homogenous "Digital Natives." It is evident that we need to develop a much better understanding of young people's technology use and experiences if we are to effectively respond to their needs, and unevidenced claims do not add to that understanding. In order to help create the conditions for that understanding, we now consider how such claims have become so widely cited despite their lack of an empirical basis, and then explore the implications of the nature of the debate for education and educational research.

The Nature of the Debate

The clear disparity between the confidence with which claims about a new generation of "Digital Native" students have been made and the lack of empirical evidence to support such claims raises the question of why they have gained such currency. Why have arguments based on a series of questionable assumptions and leaps of logic become so widely disseminated? There are, of course, vested interests at play in the dissemination of claims. Commentators and academics are eager to raise their academic and media profiles, consultants and technology vendors wish to promote their services and products, and educational administrators desire easy, quick, and simply understood policy ideas. Claims made about "Digital Natives" also fit the profile of what, in another context, Pearson (1983) described as "respectable fears"—where older generations view the activities of the young as new, fast-changing, and undermining the status quo—making them attractive to the popular media. There are a host of such interests working to portray educational problems and their solutions in terms of technology (Bayne & Ross, 2007; see also Buckingham, 2007 for a more general argument). Here, however, we shall focus on something often overlooked when discussing the promulgation of ideas (Maton, 2000; in press): the form taken by the debate itself.

As we have argued in a previous paper (Bennett, Maton & Kervin, 2008), much of the debate over digital natives can be understood as an academic form of a "moral panic" (Cohen, 1972). A moral panic is a form of public discourse that arises when a group is portrayed as representing a challenge to accepted norms and values in a society. The concept is widely used in sociology and cultural studies to explain how this public concern gains prominence and momentum far beyond the evidence to support it. The idea originated in Cohen's study of 1960s youth subcultures, which were seen as undermining the social fabric at the time. According to the model, intense media focus, couched in sensationalist language, amplifies the apparent threat posed by a group (such as a youth subculture), prompting calls for authorities to take action. Any action taken or publicly considered, and then the media reporting and debate over this, in turn amplifies the threat in a self-reinforcing cycle as it brings the activities of the group into greater public prominence. This "deviancy amplification spiral" (Cohen, 1972) creates a moral panic about the group until the need for more "news" sees it replaced by a new focus for concern. Often the focus of previous panics may resurface in a new guise, such as debate over "illegal immigrants" or "boat people" returning as concern over "asylum seekers" or "economic migrants." (Similarly, the moral panic over "Digital Natives" could be superseded by a moral panic over those lacking "Digital Wisdom" if Prensky's latest assertions are given attention.)

Many of these features can be found in the digital natives debate. Arguments are couched in dramatic terms, emphasize generational differences, appeal to commonsense rather than to research evidence, declare an emergency situation, and call for urgent action and fundamental change in order to meet this clear and present danger. For example, Prensky claims:

> Today's students have not just changed incrementally from those of the past . . . A really big *discontinuity* has taken place. One might even call it a "singularity"—an event which changes things so fundamentally that there is absolutely no going back.
>
> (2001, p. 1)

Though in the case of "Digital Natives," the notion of a fundamental change requiring urgent action has been primarily promulgated through academic and professional literature rather than the popular media, the effect is similar; it is an academic form of a moral panic.

We should emphasize that claims about a "singularity" are themselves anything other than a singularity. Such claims are common in social science. Fundamental social change has been variously described as creating a "status society," "service society," "postindustrial society," "postmodern society," "knowledge society," and so on. Indeed, Beniger (1986) lists seventy-five such announcements of fundamental social change for the period 1950–1985. Similarly, successive generations of students have been regularly described as fundamentally dissimilar and ascribed different characteristics—"baby boomers," "generation X," "generation Y," etc. Indeed, moral panics over new students are a recurrent paradigmatic phenomenon in education (Hickox & Moore, 1995; Maton, 2004). During the late nineteenth century, for example, the expansion of formal state education was accompanied by concerns over the entry of middle-class and female students (Lowe, 1987). Similarly, policy debates in higher education during the early 1960s focused on the knowledge, interests, and aptitudes of new working-class students that expansion was expected to bring into universities (Maton, 2004, 2005).

What is problematic about declarations of fundamental change in the digital natives debate, such as Prensky's claim quoted above, is that they embody "historical amnesia" (Maton & Moore, 2000). That is, they obscure such past examples of claims of generational difference and calls for change in education. They proclaim a rupture or radical break with the past that

> renders the field unable to address the very claim upon which this phenomenon is based, namely social and intellectual *change*. By erasing the past, social and intellectual change is rendered an article of faith rather than constructed as an object of inquiry . . . it sets the present adrift from the past, which indeed becomes a "foreign country"—in fact, an *incommensurably* different culture. The old and the young . . . are held to literally inhabit different worlds.
>
> (Maton & Moore, 2000)

Prensky (2001), for example, claims that "digital immigrant instructors . . . are struggling to teach a population that speaks an entirely new language." This is said to be "obvious to the Digital Natives—school often feels pretty much as if we've brought in a population of heavily accented, unintelligible foreigners to lecture them." Only those suffering from amnesia about the history of education could view such sentiments (even if they were proven to be true, which they have not been) as an entirely new phenomenon. They are the same kind of claims made, for example, about a generation of students immersed in the emerging commercial culture of the late 1950s and early 1960s. In the UK, concern was widespread about the effects of a perceived gap between children's everyday and school lives, which meant they were having to "live with a foot in both these worlds" (National Union of Teachers, 1960, p. 26). When such precedents are erased in the digital natives debate, the apparent "newness" of the current situation is further amplified and accordingly the apparent threat appears even more powerful.

In similar fashion to the "deviancy amplification spiral" of moral panics, the debate has also often been characterized by what can be termed a "certainty-complacency spiral" concerning empirical evidence (Maton, in press). Here, belief and commonsense perceptions replace evidence and rigorous research. Rather than being advanced as conjectures to be tested, claims are made without evidential support and then repeated unquestioningly as if they were proven facts. Citations (in the form of quotes and referencing) then give the impression of pointing to evidence rather than to unevidenced assertions. Repetitions of the claims made about digital natives thereby iteratively amplify and reinforce the sense of certainty that evidence for this group, its defining characteristics and experiences of education, actually exists. Through sheer weight of repetition, the notion that there are digital natives and the argument that education needs to change to accommodate them can thereby come to appear to have bases that a reading of the research literature shows does not exist (Bennett et al., 2008). Such complacent, uncritical acceptance of the veracity of claims in turn encourages further certainty, as the number of publications adopting the term grows. So, as the number of articles, conference papers, blogs, or newspaper articles using the term "Digital Natives" grows, the more certain and the more complacent those adopting the term can become that it connotes a real phenomenon based on empirical evidence.

This is not to say that everyone using the term reinforces complacency—real research, as illustrated above, has done much to question assumptions underlying the notion of "Digital Natives." However, the term was disseminated and claims widely repeated before the results of such research were able to bring a calmer and more rational tenor to the debate. This difference between the speed with which unevidenced or insufficiently based claims can be made and the time required for rigorous research and peer-reviewed publication has proven problematic for reasoned discussion. Sensationalized, ungrounded claims can get halfway around the world before research has a chance to gain ethical clearance. In the resulting intellectual vacuum, rational debate is sidelined by the urgency and stridency of calls for change. Those who pause for thought or raise questions can be described as unwilling to face the impending crisis or as reactionaries in denial. This certainty-complacency spiral is thus underpinned by the *doxa* of a field of research—its taken-for-granted assumptions that "go without saying"—and the shared interests of its members (cf. Maton, 2005), such as the centrality of technology for solving contemporary educational problems. Couching this case in terms of fundamental change also privileges those who make the claims:

> To question the break is to be assigned to the other side of the divide and thus have no access to legitimate knowledge of the post-apocalyptic world.

> Those who cannot see what they see . . . have by definition nothing to say about it . . . One either "gets it" or one doesn't.
>
> (Maton & Moore, 2000)

We are not suggesting a conscious suppression of skepticism is taking place; in fact, the sociological concept of "*doxa*" highlights the *unconscious*, shared assumptions of social fields of practice. Nor do we claim that everyone involved in the debate exemplifies this position. Indeed, the research discussed earlier provides examples of scholarly work not characterized by these features. Rather, we are arguing that the claims that energize and underpin the debate as a whole are characterized by these structural features of historical amnesia, moral panic, and a certainty-complacency spiral, which serve to restrict the space for rational debate and downplay the need for a transparent evidence base on which to make claims.

Understanding the form of the debate is not merely an academic exercise. Rather it highlights some of the reasons why the notion of "Digital Natives" has become widely repeated despite its flimsy foundations and why it has been difficult to move discussion onto a more rational, empirically grounded footing. We are not claiming that the notion of "Digital Natives" is entirely unfounded, if beset with a host of appropriate caveats. There may indeed be a small subset of young people who are highly adept with and interested in digital technologies, but there is mounting evidence to suggest that patterns of access and use are varied and complex, influenced by a range of factors including but certainly not limited to age. We are, therefore, calling for a much more measured approach. If we are to ascertain whether "Digital Natives" do indeed represent an educational emergency, a moral panic, both or neither, we need systematic research. To paraphrase and invert the famous eleventh thesis on Feuerbach by Marx, all too often people have tried to change education in various ways. The point, however, is to understand it, so we know what requires change, what is possible to change, how to change it, and with what effects for whom (see Maton, 2002).

Implications for Education and Educational Research

Having discussed the lack of evidence for the original claims made about "Digital Natives" and explored how these have become prevalent, the question remains of their implications for education and educational research. Clearly the debate as a whole has been useful, albeit secondarily and inadvertently, in drawing attention to the high degree of variability in ICT access, use, skill, knowledge, and interest among young people (e.g., Helsper & Eynon, 2010; Kennedy et al., 2009; Livingstone & Helsper, 2007; Margaryan & Littlejohn, 2008; Maton & Bennett, 2010; Salaway, Caruso, & Nelson, 2008). The available evidence suggests that policy-makers and educators need to be mindful of diversity within the student body and wary of generalizations about technology skills that have the potential to do significant harm if they cause that diversity to be overlooked. In particular, educators must be aware of the different types of opportunities and technology experiences students have had. Furthermore, while some young people may be confident in using technology, their understandings of how that technology works and how it might help them *learn* may be extremely limited (e.g., Coombes, 2009; Kennedy et al., 2009; Singh, Mallan & Giardina, 2008). These findings raise questions about what schools can and should be doing in response to these differences. It also raises the possibility that responding to the diversity of technology access, use, experience, and orientation may in fact be a greater challenge than if younger generations were indeed more homogenous in their composition.

Another effect of the wider debate, related to but distinct from the digital native argument, has been to amplify the argument that emerging technologies are changing society in ways that education needs to account for. Web 2.0 technologies are a case in point. It is argued that freely available online software tools, collectively termed Web 2.0 (Cormode & Krishnamurthy, 2008), are providing new opportunities for collective knowledge creation through networked collaboration, eroding differences between producers and consumers to create a new breed of "produsers" (Bruns, 2008; Goggin, 2004), and so creating new notions of authorship and sources of authority (Manovich, 2001). Recent studies suggest that a significant number of young people do engage in this type of knowledge creation as part of their daily lives, creating blogs, wikis, and multimedia to share online with family, friends, and their networks beyond and participating in online communities (Conole et al., 2006; Green & Hannon 2007; Lenhart et al., 2007). The perceived popularity of these activities has led to concern that education is not keeping pace with shifts in broader society, prompting claims that these forms of knowledge creation should be integrated into teaching and learning (e.g., Green & Hannon, 2007). This is not, however, simple. Recent studies of integrating Web 2.0 technologies into educational settings suggest that despite the "newness" of the technologies and their apparent departure from previous forms, there are challenges in repurposing everyday technologies for formal education (e.g., Kennedy et al., 2009). Some may argue that the integration undertaken in these case studies falls short of radically changing education to be more like the everyday world, but the very issue highlighted by such studies is that the context of formal education, with its particular values and practices, is different from informal and non-formal learning contexts. This point has been forcefully made for some time by social realist sociology of education: knowledge practices such as learning in formal education have a different form, related to their different purpose, to knowledge practices outside those contexts (see Bernstein, 2000; Maton & Moore, 2010). Wishing away this difference by arguing for the simplistic transfer of everyday practices into educational contexts does little to solve educational problems. From what we know of the history of technology in education (e.g., see Cuban, 2001), it is far more likely that if Web 2.0 and other emerging technologies are incorporated into education it will be as another tool rather than an impetus for radical change. It may be that the most significant implication of these technologies for education lies in the need to incorporate their use into an expanding set of literacies needed by young people to become active participants in society (Buckingham, 2007; Jenkins, 2009).

This moves the focus of the discussion to what formal education should be, which is the underlying point made by Prensky, Tapscott, and others. They are right in that the characteristics of students and how they learn should inform processes of teaching and educational organization, but they are misguided in using the "Digital Native" idea as the basis for their argument. Many commentators and researchers have argued for a re-imagining of education, much of it based on a call for constructivist pedagogies. Such approaches, however, are far from proven techniques, and debate and research continue to call into question blanket assumptions that discovery learning and facilitative approaches are effective for all students across all areas of education (Chen et al., 2011; Hattie, 2009; Kirschner, Sweller & Clark, 2006). Ultimately it is well-founded, transparent empirical research that promises to provide the best guidance for how education should occur rather than unsubstantiated or unclearly evidenced claims. It is not merely an academic penchant for nuance and accuracy that demands this. It should be the very least we demand of a high quality education system.

This is, however, more than just a call for more empirical evidence. The "Digital Natives" debate is not only based on highly limited evidence, it is based on fundamentally flawed premises: the significance of generational difference over other social factors, a technologically deterministic and asociological account of how people are shaped by their upbringings, an ahistorical account of social change, and a reductionist account of educational change. Attempting to finesse or nuance an idea that is based on such deep fundamental flaws is simply to wallpaper the walls of a house repeatedly when the cracks that keep appearing are due to faulty foundations. What is required is a reframing of the debate away from the notion of "Digital Natives."

This brings us to more recent attempts by instigators of the debate to maintain its momentum. Do they actually move us forward? Typically they are taking the form of proclaiming that familiarity with technology rather than age is the key feature announcing a new kind of learner (e.g., Dede, 2005; Oblinger & Oblinger, 2005; Prensky, 2009). The claim is that technically adept learners (of any age) possess characteristics that distinguish them from the rest of the population. This is the idea of digital natives in a new guise. The form taken by the argument also remains the same: insufficiently evidenced and often difficult to falsify assertions based on an extremely simplistic, asociological understanding of social structure and its impact on the consciousness of individuals. Prensky, for example, has recently proclaimed:

> As we move further into the 21st century when all will have grown up in the era of digital technology, the distinction between digital natives and digital immigrants will become less relevant.
>
> (2009, ¶1)

For Prensky (see also Chapter 2, this volume), it is not that the distinction is less relevant because empirical evidence shows it to be so, but because now everyone is fulfilling the conditions of being a "Digital Native," namely growing up in the era of digital technology. He argues we need to "imagine a new set of distinctions" (¶1), this time based on "digital wisdom." Though "digital wisdom" is extremely vague, the central tenet of Prensky's claims is clearly stated:

> The brains of wisdom seekers of the future will be fundamentally different, in organization and in structure, than our brains are today.
>
> (2009, ¶1)

This will be due, he asserts, to interaction with and enhancement by digital technology. The new kind of person (which he labels "homo sapiens digital" rather than "Digital Native") will be, he claims, capable of all kinds of insights and understandings unavailable to those with "unaided minds" (¶7).

The question we asked is: does this move the debate forward? Again, empirical evidence is extremely limited; rather than a projection of potential futures based on a careful analysis of existing trends, this is an astrological forecast based on imagining—it is research as science fiction (which is name-checked, see ¶7). Again, technological determinism remains central to assertions: digital technology is the primary driver of biological, psychological, epistemological, and social change. Again, claims exhibit historical amnesia, ignoring precedents to which they bear a remarkable similarity, such as McLuhan's well-known accounts in the 1960s of changes potentially wrought by the rise of new media (1962, 1964). Again, these assertions draw a strong line between those in the know and those who are about to be left behind. And, again, those who question the fundamental break are portrayed as relics of a soon-to-vanish world, this time with a religious twist pronouncing the need for conversion: "I believe it is time for the emerging digitally wise among us, youth and adults alike, to embrace digital enhancement and to encourage others to do so" (2009, ¶7).

This is not only the digital natives debate relabeled; it models educational technology research as a faith-based religion (see Maton, in press). As social realist sociology of educaton shows, claims made are never just messages about their specific topic, they are also messages about the way the field should measure achievement—they are "languages of legitimation" (Maton, 2000; in press). Engaging seriously with such assertions is thus to also proffer a particular understanding of how the intellectual field of educational technology should operate. Rather than state what the contents of a future research program should be for the intellectual field, our point here is to highlight the basis for generating such a program. While studies taking the notion of "Digital Natives" as a launching pad have offered insights into the diverse nature of educational access and use, and do serve as models of reasoned, evidence-based research, the notion itself has shed little light on issues of education and technology. There is little in attempts to relaunch these ideas with different names to suggest that they would serve as a more fruitful starting point for research. More significantly, to take seriously such claims is to take seriously not simply such vague notions as "digital wisdom" but also the idea that the research agenda of an intellectual field should be driven by unevidenced (or opaquely evidenced) and unfalsifiable claims that erase the past and emphasize belief and faith over reason and rigor.

It would be remiss, however, to close without making at least one suggestion for reframing research in ways that could advance understanding and inform educational practice. A key issue that studies of young people's experiences with technology highlight is the question of how these are integrated into the array of different contexts and practices in daily life. More specifically, this is partly a question of similarities and differences between everyday and educational practices using technology. This necessarily shifts the focus of research from generational issues to questions of knowledge and experiences. It also takes into account differences between these various and varied social contexts, rather than assuming that whatever is (proclaimed as) happening in wider society should be reflected inside education. This would provide a more sophisticated understanding of different opportunities and choices available, which both explain variation in young people's technology experiences and influence their future experiences. In doing so, formal education would comprise a series of contexts that are part of a young person's world, and avoid the dichotomous inside/outside education thinking that dominates much of the current discussion (Bayne & Ross, 2007). Educators can almost certainly do more to leverage off technology experiences from formal settings, but understanding formal educational contexts in relation to the myriad contexts of young people's lives requires more sophisticated thinking than the pitting of one against the other.

Conclusion

The argument that technology is changing our society is the weakest of truisms on which to rest arguments for radical change to current systems and practices. It may not be as sexy to proclaim evolution rather than revolution, or to highlight diversity rather than paint stark differences, because such notions require measured, rational, and sophisticated thinking, and a tolerance for ambiguity and careful consideration rather than sloganeering. Yet this is what the evidence points to, and this is the thinking demanded of us. Moreover, such thinking needs to be based on research rather than merely imagining.

This chapter raises three keys points. First, the notion of "Digital Native" is a misperception of young people's technology use that idealizes and homogenizes their skills and interests. Available evidence of young people's technology access and use is limited in scope and depth but suggests diversity rather than conformity. Second, the impact of these overgeneralizations has been to generate an academic form of moral panic that disregards the past and encourages intellectual complacency. The effect of this has been to discourage genuine debate about significant issues. Finally, the implications for education and educational research are likely to be better understood by establishing a more sophisticated footing for discussion and expanding the research effort. This requires abandoning not only the notion of "Digital Natives" but, just as importantly, the basis of such claims, whatever the terminology (or relabeling) they are couched in.

The consequences of developing a better understanding through sound and transparent research is that we have a basis for demanding and designing change, and so will avoid the rush to implement solutions to problems we do not adequately understand. The consequences of *not* developing a better understanding are far greater, because with this comes the risk that we will ignore subtle digital divides that do threaten the quality of our education systems.

References

Ainley, J., Fraillon, J., Freeman, C., & Ministerial Council for Education, Early Childhood Development and Youth Affairs. (2010). *National assessment program: ICT literacy Years 6 & 10 report 2008*. Retrieved May 14, 2010, from http://research.acer.edu.au/ict_literacy/2

Aslanidou, S., & Menexes, G., (2008). Beyond the myth of the cyberkid: Young people at the margins of the information revolution. *Journal of Youth Studies*, *4*(4), 451–469.

Barnes, K., Marateo, R., & Ferris, S. (2007). Teaching and learning with the net generation. *Innovate*, *3*(4). Retrieved May 26, 2010, from www.innovateonline.info/index.php?view=article&id=382

Bayne, S., & Ross, J. (2007). The "Digital Native" and "Digital Immigrant": A dangerous opposition. Paper presented at the Annual Conference of the Society for Research into Higher Education, Liverpool, UK, December 9–11, 2007. Retrieved August 5, 2009, from www.malts.ed.ac.uk/staff/sian/natives_final.pdf

Beniger, J. R. (1986). *The control revolution: Technological and economic origins of the information society*. Harvard: Harvard University Press.

Bennett, S., & Maton, K. (2010). Beyond the "digital natives" debate: Towards a more nuanced understanding of students' technology experiences. *Journal of Computer Assisted Learning*, *26*(5), 321–331.

Bennett, S., Maton, K., & Carrington, L. (in press). Understanding the complexity of technology acceptance by higher education students. In T. Teo (Ed.), *Technology acceptance in education: Research and issues*. Rotterdam, The Netherlands: Sense.

Bennett, S., Maton, K., & Kervin, L. (2008). The "digital natives" debate: A critical review of the evidence. *British Journal of Educational Technology*, *39*(5), 775–786.

Bernstein, B. (2000). *Pedagogy, symbolic control and identity: Theory, research, critique* (revised ed.). Oxford: Rowman & Littlefield.

Brooks-Young, S. (2006). *Critical technology issues for school leaders.* Thousand Oaks, CA: Corwin.

Brown, C., & Czerniewicz, L. (2008). Trends in student use of ICTs in higher education in South Africa. In P. Brakel (Ed.), *Proceedings of the 10th annual conference of World Wide Web applications.* Cape Peninsula University of Technology: Cape Town, South Africa.

Bruns, A. (2008). *Blogs, wikipedia, second life, and beyond: From production to produsage.* New York: Peter Lang.

Buckingham, D. (2007). *Beyond technology: Childrens' learning in an age of digital culture.* Cambridge, UK: Polity Press.

CEO Forum. (1999). *The CEO Forum school technology and readiness report.* Retrieved October 19, 2009, from www.ceoforum.org/downloads/99report.pdf

Chen, R. T-H., Maton, K., & Bennett, S. (2011). Absenting discipline: Constructivist approaches in online learning. In F. Christie & K. Maton (Eds.), *Disciplinarity: Systemic functional and sociological perspectives* (pp. 125–150). London: Continuum.

Cohen, S. (1972). *Folk devils and moral panics.* London: MacGibbon & Kee.

Conole, G., de Laat, M., Dillon, T., & Darby, J. (2006). *JISC LXP Student experiences of technologies. Final report.* Bristol: Higher Education Funding Council for England.

Coombes, B. (2009). Generation Y: Are they really digital natives or more like digital refugees? *Synergy,* 7(1), 31–40.

Cormode, G., & Krishnamurthy, B. (2008). Key differences between Web 1.0 and Web 2.0. *First Monday, 13*(6). Retrieved May 26, 2010, from http://firstmonday.org/htbin/cgiwrap/bin/ojs/index.php/fm/article/view/2125/1972

Cuban, L. (2001). *Oversold and underused: Computers in the classroom.* Cambridge, MA: Harvard University.

Dede, C. (2005). Planning for neomillennial learning styles. *EDUCAUSE Quarterly, 28*(1), 7–12.

Downes, T. (2002). Blending play, practice and performance: Children's use of computer at home. *Journal of Educational Enquiry, 3*(2), 21–34.

Eamon, M. (2004). Digital divide in computer access and use between poor and non-poor youth. *Journal of Sociology and Social Welfare, 31*(2), 91–112.

Facer, K., & Furlong, R. (2001). Beyond the myth of the "cyberkid": Young people at the margins of the information revolution. *Journal of Youth Studies, 4*(4), 451–469.

Gaston, J. (2006). Reaching and teaching the digital natives. *Library Hi Tech News, 23*(3), 12–13.

Goggin, G. (2004). *Virtual nation.* Sydney: UNSW Press.

Green, H., & Hannon, C. (2007). *Young people are spending their time in a space which adults find difficult to supervise or understand.* London: Demos. Retrieved October 19, 2009, from www.demos.co.uk/files/Their%20space%20-%20web.pdf

Gros, B. (2003). The impact of digital games in education. *First Monday, 8*(7). Retrieved February 21, 2007, from www.firstmonday.org/issues/issue8_7/xyzgros/index.html

Hargittai, E., & Hinnant, A. (2008). Digital inequality. Differences in young adults' use of the internet. *Communication Research, 35*(5), 602–621.

Hattie, J. A. C. (2009). *Visible learning: A synthesis of over 800 meta-analyses relating to achievement.* Abingdon: Routledge.

Helsper, E. J., & Eynon, R. (2010). Digital natives: Where is the evidence? *British Educational Research Journal, 36*(3), 503–520.

Hickox, M., & Moore, R. (1995). Liberal-humanist education: The vocationalist challenge. *Curriculum Studies, 3*(1), 45–59.

Howe, N., & Strauss, W. (2000). *Millennials rising: The next greatest generation*. New York: Vintage Books.

Jenkins, H. with Purushotma, R., Weigel, M., Clinton, K., & Robison, A. (2009). *Confronting the challenges of participatory culture: Media education for the 21st century*. Cambridge, MA: The MIT Press.

Jones, C., Ramanaua, R., Cross, S., & Healing, G. (2010). Net generation or digital natives: Is there a distinct new generation entering university? *Computers and Education, 54*(3), 722–732.

Kennedy, G., Dalgarno, B., Bennett, S., Gray, K., Waycott, J., Judd, T., Bishop, A., Maton, K., Krause, K., & Chang, R. (2009). *Educating the net generation—A handbook of findings for practice and policy*. Sydney: Australian Learning and Teaching Council. Retrieved October 19, 2009, from www.altc.edu.au/system/files/resources/CG6–25_Melbourne_Kennedy_Handbook_July09.pdf

Kennedy, T., Wellman B., & Klemant, K. (2003). Gendering the digital divide. *IT & Society, 1*(5), 72–96.

Kent, N., & Facer, K. (2004). Different worlds? A comparison of young people's home and school ICT use. *Journal of Computer-Assisted Learning, 20*(6), 440–455.

Kerawalla, L., & Crook, C. (2002). Children's computer use at home and at school: context and continuity. *British Educational Research Journal, 28*(6), 751–771.

Kirschner, P. A., Sweller, J., & Clark, R. E. (2006). Why minimal guidance during instruction does not work: An analysis of the failure of constructivist, discovery, problem-based, experiential, and inquiry-based teaching. *Educational Psychologist, 41*, 75–86.

Korupp, S., & Szydlik, M. (2005). Causes and trends of the digital divide. *European Sociological Review, 21*(4), 409–422.

Kvavik, R. (2005). Convenience, communications and control: How students use technology. In D. Oblinger & J. Oblinger (Eds.), *Educating the net generation* (pp. 7.1–7.20). Boulder, CO: EDUCAUSE. Retrieved March 31, 2006, from www.educause.edu/educatingthenetgen

LaRose, R., Mastro, D., & Eastin, M. S. (2001). Understanding Internet usage: A social-cognitive approach to uses and gratifications. *Social Science Computer Review, 19*(4), 395–413.

Lenhart, A., Madden, M., Macgill, A., & Smith, A. (2007). *Teens and social media. Research report*. Washington DC: Pew Internet & American Life Project.

Li, N., & Kirkup, G. (2007). Gender and cultural differences in Internet use: A study of China and the UK. *Computers & Education, 48*(2), 301–317.

Livingstone, S., & Helsper, E. (2007). Gradations in digital inclusion: Children, young people and the digital divide. *New Media & Society, 9*(4), 671–696.

Long, S. A. (2005). What's new in libraries? Digital natives: If you aren't one, get to know one. *New Library World, 106*(3/4), 187.

Lowe, R. A. (1987). *Structural change in English higher education, 1870–1920. The rise of the modern educational system*. Cambridge, UK: Cambridge University Press.

Manovich, L. (2001). *The language of new media*. Cambridge, MA: The MIT Press.

Margaryan, A., & Littlejohn, A. (2008). Are digital natives a myth or reality?: Students' use of technologies for learning. Retrieved January 6, 2010, from www.academy.gcal.ac.uk/anoush/documents/DigitalNativesMythOrReality-MargaryanAndLittlejohn-draft-111208.pdf

Maton, K. (2000). Languages of legitimation: The structuring significance for intellectual fields of strategic knowledge claims. *British Journal of Sociology of Education, 21*(2), 147–167.

Maton, K. (2002). Popes, kings and cultural studies: Placing the commitment to non-disciplinarity in historical context. In S. Herbrechter (Ed.), *Cultural studies: Interdisciplinarity and translation* (pp. 31–53). Amsterdam: Rodopi.

Maton, K. (2004). The wrong kind of knower: Education, expansion and the epistemic device. In J. Muller, B. Davies & A. Morais (Eds.), *Reading Bernstein, researching Bernstein* (pp. 218–231). London: Routledge.

Maton, K. (2005). A question of autonomy: Bourdieu's field approach and policy in higher education. *Journal of Education Policy*, *20*(6), 687–704.

Maton, K. (in press). *Knowledge and knowers: Towards a realist sociology of education*. London: Routledge.

Maton, K., & Bennett, S. (2010). *The role of ICTs at the University of Sydney: A report on the experiences and expectations of students and teaching staff*. Sydney: Office of the DVC(E), University of Sydney.

Maton, K., & Moore, R. (2000). Historical amnesia: Victims of fashion and outbreaks of "breaks" in the disciplinary map. Paper presented at British Sociological Association Annual Conference, University of York, April. Retrieved June 27, 2007, from www.autodidactproject.org/other/matonha.html

Maton, K., & Moore, R. (Eds.) (2010). *Social realism, knowledge and the sociology of education: Coalitions of the mind*. London: Continuum.

McLuhan, M. (1962). *The Gutenberg galaxy: The making of typographic man*. London: Routledge & Kegan Paul.

McLuhan, M. (1964). *Understanding media: The extensions of man*. London: Routledge & Kegan Paul.

McHale, T. (2005). Portrait of a digital native. *Technology and Learning*, *26*(2), 33–34.

National Union of Teachers (1960). *Popular culture and personal responsibility: Verbatim report*. London: NUT.

Oblinger, D., & Oblinger, J. (2005). Is it Age or IT: First steps towards understanding the net generation. In D. Oblinger & J. Oblinger (Eds.), *Educating the net generation* (pp. 2.1–2.20). Boulder, CO: EDUCAUSE. Retrieved March 31, 2006, from www.educause.edu/educatingthenetgen

Oliver, B., & Goerke, V. (2007). Australian undergraduates' use and ownership of emerging technologies: Implications and opportunities for creating engaging learning experiences for the Net Generation. *Australasian Journal of Educational Technology*, *23*(2), 171–186. Retrieved June 27, 2007, from www.ascilite.org.au/ajet/ajet23/oliver.html

Organization for Economic Co-operation and Development (OECD). (2010). *Are the new millennium learners making the grade? Technology use and educational performance in PISA*. Paris: OECD.

Otto, H., Kutscher, N., Klein, A., & Iske, S. (2005). Social inequality in the virtual space: How do young people use the Internet? Results from empirical research about online use differences and acquiring patterns of young people. Report. Retrieved May 27, 2010, from www.kib-bielefeld.de/veroeffentlichungen.htm

Palfrey, J., & Gasser, U. (2008) *Born digital: Understanding the first generation of digital natives*. New York: Basic Books.

Pearson, G. (1983). *Hooligan: A history of respectable fears*. London: Palgrave Macmillan.

Prenksy, M. (2001). Digital natives, digital immigrants. *On the Horizon*, *9*(5), 1–6.

Prensky, M. (2009). H. sapiens digital: From digital immigrants and digital natives to digital wisdom. *Innovate*, *5*(3). Retrieved February 4, 2009, from http://innovateonline.info/index.php?view=article&id=705

Prensky, M. (2010). *Teaching digital natives: Partnering for real learning*. Thousands Oaks, CA: Corwin.

Salaway, G., & Caruso, J. with Nelson, M. (2008). *The ECAR study of undergraduate Students and information technology, 2008*. Boulder, CO: EDUCAUSE.

Selwyn, N. (2003). "Doing IT for the kids": Re-examining children, computers and the "information society." *Media, Culture & Society*, *25*, 351–378.

Selwyn, N. (2008). An investigation of differences in undergraduates' academic use of the internet. *Active Learning in Higher Education*, *9*(11), 11–22.

Singh, P., Mallan, K., & Giardina, N. (2008). *Just Google it! Students constructing knowledge through Internet travel*. Paper presented at the Australian Association for Research in Education Conference, Brisbane, November 30–December 4. Retrieved October 2, 2009, from http://ocs.sfu.ca/aare/index.php/AARE_2008/AARE/paper/viewFile/263/123

Skiba, D. J. (2005). The Millennials: Have they arrived at your school of nursing? *Nursing Education Perspectives*, *27*(3), 370.

Tapscott, D. (1998). *Growing up digital: The rise of the net generation*. New York: McGraw-Hill.

Tapscott, D. (2009) *Grown up digital: How the net generation is changing your world*. New York: McGraw-Hill.

Teo, T. (2009). Modelling technology acceptance in education: A study of pre-service teachers. *Computers & Education*, *52*(2), 302–312.

Thrupp, R. (2008). *Social groups and information communication technologies*. Unpublished doctoral dissertation. Central Queensland University.

Waycott, J., Bennett, S., Kennedy, G., Dalgarno, B., & Gray, K. (2010). Digital divides? Student and staff perceptions of information and communication technologies. *Computers & Education*, *54*(4), 1202–1211.

Youn, S. (2008). Parental influence and teens' attitude toward online privacy protection. *The Journal of Consumer Affairs*, *42*, 362–388.

12

RECLAIMING AN AWKWARD TERM

What We Might Learn from "Digital Natives"

John Palfrey and Urs Gasser

Many—though not all—young people are using digital media in ways that are changing how they learn and how they relate to one another, to information, and to institutions. In this chapter, we make the case that the sum of these changes in youth media practices can be good for teaching and learning, but that they are not without complications. Along the way, we also make the case, in tension with what others in this volume have argued, that the use of the term "Digital Natives" can be a constructive way to reach parents and teachers and that it can be done in a fashion that is true to sound research about youth practices with respect to digital media.

The roadmap to this chapter is as follows. First, we explore the awkward term "Digital Natives" (as in Palfrey & Gasser, 2008), explain why we have chosen to use it in certain contexts, and describe some of the common attributes of this subset of the world's young people today. Then we will address some of the key problems faced by these young people and others in society. Last, we will end with a positive outlook. While there are problems associated with youth media practices, and challenges for large learning institutions in responding to those problems, overall we believe a bright future can lie ahead if we are smart about it and listen to sound research.

The goal of our research has been to understand how young people use technology and relate to information in a digital era and to address the implications of lives that are highly mediated by digital technologies. At the same time, we have looked hard at articulated positions about youth and digital media that might be more myth than reality. One related purpose of our work is to examine what the most important implications of these practices are for learning institutions, including universities and libraries.

In performing this research, we have built on the shoulders of giants. There are many other people who have studied this topic for a long time, such as Mizuko Ito (e.g., Ito et al., 2008), danah boyd (e.g., boyd 2007), and, at the Pew Center for Internet and American Life, Amanda Lenhart (e.g., Lenhart & Madden, 2005). While the most extensive empirical work on this topic has been done in the United States and in the United Kingdom, we have grounded our work in the extensive literature of researchers around the world (such as Buckingham, 2008; Döring, 2003; Drotner & Livingstone, 2008; Livingstone, 2009; Metzger & Flanagin, 2008). To the extent that we have relied upon the work of other colleagues, we have documented much of that reading in the form of two extensive literature reviews (Biegler & boyd, 2010; Marwick, Murgia-Diaz & Palfrey, 2010) with a forth-coming third literature review led by Urs Gasser related to youth, media, credibility, and information quality. A related piece, written in partnership with UNICEF, is a review of the literature related to youth media practice and safety around the world (Gasser, Maclay & Palfrey, 2010). Our book, *Born Digital*, also includes a Selected Bibliography that notes the texts and projects that most influenced our thinking (Palfrey & Gasser, 2008, pp. 359–369). To complement the research work of others, we have also held our own series of focus groups and interviews to try and understand what the key issues are associated with how young people use digital media.

Reconstructing "Digital Natives"

This book is devoted to the task of deconstructing the term "Digital Natives." This is a worthy and important goal. The term itself evokes strong feelings, many of them sharply negative. Over the past decade, there has been a great deal of healthy debate over the term "Digital Natives" as a means to describe the habits of youth. The use of the term, in this respect, has served an important rhetorical purpose. Many people—in fact, most academics we know—do not like the term at all and feel strongly that its use can do more harm than good. That perspective is made plain in many of the other chapters of this book, and with great force (see also Buckingham, 2008; Herring, 2008). For our part, despite its obvious demerits as a term, we decided to take a hard path: to embrace this term, in part, and to take on the difficult task of redefinition.

Our rationale for the approach of using, rather than rejecting, the term "Digital Natives" has been to lean into the public discourse. The public conversation that we encountered, outside our own sheltered academic cloister, is often framed in the context of digital natives. For many parents and educators, the idea of "Digital Natives" resonates deeply, and this resonance is not something academics should just ignore or dismiss. Our decision was to apply our own research and the work of others to understand the salience of the term and to use it as a teaching and learning device, and to insert into this discourse insights about what sound social science is telling us. The risks of doing so—in particular, of *contributing* to the use of an awkward and limited term—are plain, but we perceived the benefits to be greater. Our approach has been to ask: is there a way to use an awkward term in a constructive manner, without resorting to reductionism, and without implying technological determinism? What are the facts about youth practice and can they fit into this frame in a way that can help move the public discourse forward?

There are two subsidiary questions to answer. First, is there a generational break that divides older and younger people by how each group uses technology? The answer is "no." People have adopted new technologies at varying rates and at varying ages over time. Here, we differ significantly from Marc Prensky's (2001) original formulation of the term "Digital Natives." He uses words like "singularity," "*discontinuity*," and "*fundamentally different*" (emphases in original) to describe young people (see also Herring, 2008, p. 75). But there is no moment in history that demarks an overnight change in how people use technology or what it means for our lives or our societies. People have learned and adapted to life in a partially digitally mediated world at different rates.

Second, is there a generation of young people all using technology in the same way? Again, the answer is "no" (Hargittai, 2010). There is no extent to which one could say all youth of recent generations use technology in advanced ways. It is also not the case that those of us who are older use technology in ways identical to one another, or in ways more naïve than those of children. Instead, what we focus on is a *subset* of young people exhibiting certain *practices* that are potentially very sophisticated, rather than arguing for a *generation* all acting and thinking identically (Palfrey & Gasser, 2008, p. 15).

The core idea, what we mean when we talk about digital natives, is to allow a term to describe a subset of today's youth; the manners in which they relate to information, technology, and one another; the problems that arise from some of these practices; and the new possibilities for creativity, learning, entrepreneurship, and innovation (Palfrey & Gasser, 2008, p. 15). By identifying the youth exhibiting sophisticated usage—whether through the term "Digital Natives" or otherwise—we can then talk with them and learn about the larger social context in which their sophisticated skills and attitudes exist. The purpose of such study is ultimately to be able to extend, to a broader audience, an argument about the creative possibilities associated with how some young people use new technologies.

We identify digital natives as a population, and not a generation, of young people who use technology in relatively advanced ways. In order to be classified by this term, a young person has to meet three criteria. First, they were born after 1980. This date is, in essence, arbitrary; a date a few years in earlier or later could have worked just as well, given the evolutionary, rather than revolutionary, character of these changes. The reason we chose this particular year was to signal that these young people were born after the advent of digitally mediated social technologies, such as bulletin board systems (BBSs), and that they did not know a world in which these types of online social media did not exist. Second, they have access to digital technologies. It is important to recognize that fewer than 2 billion out of 6.8 billion people on the planet have access to digital technologies. Last, and most crucially, digital natives are those with the skills to use these digital technologies in relatively sophisticated ways (Palfrey & Gasser, 2008, p. 1).

The most important of these three factors is the third. These sophisticated skills are often referred to as a level of "digital literacy" or "new media literacy" (Jenkins et al., 2006; see also newmedialiteracies.org). These skills relate to analytical abilities that enable a young person to distinguish situations that may prove dangerous to them from those that are ordinary social situations with peers; to locate and recognize high-quality information; to manage their own identity as it forms through the use of selective information sharing and privacy settings on social network sites; and so forth.

It is not always the case that young people are growing up in environments where they are supported in their use of these technologies. This is one of the primary difficulties of the term "native." It is not true that access begets skill; education is a necessary part of the equation for young people to develop the media literacies they need to succeed in a digitally mediated world. Nor is it sufficient that they can get access to the Internet in a school or a library; we know from our research that for young people to develop sophisticated skills, it is crucial that they have a home where parents support them, schools where teachers support them, and libraries where librarians support them. The work of Henry Jenkins and Eszter Hargittai on this "participation gap" is instructive on this score (Jenkins et al., 2009; Hargittai, 2010). No amount of "reclaiming" of the term "Digital Natives" can overcome these crucial social problems associated with uneven levels of skill, education, and literacy, whether digital or not. It is a further risk of the use of the term that one might contribute to an incorrect presumption of the innate ability of youth born after a certain moment in history, a presumption that must be rebutted at every turn.

The critics of the term "Digital Natives" are quite right in many respects. Among other things, it is not enough to be born on a certain date in history and merely to have access to technology. And it is not the case that youth are born with an intuition for how to use digital tools or how to sort through online information. Some young people are born *into* a digital *world* (hence the title we chose for our book, *Born Digital*), but this digital world exists only because of the support structures that we, as parents, educators, and librarians, provide, and the technological environment that we as humans are constructing. The challenge is not even as simple as a separation between "digital haves" and "digital have-nots" that we can we try to bridge; we cannot forget that there is a vast diversity of attitudes towards and expectations of technology, and differing levels of skill and sophistication, found within the youth fitting the above three criteria. Our challenge is to find and understand the very best practices and then to try and extend the possibilities presented by such practices to people regardless of when they were born, across a range of access to digital technologies, and across a range of support structures.

Many people born before 1980, too, are skilled at using new digital technologies, often more skilled in fact than their younger counterparts. The foreignness and bewilderment suggested by the term "Digital Immigrants," the counterpart term to "Digital Natives" in its original formulation (Prensky, 2001, pp. 1–2), is not an accurate or descriptive label for many adults.[1] Many librarians, for instance, use technology just as effectively as any young person, or more so. The Pew Internet & American Life Project identifies about a third of US adults (18+) as "technology elites" whose "trendsetting ways often ripple widely in society" (Horrigan, 2003, pp. ii–iii). The majority (three-fifths) are "Wired GenXers" with an average age of thirty-six. The "Young Tech Elites," with an average age of twenty-two, are only a fifth of these technology elites. A further fifth are "Older Wired Baby Boomers," a population of "yesterday's technological elites who have maintained their sophistication over time" (Horrigan, 2003, pp. 6–9). There are, of course, older people who use technology less effectively and think about technology in less open-minded ways than do digital natives, but it is not accurate to label all adults "Digital Immigrants." The category is not a particularly helpful one, especially as there is no clear utility in identifying and labeling those among older generations who are less skillful at using technology. Without the generational essentialism of employing digital natives and digital immigrants as exhaustive categories, we observe that there is no *gap* between generations but rather *gradients* of different usage patterns.

We advance, too, an argument that there may be an emerging global culture of young people using technology in similarly sophisticated ways. This is the least strong of our assertions; there is too little in the way of sound data to support this claim, but it seems a plausible hypothesis to test. At least among young people from the elite in the societies where we spent the most time (Bahrain in the Gulf; Switzerland in Europe; China in East Asia), there are aspects of a common culture that is emerging in terms of how they use these technologies. We suspect that it does break down along lines of socioeconomic status (SES), as it does in the United States, and of course these are numerous local differences based on culture, history, language, and other factors. Despite these limitations and differences, there remain great opportunities for cross-cultural understanding in this common culture that is emerging among people around the globe if this hypothesis proves to be accurate.

As a brief statement of our methods: most of our claims rest on the findings of the studies of the growing group of highly networked researchers (and particularly researchers networked through the Digital Media and Learning Research Hub, www.DMLcentral.net) asking questions about youth media practice from a social scientific perspective. Most of our close colleagues focus on the United States, an obvious limitation. To complement what we read in the work of our collaborators and colleagues in the field, we conducted research with a diverse group of young people in terms of age, socioeconomic standing, and technological ability. Our analysis here draws in part on original research conducted in the greater Boston area. Our goal was not to undertake a comprehensive study, but rather to take an in-depth look at the way some young people are relating to information and one another on topics such as privacy, creativity, and learning, as well as gain insight into the discourse taking place among students on issues of copyright and piracy. We also spoke with informants, using the same methodology, in three other parts of the world: in Switzerland; in Bahrain; and in Beijing and Shanghai. Other researchers have used our protocols to carry out similar studies, for instance, in Japan. It is important, of course, to address up front the limitations of our study: we explored youth discourse surrounding their use of digital technologies within a particular and limited population, one not representative of digital natives in the US as a whole. While our findings begin to uncover and describe how youth are approaching these issues and the complex dynamics at hand, it is not possible to extrapolate our findings to the greater United States population at large. We rely heavily and primarily, here and elsewhere, on the findings of other researchers using a broad range of methods, from the highly qualitative to the quantitative.

Specific Attributes of this Population of Today's Youth

There are a series of common practices and associated attributes we refer to when we talk about those in the population of digital natives. These attributes are often familiar to many educators, parents, and librarians, which is part of the reason why the term resonates for some people thinking about issues of youth and technology. We will discuss four of the most common practices to set the stage for the challenges and opportunities: using technology to express identity, multitasking (or "task-switching"), expecting information to be in a digital format, and moving from consumers to creators of publicly accessible information.

The first practice is the extent to which digital natives use technologies in ways that express their identity. They will express themselves in social networks such as Facebook and MySpace, environments in which they are shaping an identity. As one seventeen-year-old female high school student in the northeast of the United States told us, "I personally am like, you know, I'm very careful about what I put on MySpace and Facebook in like making sure that that's what—that's who I feel I am" (unpublished focus group data, 2007). They choose how to express themselves by the photographs that they upload to these social networks, but it is important to note that these expressions are not distinguished from creating their identity in the offline space (Palfrey & Gasser, 2008, p. 19). The notion that there is a separate world, a separate set of online identities, makes little sense to many of those growing up immersed in digital technologies.

For youth in a digital era, it all converges, by and large. It is not online life and offline life—it's just life. It is where social life is playing out, and often times the identity-shaping happens in a way that is identical to the kind of traditional role-playing young people have been carrying out in the process of shaping their identities. The difference is perhaps the multiplicity of identifies formed in these online spaces (Palfrey & Gasser, 2008, p. 20).

Though digital natives think that they are creating multiple identities in this converged space, there is also an ability for the onlooker to see all of these identities at once. This paradox is an interesting, and profound, change made possible by the use of Internet and social forms of digital media. Previously, if onlookers had to find and look at these identities seriatim, then the identities would not be visible all at once, and onlookers could not see multiplicity. Though these young people may think there is more control and experimentation in terms of their identities today, it may be that they have far less ability to maintain multiple identities than they think.

The second practice of digital natives, which feels familiar to many who teach young people, is multitasking or switch-tasking (Lenhart, Hitlin & Madden, 2005, p. 22). Very often, when educators talk about this issue of young people and technology, this is the first thing mentioned. Some young people always have iPod earbuds in their ears as they walk across the street (and we fear we might run them over because they cannot hear us). They may be talking on their cell phone at exactly the same time. In our law school classes, when we look out on groups of students (and of course, most Harvard Law School students will come from backgrounds where they have access to technology and strong support structures), we see a sea of laptops, with few if any of the students looking up at the teacher.

In the context of a school environment, it is a very different experience to look out on a group of people who are looking into their mobile device or laptop than it is to look out on a group of people looking at you as the teacher. In such cases, the term "Digital Natives" is particularly appropriate to describe how us teachers relate to students with certain attitudes towards technology. As teachers, we have the experience of seeing students in the audience smirking and laughing, and realizing they are instant messaging one another back and forth. But they are often doing more than one thing at once—or, more accurately, switching back and forth between various tasks one after another ("switch-tasking" rather than multitasking).

In our work as teachers, we have made a practice of occasionally sitting in the back of classes taught by our colleagues to observe the teaching and the activities of students online during class. It is an illuminating experience. From the back of the room, one can see what most students do on their laptops during class. One such recent class was an early iteration of what is now a required first-year course for students at the Harvard Law School. What we observed, for anecdotal purposes only, was a mix of practices. For about the first twenty minutes, we saw only Word documents on the screens. Students were actually taking notes.

And then, at about minute twenty-one, students began to deviate in their behavior. Different screens started coming up; it would be, for some students, their email, for others, instant messaging. At about minute forty-one, the most popular thing was people looking at slide shows of the ball gowns Michelle Obama had worn for the Inauguration of her husband, United States President Barack Obama. By the end of the class period, we saw online shopping.

We do not need major pedagogical studies to know that if students are doing their email while their professor is trying to teach them the rules of evidence, they are not going to learn as well as if they are paying full attention to the class material. Teachers know that distractions in the classroom, whether digital or not, tend not to be great for learning (Fried, 2006). But where we have to dig deeper is to understand what students are in fact doing when they are engaged with digital media in the classroom. A lot of what is actually happening is not multitasking, but this notion of "task-switching" or "switch-tasking." Young people who use technology extensively can actually become quite good at switching between different things at different points and doing all tasks effectively.

We are not condoning, through bringing up task-switching, looking at Michelle Obama's ball dresses during evidence class. That is not the point. The point is that there are processes taking place in classrooms that may not be as bad as we, as educators and librarians, may think in terms of learning. There might even be things going on that we could embrace and use to advantage, to improve the system of education. Some behaviors that we see in young people, related to their digital media use, are things we want people to be able to do. Students exhibit a broad range of behaviors, inside and outside of class, that affect their learning. As teachers, we need to be open-minded, seeking to find ways to limit behavior that constrains our students' learning while building upon their creative and innovative learning practices.

The third practice—and the associated attitude—of these young people involves their relationship to digital media. Many young people presume that material they interact with is going to be in a digital format in most cases. On a recent vacation, we had forgotten to bring a digital camera, so we bought a disposable camera at a souvenir store. One of our children took some pictures, turned the camera over and said, "Mom and Dad, I don't get it. Where is the picture on the back of this thing?" She did not expect, and was confused by, the absence of a digital image on the back of the camera. She is not accustomed to having to print out a roll of film, bring it to a store, and only get the prints back three days later after paying twenty dollars. Images are presumed to be digital, something to delete or upload or manipulate.

The same is true of video. Children love to look up silly videos of sneezing pandas on YouTube. For some children, they would much rather type in "sneezing pandas" in YouTube than watch television because a three-minute video of baby pandas in China is far more entertaining to them than anything on television. It is not surprising that in 2008, YouTube surpassed Yahoo! to became the search entity with the second-most number of search queries in the US, second only to Google (comScore, Inc., 2008).[2] It is still too early to tell whether online video, or television programming accessible on-demand online, will replace the television set. The Nielsen Company has been measuring trends about the relationship between television and the Internet since 2008, and the results from this period seem to indicate not (The Nielsen Company, 2008–2010). But this brings us back to digital natives not referring to all youth. For one of our children, the new medium of the Internet plays part of the role television has played for those of us who grew up in another era. She expects video to be delivered in a digital format over which she has greater control. Data show that this is true for some kids, but not for others, in this digital era.

In the context of print, we observe similar changes in expectations. Books that we write today are not just available on the shelf; they are often searchable within Google if they are digitized. The presumption is that one can process new works through digital media; search through them using search engine algorithms; and share them with peers over the Internet as well, instead of by passing on hard copies. The materials are meant to be social.

One of the key elements of this iteration of the Web—Web 2.0, or the read/write web, or the social web—is that materials are often shared in digital public places and are visible to any potential onlooker (boyd, 2007). Digital natives take photographs on smart phones or PDAs, upload the images to Flickr, Photobucket, or Facebook and tag them with the names of the friends who appear in those images. The presumption is always towards sharing information and knowledge with others. The notion of Wikipedia makes this idea very clear, too; the idea of a community working together on collective knowledge creation. It is a shared environment and a social environment when it is at its most successful.

The fourth practice, and the one that makes academics the most excited, is the related notion that some young people are not just *consumers* of information, but in some cases they are also *creators* of information (for a general discussion not specific to youth, see Searls & Weinberger, 2009). The move from consumers to creators is not complete, but we see great promise in the trajectories involved. In our research, we came to the project with a normative assumption: we hoped to find everybody creating remix videos on hot political issues on Saturday afternoons, but this turns out not to be true. There are many young people without the technical knowledge of how to create such media, and there are even plenty of couch potatoes out there. Still, according to a Pew study, a full *half* of teenagers have created content. They have done things such as:

> . . . create a blog; create a personal webpage; create a webpage for school, a friend, or an organization; share original content they created themselves online; or remix content found online into a new creation.
>
> (Lenhart & Madden, 2005, pp. 1–2)

But the "participation gap" again emerges; teens in urban areas and with access to high-speed connections are most likely to be content creators. The practices of certain digital natives help us imagine a world where anyone can learn to become a creator of information or code that can help to transform their lives and societies. And even less creative forms of content creation, such as posting status updates on popular social networking sites or leaving comments on a friend's blog, are likely to have a positive effect on information literacy skills of young users as recent information quality-related research suggests (Gasser, Cortesi, Malik & Lee, forthcoming).

A variant of this creativity, which we see in the classroom, is that some people are excellent at working together and working in teams. This is a skill that we in legal education (and many other fields of education besides) have failed to nurture. As legal educators, we prepare lawyers to go into the practice of law; with very few exceptions, this means working with a group of other lawyers on a case. It is very rare for a lawyer to spend all her time sitting alone in a room, drafting a response to a judge in a legal matter. That lawyer is much more likely to be working with a senior associate and a partner and five other junior associates, or perhaps a smaller team at the public interest equivalent. Despite this reality of legal practice, we almost always teach young people to learn on their own in the quiet of the library carrel and then demand that they take an exam on their own. We round out the process by giving them a grade with no feedback. This is where digital natives connect with legal education: when we put skilled students into a team-based environment, especially in ways that are mediated by digital technologies, they can come up with wonderful means of working together and putting together terrific work products. They are extremely good at using lightweight collaboration tools such as Google Docs or Etherpad, or wikis, or video-editing software.

Our students are often unhappy at first when one assigns them to perform a group project. They immediately realize (accurately) that they are likely to be faced with a free-rider problem: one of their classmates will not work as hard and yet all of them will get the same grade. But in teams at law firms or in any other work setting in our field, that will happen, too, and it usually works itself out over time. We find surprising results when we get young people to work in creative teams in ways that use digital technologies, inside and outside of the classroom, inside and outside of the library. We need to find ways to leverage the skills possessed by our students. Technologies can help meet our pedagogical goals if we are creative and clever.

Problems Associated with Youth Media Practice

What are the problems potentially associated with these changes in culture, practices, and relationships to information? We raise five such concerns: safety, privacy, intellectual property, information quality, and information overload. These problems are real, but they are not quite as crisp, or as different from what we've seen before, as they are made out to be in the mainstream media. There are many myths about these problems we seek to debunk. These problems are more general than the discussion of digital natives; in fact, we might label an individual as a digital native based on her or his ability to manage such problems far more skillfully than her or his peers.

First, take safety. The idea is to figure out where the safety issues are for kids, which are real concerns in the United States, and then whether we could bring technologies to bear on them to help make kids safer (Schrock & boyd, 2008). A commonly articulated (Marwick, 2008) fear is associated with the premise of the television program, "To Catch a Predator," the notion that young people will meet someone on Facebook or MySpace and then meet that person in offline space, where terrible harm is done to them (Palfrey & Gasser, 2008, p. 83). Unfortunately, this does happen. It is terrible when it does. It is a parent's worst nightmare; we do not diminish the real risk of it happening. What we have to be honest about, and learn from, is that it does not happen more in a digital era than it did before; nor are all young people equally at risk of it happening to them. The data show that the overall risk of this happening, despite the advent of the Internet, is falling, not rising (Schrock & boyd, 2008, p. 14). It is not the case that the Internet or digital media has made this problem spiral out of control and become an epidemic. The problem is largely the same as it was before the digital era. Known cases of sexual assault involving predatory older strangers are very rare; as uncomfortable as it is, Internet-initiated sex crimes where the adult perpetrator is known to the youth victim are still a much larger problem (Schrock & boyd, 2008, p. 15).

What has changed in the digital era is not the prevalence of predation by strangers occurring, but rather that sometimes the place where the first meeting occurs is no longer the playground in the real world. The public spaces in which our youth are growing up has moved from physical environments to these online environments in which kids are shaping their identity and expressing themselves and so forth. It also turns out that the kids most at risk are kids who are most at risk in real space, too. They often have difficult home lives or other problems that they are fighting (Schrock & boyd, 2008, p. 46). It is important that we focus on the extent to which this is not all that much different because of the Internet. It may be that the first meeting happens online, but the core problem—of sexual predation—is fundamentally the same.

There is another safety issue, but this one has a basis in some of the data collected about youth media practices: some studies show an uptick in bullying that is happening online (Schrock & boyd, 2008, pp. 22–23). In other words, some researchers argue that the extent to which young people, peer-to-peer, are doing harm to one another through networked digital media is on the rise.

There are a couple of caveats to this apparent increase in harms. First, much turns on how we define bullying; the bullying described in these studies relates to psychological harms inflicted by peers, not the iconic image of the lunch-money-stealing bully (Schrock & boyd, 2008, p. 22). Second, changes in data collection methods might also have an effect (Schrock & boyd, 2008, p. 9). But most importantly, for the first time, adults can see some of these harms happening. Two decades ago, parents could not see bullying as it happened on the playground. Now, if these acts take place in a social network online, there is potentially a digital record of communication for adults to see either after the fact or even as it happens. The new online visibility may be affecting reporting: when many studies show a clear uptick in the occurrence of bullying online, the question is whether that is a real rise in bullying or if in fact it is just a transfer of the bullying that has always happened in real space into these online environments where it is more visible and measurable. If we were to see a rise in incidences of online predation, we might present the same critique, but it so happens that debunking the myth of increased predation is easier because the data already shows a decrease in incidences. Still, this data is not unambiguous either; measuring the prevalence of *any* online harm is difficult because so many incidences may go unreported (Schrock & boyd, 2008, p. 60). There is no doubt that real harms are being caused; but we should keep in mind that it is far from clear that there is an overall increase in these harms now that interactions are digitally mediated.

The second issue that comes up is privacy. One of the myths we take up in our research is the idea that "young people don't care about privacy" (Palfrey & Gasser, 2008, pp. 53–82; see also Marwick, Diaz & Palfrey, 2010, p. 4, for expanded discussion). There is evidence that many young people do share too much information about themselves in these online environments. But it is not the case that they do not care about privacy (boyd & Hargittai, 2010). They do care about privacy; certainly, they care about privacy from their parents and teachers and other authority figures (Marwick, Diaz & Palfrey, 2010, pp. 14–15). They are not always equipped, though, with the skills to protect their own information in the way that they would like. Our colleague danah boyd, in particular, has done a lot of compelling work on this topic. Her work shows the extent to which young people often make a series of common mistakes when they are posting material online, such as the unintended audiences that may get access to their postings or the persistence of the information over long periods of time (boyd, 2007). That is, these are "mistakes" in the terms of the young people themselves, actions that frustrate their own goals and preferences, and not something we are imposing with our interpretation or something we need to teach them to care about.

The one positive note on this front is that young people we talked to who had been online longer are much smarter about it. In fact, they are much smarter than many adults are about privacy. We perceive that this is a persistent problem only insofar as not all youth have the sophistication of those identified as digital natives. Kids who are given the proper scaffolding—through the support of education and parenting and the work of technology companies—will come to realize the risks they are running associated with their behavior. We believe that youth can get much smarter about using privacy controls; this may come about partially through young people becoming better at hiding from adult benefactors the information that these benefactors would like to oversee and monitor, but it also means that youth will be able to avoid effectively the scenarios their adult benefactors fear without needing intervention and regulation from adults.

The third of the problems is the notion that young people do not pay for the information and the media that they enjoy online (Palfrey & Gasser, 2008, pp. 131–153). The prevalent view is that when it comes to music and movies, for instance, young people tend to go online and steal them. Unfortunately, it turns out that's not exactly a myth we can debunk. This is an example of a practice that characterizes not just those we would identify as digital natives, but in fact most young people: according to Pew data from 2005, half of online teens[3] admit to downloading music, with another third admitting to have done so in the past, giving a total of two-thirds of online teens who download music (Lenhart & Madden, 2005, pp. iii, 10). And that's only the number of teens who admit to doing so. We see here a dramatic difference between youth and older populations: the numbers of online older users who admit to downloading music is 40 percent for users aged eighteen to twenty-nine (note: when this study was conducted in 2005, anybody younger than twenty-five would have been born after 1980), 18 percent for users aged thirty to forty-nine, 13 percent for users aged fifty to sixty-four, and 6 percent for users aged sixty-five and above (Madden & Rainie, 2005, p. 7).

In our focus group research, most of the young people we spoke to knew that it was unlawful to steal the music online on LimeWire or the other peer-to-peer services they used. They made clear to us that they knew what they were doing was a violation of the copyright laws of the United States and most other countries (Palfrey & Gasser, 2008, p. 137). We do it anyway, they said. We are "sticking it to The Man," they told us. There was this sense, consciously, that this practice was something that everybody did. And while they perceived their acts to be unlawful, they also perceived them to be justified. This attitude may not be unique to younger users, and older users who download music may well have similar perceptions.

The area where there was much less knowledge, and in fact outright confusion in most cases, was remixing. We asked them questions about what they do with the copyrighted materials of other people in their own work. Could they make new works with the copyrighted materials of others in the context of a museum or library or school? This is something that we are very interested in as a matter of public policy. We are eager to see more of this "semiotic democracy" emerging—the practice of the remaking of culture by young people. What is clear is that young people often do work other people's materials into their own, but they are extremely confused about the law in this area. They have no idea what their rights are to remix copyrighted works. We saw the same dynamic in talking to parents and teachers. They are mystified, too, as to what the rights of remixers are, and they are often just as mystified as to whether the practices of their children and students are lawful or unlawful. Copyright used to apply only to those who created maps, books, and charts 200 years ago. Now it applies to everybody, particularly our kids, as they are going through life in this digitally mediated way—and yet the doctrine of copyright is only more complex, not less so, than it was when it applied to many fewer people (Palfrey & Gasser, 2008, p. 138).

The fourth issue is the problem of the quality of information in a digital-plus world. Quality—or closely related concepts such as credibility, reliability, trustworthiness, or authority—is something plainly on the minds of librarians. We know that young people do not wake up first thing in the morning and read the *Wall Street Journal* or the *Washington Post* cover to cover while they drink a cup of coffee; likewise, we know they don't come home at the end of the day to turn on the evening news, to watch Walter Cronkite or Katie Couric tell them what had happened over the course of the day. Those sources of information traditionally presented by authority and social norms as "high-quality" are no longer the only, or even necessarily the dominant, sources of information for young people. Also, the point is not that young people should turn to the *Wall Street Journal* or the *Washington Post* as automatic high-quality source. The point is that these are no longer the only accessible sources. There are a greater number and a greater variety of sources for librarians to teach young people how to analyze, but it takes a different set of skills to navigate this more complex information environment. We know also that when somebody is looking up something for a project as a research matter, they rarely go first to the physical library. They go to a teacher or a friend or to Google first; put another way, they are more likely to "Ask Jeeves" than to ask a reference librarian (Palfrey & Gasser, 2008, p. 239). When they perform a search, many of the young people we talked to would head for the Wikipedia page on their topic after using a search engine. When they got to the Wikipedia page, we then saw a range of practice. We saw young people on one end of the spectrum who would cut and paste what they saw in Wikipedia, stick it in their term paper, and hand it in. One hopes that they did not get a very good grade; but from their perspective, at least it was an efficient way to get the work done. On the other end of the spectrum, we found skeptical kids who would say that they didn't trust anything they found on Wikipedia, because their classmate may have just been there two minutes before and introduced a false fact just to mess them up (Palfrey & Gasser, 2008, pp. 160–161). This issue highlights, in particular, the importance of information literacy—the ability to recognize what information is most effective for a particular need, and to find such information online. It turns our attention again to the idea of the "participation gap" (Jenkins et al., 2006); there is variation in the skills that young people bring to the digital world, and these skills are growing in importance with each passing year.

The last of the issues is information overload: the feeling of being overwhelmed with the amount of information with which one is confronted. While information overload is not in itself a disorder, it can cause anxiety that has physical effects (Akin, 1998). Young people get a great deal of information from a broad range of sources, often spending an enormous amount of time connected to the digital world, and there is the possibility that during that time they will experience information overload. Denise Agosto has studied how experiencing overload may cause a young person to give up a task. While this might cause him or her to get off the Internet and spend a little bit of time disconnected from the digital world, we should not see this as a good thing, as it also means a less-than-optimal resolution for the young person's task (Agosto, 2002, pp. 22–23). The issue here is the same as the quality issue: our students need the skills to cope with this new, and often intense, means of interacting with news and information.

Opportunities for a Brighter Future

We promised to conclude with a positive outlook. Much of this story is hopeful. There are huge opportunities in what young people are already doing in these online public environments. Young people are expressing themselves and interacting with one another in ways from which they learn. Essential to this story is that we figure out how to impart good media literacy skills—the ability to sort credible information from less credible information online; to share only what you mean to share about yourself; to avoid violating the intellectual property of others; and so forth—to young people across the board, such that they are learning good and positive things through these interactions. The New Media Literacies Project is a great example of this potential. At the Harvard Graduate School of Education, Howard Gardner's Project Zero has an initiative called Good Play that is another great example of this, as is Common Sense Media. There are an emerging series of strong curricular elements now for how we can teach kids to navigate these digital environments in healthful ways.

On the intellectual property front, just as there are concerns, there is also the creative side of what kids are doing online. Some of them, the most sophisticated kids, are making extraordinary things online. Whether it is on their social network profiles, or through podcasts, or creating and remaking videos, these young people are shaping our—and their—culture (Palfrey & Gasser, 2008, pp. 111–129). By and large, this practice is something that will be good for global society, if we embrace it in the right ways.

On the quality front: this is the place where librarians and teachers are most crucial (Palfrey & Gasser, 2008, p. 181). It is the case that there are many more sources of information that kids can turn to in their everyday learning. It is tricky to figure out how to teach them to navigate this complex environment—but it is also a huge opportunity. Young people also have the chance to become *involved* in the making of culture and the making of the knowledge base. They have a chance at a much richer, much more participatory way of learning and interacting with the world than their grandparents did. It is not obvious what kinds of institutions we need to build to be intermediaries here between kids and information. It is obvious, though, that they love these social information platforms. They love YouTube and Facebook and they do make interesting things when they are given the opportunity and the encouragement and the skills to do so.

On information overload: this is much more an opportunity than it is a problem. Again, the importance of librarians and museums and curators and archivists, along with all parents and teachers, is obvious in this context. We need new kinds of guides to young people, to give them handholds in terms of what they ought to be looking for and what they ought to discard as less useful information. We should embrace the extent to which the global Internet provides the chance to create the digital Library of Alexandria that we have dreamed about. It is astonishing that from any place in the world one can get access to the store of the world's knowledge—and, in fact, to add to it—through a web browser or even a mobile device. It will take the success of projects such as Brewster Kahle's Internet Archive, Carl Malamud's Law.Gov, and many related experiments in libraries and other cultural institutions around the world to make it so. But the opportunity lies plainly before us. We are incredibly hopeful that, before too long, we can create a global information environment that is vastly richer than the one we have today.

The net result of this research is that there is more on the opportunity side of the ledger than there is on the challenge side, especially in the context of learning, innovation, and activism. What matters most is not the labels—whether "Digital Natives," "Millennials," "Digital Youth," "Youth" with no modifier at all, or otherwise—we use to describe these practices of youth, but rather whether we are doing our research carefully and working together, in the public interest, based on sound findings. The language that we use matters, of course; the critics of these terms make sound and important points. Most important is that we share a common commitment to understanding of what is going on with new media practices and, in turn, that we work together to seize the opportunities, and mitigate the challenges, associated with media practices of youth and adults alike.

It will take a lot of hard work, hand-in-hand with young people, to make visions of a brighter future, in a hybrid age of digital and analog life, a reality. The role of teachers, parents, and information professionals—whatever the next name of a librarian or museum curator will be—is only growing in this fast-changing environment. We need to strive to understand youth (and adult) practice with respect to information as it changes based on sound data; to chart a common path forward; and then to work hard, together, to make it come to pass. With the help of our children and our students, we can design and craft a much better information environment not just for today's youth, but for society at large and for future generations.

Notes

1 David Weinberger also suggests the category of "Digital Settlers" for those like himself who were there at the beginning of the digital revolution and helped shape it (Weinberger, 2008). This is a particularly appropriate extension of the "digital nationality" metaphor as it obviously refers to the practices and achievements of a select *population*, and not the characteristics of an entire *generation*.

2 In the November 2008 ranking from comScore, Inc., YouTube first overtook Yahoo! to become the search entity with the second-most number of search queries in the US. YouTube has remained in this rank since. While YouTube is owned by Google Inc., comScore, Inc. considers "Google Sites" as a "core search entity," while Google and YouTube are "expanded search entities." The comparison made is between the Google expanded search entity and the YouTube expanded search entity. As a whole, Google sites had 63.5 percent of all searches in November 2008, followed by Yahoo! Sites with 20.4 percent.

3 "Online teens" are 8 million teens out of the total 12 million US teens (Lenhart & Madden, 2005, pp. i, 1).

References

Agosto, D. E. (2002). Bounded rationality and satisficing in young people's web-based decision making. *Journal of the American Society of Information Science and Technology, 53*, 16–27.

Akin, L. (1998). Information overload and children: A survey of Texas elementary school students. *School Library Media Quarterly Online, 1*, 1–11. Retrieved September 10, 2010, from www.ala.org/ala/mgrps/divs/aasl/aaslpubsandjournals/slmrb/slmrcontents/volume 11998slmqo/akin.cfm

Biegler, S., & boyd, d. (2010). Risky behaviors and online safety: A 2010 literature review (DRAFT). Retrieved September 10, 2010, from www.zephoria.org/files/2010Safety LitReview.pdf

boyd, d. (2007). Why youth [heart] social network sites: The role of networked publics in teenage social life. In D. Buckingham (Ed.), *Youth, identity, and digital media* (pp. 119–142). Cambridge, MA: The MIT Press.

boyd, d., & Hargittai, E. (2010). Facebook privacy settings: Who cares? *First Monday, 15*(8). Retrieved September 10, 2010, from www.uic.edu/htbin/cgiwrap/bin/ojs/index.php/fm/article/view/3086/2589

Buckingham, D. (Ed.) (2008). *Youth, identity, and digital media*. Cambridge, MA: The MIT Press.

Buckingham, D. (2008). Introduction. In D. Buckingham (Ed.), *Youth, identity, and digital media* (pp. 1–24). Cambridge, MA: The MIT Press.

comScore, Inc. (2008, December 19). Press release: comScore releases November 2008 U.S. search engine rankings. Retrieved September 10, 2010, from www.comscore.com/Press_Events/Press_Releases/2008/12/US_Search_Engine_Rankings

Döring, N. (2003). *Sozialpsychologie des Internet, 2nd ed.* Göttingen: Hofgrede.

Drotner, K., & Livingstone, S. (Eds.) (2008). *The international handbook of children, media, and culture*. Los Angeles & London: Sage.

Fried, Carrie B. (2006). In-class laptop use and its effect on student learning. *Computers & Education*, 50, 906–914.

Gasser, U., Maclay, C., & Palfrey, J. (2010, June 15). Working towards a deeper understanding of digital safety for children and young people in developing nations:

An exploratory study by the Berkman Center for Internet & Society at Harvard University, in collaboration with UNICEF. Berkman Center Research Publication. Retrieved September 10, 2010, from https://cyber.law.harvard.edu/publications/2010/Digital_Safety_Children_Young_People_Developing_Nations

Gasser, U., Cortesi, S., Malik, M., & Lee, A. (forthcoming). *Youth and digital media: From credibility to information quality: A review of selected literature.*

Hargittai, E. (2010). Digital Na(t)ives? Variation in Internet skills and uses among members of the "Net Generation." *Sociological Inquiry, 80*(1). Retrieved September 10, 2010, from http://webuse.org/p/a29

Herring, S. C. (2008). Questioning the generational divide: Technological exoticism and adult construction of online youth identity. In D. Buckingham (Ed.), *Youth, Identity, and Digital Media* (pp. 71–94). Cambridge, MA: The MIT Press.

Horrigan, J. B. (2003). *Consumption of information goods and services in the United States.* Washington, DC: Pew Internet & American Life Project. Retrieved September 10, 2010, from http://pewinternet.org/~/media//Files/Reports/2003/PIP_Info_Consumption.pdf.pdf

Ito, M., Horst, H. A., Bittanti, M., boyd, d., Herr-Stephenson, B., Lange, P. G., Pascoe, C. J., Robinson, L., Baumer, S., Cody, R., Mahendran, D., Martinez, K., Perkel, D., Sims, C., & Tripp, L. (2008). *Living and learning with new media: Summary of findings from the digital youth project.* Retrieved September 10, 2010, from www.macfound.org/atf/cf/%7BB0386CE3-8B29-4162-8098-E466FB856794%7D/DML_ETHNOG_WHITEPAPER.PDF

Jenkins, H., Purushotma, R., Clinton, K., Weigel, M., & Robison, A. J. (2009). *Confronting the challenges of participatory culture: Media education for the 21st Century.* Retrieved September 10, 2010, from www.newmedialiteracies.org/files/working/NMLWhitePaper.pdf

Lenhart, A., & Madden, M. (2005). *Teen content creators and consumers.* Washington, DC: Pew Internet & American Life Project. Retrieved September 10, 2010, from www.pewinternet.org/Reports/2005/Teen-Content-Creators-and-Consumers.aspx

Lenhart, A., Hitlin, P., & Madden, M. (2005). *Teens and Technology.* Washington, DC: Pew Internet & American Life Project. Retrieved September 10, 2010, from www.pewinternet.org/Reports/2005/Teens-and-Technology.aspx

Livingstone, S. (2009). *Children and the internet.* Cambridge, UK: Polity Press.

Madden, M., & Rainie, L. (2005, March). *Pew Internet Project data memo: Music and video downloading moves beyond P2P.* Washington, DC: Pew Internet & American Life Project. Retrieved September 10, 2010, from www.pewinternet.org/~/media//Files/Reports/2005/PIP_Filesharing_March05.pdf.pdf

Marwick, A. (2008). To catch a predator? The MySpace moral panic. *First Monday, 13*(6), article 3.

Marwick, A. E., Murgia-Diaz, D., & Palfrey, J. (2010, March 29). *Youth, privacy and reputation (literature review).* Berkman Center Research Publication No. 2010–5, Harvard Public Law Working Paper No. 10–29.

Metzger, M. J., & Flanagin, A. J. (Eds.) (2008). *Digital media, youth, and credibility.* Cambridge, MA: The MIT Press.

The Nielsen Company. (2008–2010). *Three screen report.* Retrieved January 15, 2011, from www.nielsen.com/content/corporate/us/en/search.html?q=three+screen+report

Palfrey, J., & Gasser, U. (2008). *Born digital: Understanding the first generation of Digital Natives.* New York: Basic Books.

Prensky, M. (2001). Digital natives, digital immigrants. *On the Horizon, 9*(5), 1–6.

Schrock, A., & boyd, d. (2008). Online threats to youth: Solicitation, harassment, and problematic content. *Research Advisory Board Report for the Internet Safety Technical Task Force*. Retrieved September 10, 2010, from www.danah.org/papers/ISTTF-RAB LitReview.pdf

Searls, D., & Weinberger, D. (2009). Markets are conversations. In R. Levine, C. Locke, D. Searls, & D. Weinberger, *The Cluetrain Manifesto: 10th Anniversary Edition* (pp. 75–114). New York: Basic Books.

Weinberger, D. (2008). Digital Natives, Immigrants and others. *KMWorld, 17*(1). Retrieved September 10, 2010, from www.kmworld.com/Articles/News/News-Analysis/Digital-natives,-immigrants-and-others—40494.aspx

CONTRIBUTORS

Shakuntala Banaji works at the London School of Economics, UK. She lectures in Media and Cultural Studies, and has undertaken research into young people and film, creativity and education, pedagogy, civic participation, and online media cultures and has been part of several large-scale research projects including CivicWeb: Young People, the Internet and Civic Participation (2006–2009); Children in Communication about Migration (CHICAM 2001–2004); and Rhetorics of Creativity (2005–2006). Her new edited collection *South Asian Media Cultures* was published in 2010 by Anthem Press.

Sue Bennett is an Associate Professor in the Faculty of Education at the University of Wollongong, Australia, and the coordinator of the Cognition and Learning Design Laboratory. Sue's research is concerned with understanding the impact of information and communications technologies on education. Her body of work encompasses a wide range of research questions relevant to school and university education. One current focus is on investigating the "Digital Native" idea through large-scale collaborative research studies inquiring into students' experiences with and perspectives on information and communication technology in everyday life and in education.

Rolf Dalin, M.Sc., is a statistician whose main function is to provide research support in various subject fields, especially in the line of evidence-based practice development in social welfare at Mid Sweden University and with a research and development unit in the Association of Local Authorities in Västernorrland. He is also the developer of *Statistics for Scientific Work*, an international course package for statistical methods in empirical research. Recent publications have appeared in the *Scandinavian Journal of Disability Research* and *Managing Service Quality*.

Ola Erstad is Professor at the Institute for Educational Research, University of Oslo, Norway. He has been working both within the fields of media and educational research. He has published on issues of technology and education, especially on media literacy and digital competence. Media education has been a special interest, and he is active in different networks on media education in the Nordic countries. He is leader of a research group at the Faculty of Education, Oslo, called "TransAction-Learning, Knowing and Identity in the Information Society" and is leading a research project called "Local Literacies and Community Spaces—Investigating Transitions and Transfers in the 'Learning Lives' of Groruddalen," funded by the Norwegian Research Council. Recent chapters have appeared in *Digital Literacies* edited by Lankshear and Knobel (2008), and *Digital Storytelling, Mediatized Stories—Self-Representations in New Media* by Lundby (2008).

Urs Gasser is Executive Director of the Berkman Center for Internet & Society at Harvard University. He was previously a law professor at the University of St. Gallen in Switzerland and director of its Research Center on Information Law. Dr. Gasser is the author or editor of more than seven books and sixty articles. His work spans intellectual property, information law, corporate law, and international and comparative law. Dr. Gasser is a graduate of the University of St. Gallen (S.J.D. 2001, J.D. 1997) and Harvard Law School (LL.M. 2003). For his academic work, he has received several awards, including Harvard's Landon H. Gammon Fellowship for academic excellence and the "Walther Hug-Preis Schweiz," a prize for the best doctoral theses in law nationwide, among others.

Chris Jones is a Reader in the Institute of Educational Technology at The Open University in the UK. He teaches on the Masters program in Online and Distance Education (ODE) and coordinates the ODE strand of the Doctorate in Education (Ed.D.). His research focuses on networked learning and the utilization of the metaphor of networks to the understanding of learning in tertiary education. Chris has a longstanding interest in collaborative and cooperative methods of teaching and learning and in Communities and Networks of Practice. Chris is the principal investigator for a UK Research Council funded project "The Net Generation Encountering E-learning at University." He was previously a co-leader of the European Union funded Kaleidoscope Research Team "Conditions for Productive Networked Learning Environments." Chris has published two edited collections, most recently *Analysing Networked Learning Practices in Higher Education and Continuing Professional Development* (2009), and over 60 refereed journal articles, book chapters, and conference papers connected to his research.

Terry S. Judd is a Senior Lecturer and educational researcher in the Medical Education Unit at the University of Melbourne in Australia. Terry has been designing and developing educational software to support learning and teaching within the tertiary sector since 1995. His research has focused on understanding how and why students use educational technology, and his expertise lies in understanding the behavioral and technical considerations associated with the development and implementation of technology in learning and teaching environments. He has developed a range of innovative techniques for electronically collecting and analyzing behavioral data to support this work and is well-published in this area.

Gregor E. Kennedy is an associate professor and researcher in Health Informatics and Virtual Environments in the Faculty of Medicine, Dentistry and Health Sciences at The University of Melbourne, Australia. He has been conducting research in education and educational technology for over fifteen years. He recently led a number of large-scale, empirical investigations of "Net Generation" students now entering university and these have provided significant insight into how students' use technology and emerging technology based-tools in higher education. Gregor has published widely in the area of educational technology and student learning, and has been an invited speaker in a number of national and international forums.

Mike Levy is Professor of Applied Linguistics and Head of the School of Languages and Linguistics at Griffith University, Australia. His research focuses upon computer-assisted language learning (CALL) and includes studies on the role of technology in *ab initio* language learning, teacher education and learner training, mobile learning for Italian, and distance education for Mandarin Chinese. His publications include *CALL Dimensions* with Glenn Stockwell (Erlbaum, 2006) and *Teacher Education in CALL* with Philip Hubbard (Benjamins, 2006). He is also Chair of the Conference Planning Committee for WorldCALL (www.worldcall.org).

Rachael Levy is a Post Doctoral Fellow in the School of Education and member of the Centre for the Study of New Literacies at the University of Sheffield, UK. Her main research and teaching interest is in the areas of literacy, early childhood education, and the study of new literacies. She has published papers in the *Journal of Early Childhood Literacy*, *Journal of Research in Reading*, and the *Cambridge Journal of Education* and is currently writing a book based on her doctoral research. She is also editor for the *UKLA* minibooks series and recently won the *UKLA* postgraduate award for her thesis *Becoming a Reader in a Digital Age*.

Rowan Michael is a Lecturer of English in the School of Languages and Linguistics at Griffith University, Australia. He has previously taught English and Chinese at schools and universities in Australia, China, and Kazakhstan. Rowan's research interests include language teacher training at a distance, language teaching and learning (Chinese & ESL/EFL), and interaction in online environments. His publications include *Developing Northwest China through Distance Education* (2010).

Karl Maton is Senior Lecturer in sociology at the University of Sydney, having previously taught at the University of Cambridge, The Open University (UK), Keele University, and Wollongong University. Karl has published extensively in sociology, cultural studies, education, linguistics, and philosophy, and his Legitimation Code Theory is now being widely used by researchers in Australia, France, South Africa, and elsewhere for studies in sociology, education, linguistics, and philosophy. He recently co-edited *Social Realism, Knowledge and the Sociology of Education: Coalitions of the Mind* (with Rob Moore, 2010) and *Disciplinarity: Systemic Functional and Sociological Perspectives* (with Fran Christie, 2011). Karl's book, *Knowledge and Knowers: Towards a Realist Sociology of Education*, is to be published by Routledge.

John Palfrey is Henry N. Ess Professor of Law and Vice Dean for Library and Information Resources at Harvard Law School. He is the co-author, with Urs Gasser, of *Born Digital: Understanding the First Generation of Digital Natives* (Basic Books, 2008). He is also co-editor of *Access Denied: The Practice and Politics of Internet Filtering* (The MIT Press, 2008) and *Access Controlled: The Shaping of Power, Rights, and Rule in Cyberspace* (The MIT Press, 2010). His research and teaching is focused on Internet law, intellectual property, and international law. He practiced intellectual property and corporate law at the law firm of Ropes & Gray. He is a faculty co-director of the Berkman Center for Internet & Society at Harvard University.

Marc Prensky is an international speaker, writer, and consultant in education and learning. He is the author of three books: *Teaching Digital Natives: Partnering for Real Learning* (Corwin, 2010), *Don't Bother Me Mom—I'm Learning! (How Computer and Video Games Are Preparing Your Kids For Twenty-first Century Success—And How You Can Help!)* (Paragon House, 2006) and *Digital Game-Based Learning* (McGraw-Hill, 2001). Marc has written almost 100 articles on education and learning, including multiple articles in *Educational Leadership*, *EDUCAUSE*, *Edutopia*, and *Educational Technology*. He has designed and built over 100 software games in his career, including worldwide, multi-user games and simulations that run on all platforms from the Internet to handhelds to cell phones. Marc also writes a column for *Educational Technology* magazine, and for *Greentree Gazette*, a publication for leaders in academia. Marc's background includes Masters degrees from Yale, Middlebury, and The Harvard Business School (with distinction).

Toshie Takahashi is a faculty fellow at the Berkman Center for Internet and Society at Harvard University. She is also Associate Professor in the Department of Communication and Media Studies, Rikkyo University, Japan. Earlier in 2010, she was also appointed visiting research fellow at the Department of Education at the University of Oxford. Her current research is an ethnography centered on cross-cultural research into youth engagement with digital media in the USA, UK, and Japan. She focuses on the social and cultural implications: identity, digital literacy, connectivity, and risk in the globalized world. Professor Takahashi is Deputy Head of the Audience Section of the IAMCR and holds a Ph.D. in Media and Communications from the London School of Economics and an MA in Sociology from the University of Tokyo.

Michael Thomas is Senior Lecturer in language learning technologies and international digital business communication at the University of Central Lancashire, UK. His research interests are in ICT in education and digital literacies. His publications include *Handbook of Research on Web 2.0 and Second Language Learning* (2009), *Interactive Whiteboards for Education: Theory, Research and Practice* (with E. C. Schmid) (2010), *Task-Based Language Learning & Teaching with Technology* (with H. Reinders) (2010), *Digital Education: Opportunities for Social Collaboration* (2011) and *Online Learning* (2011). He is editor of the *International Journal of Virtual and Personal Learning Environments* and has guest edited special editions of the *Australasian Journal of Educational Technology* and the *International Journal of Emerging Technologies and Society*.

Sheila Zimic is a doctoral student in Informatics at Mid Sweden University. Sheila is using the national representative study conducted by the World Internet Institute (a partner of World Internet Project) in her research on young people's Internet use with a focus on digital competence and digital participation. The overall aim of her research is to question the deterministic images of young people in the digital society. Sheila is also a member of the multidisciplinary research group *CITIZYS* at Mid Sweden University. A previous publication on the "Net generation" has recently appeared in the journal *Digital Culture & Education*.

INDEX

Taylor & Francis

eBooks

FOR LIBRARIES

ORDER YOUR FREE 30 DAY INSTITUTIONAL TRIAL TODAY!

Over 23,000 eBook titles in the Humanities, Social Sciences, STM and Law from some of the world's leading imprints.

Choose from a range of subject packages or create your own!

Benefits for you

- Free MARC records
- COUNTER-compliant usage statistics
- Flexible purchase and pricing options

- Off-site, anytime access via Athens or referring URL
- Print or copy pages or chapters
- Full content search
- Bookmark, highlight and annotate text
- Access to thousands of pages of quality research at the click of a button

For more information, pricing enquiries or to order a free trial, contact your local online sales team.

UK and Rest of World: **online.sales@tandf.co.uk**

US, Canada and Latin America:
e-reference@taylorandfrancis.com

www.ebooksubscriptions.com

ALPSP Award for BEST eBOOK PUBLISHER 2009 Finalist

Taylor & Francis eBooks
Taylor & Francis Group

A flexible and dynamic resource for teaching, learning and research.